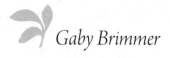

Gaby Brimmer

WIT!!DRAWN

HBI SERIES ON JEWISH WOMEN

Shulamit Reinharz, *General Editor*
Sylvia Barack Fishman, *Associate Editor*

The HBI Series on Jewish Women, created by the Hadassah-Brandeis Institute, publishes a wide range of books by and about Jewish women in diverse contexts and time periods. Of interest to scholars and the educated public, the HBI Series on Jewish Women fills major gaps in Jewish Studies and in Women and Gender Studies as well as their intersection.

For the complete list of books that are available in this series, please see www.upne.com

Gaby Brimmer and Elena Poniatowska, *Gaby Brimmer*

Harriet Hartman and Moshe Hartman, *Gender and American Jews: Patterns in Work, Education, and Family in Contemporary Life*

Dvora E. Weisberg, *Levirate Marriage and the Family in Ancient Judaism*

Ellen M. Umansky and Dianne Ashton, editors, *Four Centuries of Jewish Women's Spirituality: A Sourcebook*

Carole S. Kessner, *Marie Syrkin: Values Beyond the Self*

Ruth Kark, Margalit Shilo, and Galit Hasan-Rokem, editors, *Jewish Women in Pre-State Israel: Life History, Politics, and Culture*

Tova Hartman, *Feminism Encounters Traditional Judaism: Resistance and Accommodation*

Anne Lapidus Lerner, *Eternally Eve: Images of Eve in the Hebrew Bible, Midrash, and Modern Jewish Poetry*

Margalit Shilo, *Princess or Prisoner? Jewish Women in Jerusalem, 1840–1914*

Marcia Falk, translator, *The Song of Songs: Love Lyrics from the Bible*

Sylvia Barack Fishman, *Double or Nothing? Jewish Families and Mixed Marriage*

Avraham Grossman, *Pious and Rebellious: Jewish Women in Medieval Europe*

Iris Parush, *Reading Jewish Women: Marginality and Modernization in Nineteenth-Century Eastern European Jewish Society*

Shulamit Reinharz and Mark A. Raider, editors, *American Jewish Women and the Zionist Enterprise*

AN AUTOBIOGRAPHY

Gaby Brimmer

IN THREE VOICES

Gaby Brimmer &
Elena Poniatowska

Translated by TRUDY BALCH
Foreword by JUDITH E. HEUMANN
& JORGE PINEDA
Introduction to the English-language Edition
by LAURI UMANSKY
Afterword by AVITAL BLOCH

⋮ BRANDEIS UNIVERSITY PRESS
Waltham, Massachusetts

Published by
UNIVERSITY PRESS OF NEW ENGLAND
Hanover & London

BRANDEIS UNIVERSITY PRESS

Published by University Press of New England,

One Court Street, Lebanon, NH 03766

www.upne.com

© 2009 by Brandeis University Press

Printed in the United States of America

5 4 3 2 1

Originally published as *Gaby Brimmer*

©1979, GABY BRIMMER-ELENA PONIATOWSKA

D.R. © 1979, sobre la presente edición

 EDITORIAL GRIJALBO, S. A.

 Calzada San Bartolo Naucalpán, 282, México, D. F.

© 1988, EDICIONES GRIJALBO, S. A.

 Aragó, 385, Barcelona

The HBI Series on Jewish Women is supported by a generous gift from Dr. Laura S. Schor.

University Press of New England is a member of the Green Press Initiative. The paper used in this book meets their minimum requirement for recycled paper.

Library of Congress
Cataloging-in-Publication Data

Brimmer, Gabriela, 1947–

Gaby Brimmer: an autobiography in three voices / Gaby Brimmer and Elena Poniatowska; translated by Trudy Balch; foreword by Judith E. Heumann and Jorge Pineda; introduction to the English-language edition by Laura Umansky; afterword by Avital Bloch. — 1st ed.

 p. cm. —

(HBI series on Jewish women)

ISBN 978-1-58465-758-3

(pbk.: alk. paper)

1. Brimmer, Gabriela, 1947–
2. Cerebral palsied — Mexico — Biography. 3. Jews — Mexico — Biography. 4. Disability awareness. I. Poniatowska, Elena. II. Balch, Trudy. III. Title.

RC388.B67   2009

362.196'83600922 — dc22

2009007659

CONTENTS

: *Judith E. Heumann & Jorge Pineda*

FOREWORD

*Judith E. Heumann and Jorge Pineda met Gaby Brimmer at different stages in their
lives and careers, before they married in 1992. Jorge, an accountant by profession, recounts
that it was Gaby who spurred him on to activism. Judy, on the other hand, had already
made activism her career. By the time she met Gaby, she had held posts with the Berkeley,
California–based Center for Independent Living and the California State Department
of Rehabilitation, and had cofounded the World Institute on Disability. Today, Jorge
is the accountant for the National Council on Independent Living, while Judy is the
director of the District of Columbia Department on Disability Services. Both found
Gaby unforgettable.*

JORGE
Like Gaby, I was born and raised in Mexico City. I have used a wheelchair or
crutches all my life, because complications during my birth left me paraplegic.
I went to the same "special" school Gaby attended; unlike her, however, I didn't
have to pressure the education authorities into giving me a battery of tests
before they'd let me go on to regular public schools. Perhaps it was because
our disabilities were perceived differently. In those days, most people thought
that having cerebral palsy automatically meant being mentally disabled, too
(in fact, many people still think so today) and they doubted Gaby was capable
of going on with her education. Well, they couldn't have been more wrong!

　I didn't feel discriminated against until I tried to get a part-time job while
I was still in college, in the late 1970s. At my first interview, the owner of
the company—and today I don't even remember what kind of company
it was—took one look at me and said no. I wouldn't be able to do annual
inventories if I was on crutches, he told me. (In Mexico, accountants must
personally take inventories at the end of each fiscal year to calculate a company's cost of goods sold, which figures into the calculation of overall profits.)
No matter how many doors I knocked on, the answer was always the same.
Eventually an accounting firm offered me part-time work, and later another

one did. After I graduated, I got a job at an institute that trained construction workers because a friend of my family recommended me to the director. Five years later I got a new job at a clothing factory, through the husband of a childhood friend. Also, the owner/manager of the factory was disabled, which must have helped.

The night I met Gaby — at an exhibition of art by students from our old school, in the late 1980s — changed my life. We quickly became friends, and my conversations with her made me realize how many people with disabilities never got to live the lives they wanted because there were no laws to protect their rights and not enough leaders to fight for them. I started going to the once-a-month Saturday meetings at her house, where we began putting together the organization Gaby had dreamed of for so many years. Unlike other disability groups in Mexico in those days, Gaby said, this group would not isolate or marginalize people with disabilities from the "normal" world. It would open up sources of work that could lead to some kind of financial independence, and it would press the government to pass laws ensuring equal treatment for people with disabilities.

By 1989, Gaby's dream became a reality. The ADEPAM (Asociación para los Derechos de Personas con Alteraciones Motoras, or Association for the Rights of People with Motor Disabilities), as it became known, even got offices of its own, "lent" to us by a generous benefactor who let us use a house she owned as long as we kept it in good condition. I had been the ADEPAM's treasurer from the start, and even before we were recognized officially, I had cut back my hours at my regular job so that I could concentrate more on helping to run the organization. It seemed a hopeful time: Mexico's political atmosphere had begun to open up, and the country's political parties had started to take more interest in disability issues.

Still, change was slow, often hampered by a lack of influence at high levels and, unfortunately, political corruption that muffled our efforts to speak out. This frustrated Gaby and me to no end, but she wouldn't give up. We had to keep raising our voices, she said. We had to fight so that people with disabilities in Mexico would get equal rights and become full members of society.

JUDY

One day, in the mid-1980s, Gaby was in California visiting one of her cousins, and she came over to my house in Berkeley. I introduced her to a good friend of mine, Hale Zukas. Hale and I had worked together for many years, first at the Center for Independent Living and later at the World Institute on Disability. He was a public policy wonk, tremendously involved in local and national politics. Like Gaby, he had cerebral palsy and used a communication board to speak. Gaby used her foot to spell out words on her communication board, which sat on the footrest of her wheelchair, while Hale used a wand attached to a headpiece, with the board mounted on his wheelchair's arm. What a pair — two fighters who had personally proved to themselves and to others that they would not be limited by society's paternalistic view of what they could or could not achieve. I asked them whether they were interested in using a communication device that would enable them to type in their words and have them spoken with synthetic speech. No way, they said. Their means of communication was empowering for them; it was a part of their personas. What a wild discussion we had, all of us laughing as they told me my idea was ridiculous, and I countered that they were unwilling to come into the twentieth century. But in the end, my deep admiration for them overwhelmed me. These two brilliant people had fought and continued to fight winning victories, proving to all that their capacity to make major contributions to society should have been able to end discrimination with one fell swoop of their foot or wand. Unfortunately, such was not true, but fortunately, their inner strength was unwilling to give up.

In June 1997, twenty-two U.S. government agencies, including the Department of Education and the Social Security Administration, joined with the World Institute on Disability, Mobility International USA, Rehabilitation International, and numerous other public- and private-sector organizations to hold a conference on disabled women: the International Leadership Forum for Women with Disabilities. We were able to get a scholarship for Gaby to attend. More than six hundred disabled women came from more than eighty countries. Women who had spent years fighting for the rights of disabled women — and men — gathered to speak out about the problems and the solutions they were working on as they fought for equality. It was an amazingly powerful meeting. U.S. Secretary of State Madeleine Albright, Secretary of Health and Human Services Donna Shalala, and Secretary of Education Richard Riley all addressed the group. Gaby was there — one of the powerful disabled women who made a difference every day of her life.

I am only sorry she couldn't have lived to be a part of the Mexican delegation that fought for the passage of the United Nations Convention on the Rights of Persons with Disabilities. It was approved in 2006, and Jorge and I can both imagine how she would have beamed with joy.

JORGE *&* JUDY

Gaby's legacy will live on as the international disability rights movement grows, and as our history gets passed on to new generations of disabled people who are fighting for their own liberation and the rights of millions of others. We are delighted to help tell her story.

: *Lauri Umansky*

INTRODUCTION TO THE
ENGLISH-LANGUAGE EDITION

By 1955, when Gabriela Brimmer reached the age of eight, she had already been taken to medical specialists in Mexico and on both coasts of the United States. She had spent hundreds of hours receiving "treatments" for cerebral palsy, including a lonely stay of several months at the Cerebral Palsy Institute in Baltimore. She had been brought to neurologists, physical therapists, and speech pathologists. In the hospital, her hands had been submerged in ice water to "relax her spasms and make her nerves loosen up." With her legs fitted into hip-to-foot braces, she had performed daunting exercise regimens that took hours a day to complete. At one point, Gaby had walked a few steps across the garden of her spacious home in Mexico City.

But *Gaby Brimmer*, the eponymous book coauthored with renowned Mexican writer Elena Poniatowska, is not the triumphal tale of a heroic figure who overcomes a "tragic handicap." Unlike the standard narrative — still, and certainly in 1979 when the book first appeared in Spanish — that presents disability as an affliction, an illness, a misfortune to be overcome through grit, persistence, and medical intervention, *Gaby* offers a complex and prescient view of disability as a series of negotiations between people with particular impairments and the societies in which they live.

The book began to take form when Gabriela Brimmer asked a family friend, who was participating in a writing workshop given by Elena Poniatowska, to relay a message to Elena: "Come visit me." A celebrated journalist, novelist, and intrepid champion of the radical movements that shook Mexico in the 1960s and 1970s, Elena went to the Brimmers' home in the southwestern part of the city.[1]

She went, she says, because she was asked and because she felt a personal tug toward people with disabilities.[2] Her nephew Alejandro had been injured badly in a car accident six years earlier and all but consigned to death by the medical establishment. Kitzia, his mother and Elena's sister, defied the doctors by bringing him home and launching "a struggle that is still going on, against doctors, nurses, clergy who speak to her of Christian acceptance." Kitzia spoke to her son and eventually he communicated back, first by smiling, then later by spelling out words on a hand-drawn alphabet board. "Perhaps this is why I went to see Gaby and wanted to meet her when she sent for me," writes Poniatowska. "I could not ignore an indirect call — or maybe a very direct call — from Alejandro."

And why did Gaby seek out Elena? One might ask instead what left-leaning aspiring writer in Mexico would *not* have sought out Elena, given the opportunity. Hélène Elizabeth Louise Amélie Paula Dolores Poniatowska Amor, born in 1932 in France to a father descended from Polish royalty and a French-born mother of Mexican ancestry, fled war-torn Europe with her family, arriving as a linguistic and cultural outsider in Mexico City in 1942. She was educated through high school in exclusive private schools in Mexico and the United States, after which she began her journalistic career as a society page writer for the Mexico City daily newspapers *Excélsior* and *Novedades*. Elena soon developed a pointed, somewhat saucy, interview style, as she also branched out to write short stories, novels, and social chronicles.[3] Despite her elite upbringing, she felt drawn to the disenfranchised of Mexican society, perhaps because she as a woman in a male-dominated profession and as an immigrant to her ancestral homeland understood something of life on society's margins.[4]

Her politics drifting leftward, Elena became an advocate of the common people, the oppressed, the downtrodden, as she wrote the spoken words or testimonies of people whose voices would not otherwise be heard. Petite and glamorous, and absolutely fearless, she had become by the mid-1970s one of Mexico's most famous writers, known as a feminist and a voice of conscience against a repressive governmental regime. Her 1971 book *La noche de Tlatelolco* (titled *Massacre in Mexico* in the English version), which weaves together the voices of scores of witnesses to the brutal suppression of the student movement of 1968 in Mexico City, catapulted her to near-iconic status among the movement's sympathizers.[5]

Gabriela Brimmer most assuredly counted herself among those sympathizers. Although she had not yet enrolled in the Universidad Nacional Autónoma de México (UNAM) in 1968, she had grown up under the political tutelage of a self-avowed Marxist father, had joined her older brother

Enrique "Henry" Brimmer (called David in *Gaby*) at the summer camps of the Marxist Zionist Hashomer Hatzair movement, and as a young adult had passionately embraced the ideals of Latin American revolution, especially as personified by Ernesto "Che" Guevara. Indeed, Gaby gave the name "Che" to the typewriter that she used for verbal communication by typing with the big toe of her left foot.

Gaby also defined herself as a writer. She spoke to people by typing or by pointing with her toe to letters on an "alphabet board" in order to spell out words, and she carried on a far-flung correspondence with family and friends, spending many hours a week composing letters. She had published poems and articles in the journals of disability and other organizations in Mexico and the United States, and her most fervent wish was to establish herself as a journalist. "I could write for a newspaper," she said. "Review books and even records because I listen to a lot of music, and do articles about literature."

Gaby's mother, Sari, not only supported her daughter's writing efforts; she believed that telling Gaby's story would help to topple the barriers of prejudice and discrimination that circumscribed the lives of Gaby and others with disabilities. Gaby remembered Sari saying, "It is not only for you; it is for all your friends who need to be listened to. The media ignorance is frightening. In this country there is a lot of ignorance."[6] Sari saw Elena as someone who could make Gaby known to the world by helping to publish the "manifesto of her life."[7]

Whatever the Brimmers' motives for meeting Poniatowska, Gaby found the grande dame of Mexican letters to be charming and approachable when she came to visit in May 1977. Elena used the familiar "tú" form of address and asked to see how Gaby worked with the electric typewriter at the foot of her wheelchair. Gaby responded by typing, "ELENA TE AMO POR SER TÚ." (Elena, I love you for being you.)[8] They discussed Elena's children and her nephew Alejandro. As Gaby later recalled, upon leaving, Elena told Sari that she intended to write an article about Gaby for *Novedades*; she also said, "Tell Gaby I love her very much."[9]

For her part, Poniatowska found her initial encounter with Gaby to be jolting. "The first time I saw Gaby, I didn't even dare to look at her," she writes in her introduction to the book. "I was disconcerted by her spasms, by the fact that she would arch up in her chair or throw her head all the way back, as though her entire body were coming apart." Although Elena had spent many hours with her nephew since the accident, she had limited experience inter-acting with people with disabilities. Her discomfort placed her squarely in the mainstream of nondisabled people.

That day, Elena also met Gaby's "two mothers," Sari Brimmer (née Dlugacz) and Florencia Morales Sánchez. The men of the household were gone: Miguel, Gaby's father, had died of a heart attack in 1967, and Henry also left that year, going first to Israel, then to Berkeley to study. Sari, born to a prosperous Jewish family, grew up in Vienna.[10] Her family, and Miguel's, fled within a year of the *Anschluss* in 1938. The families formed an American diaspora, securing whatever visas they could. Both sets of parents and a Brim-mer brother went to Mexico City; one Dlugacz sister went to San Francisco; and another, with Sari and Miguel, went to Chile. There Miguel worked as a manager on a ranch. When their first child died a few days after birth, they decided to leave for Mexico, where Miguel established a sweater and wool goods factory, and Sari, a leather goods boutique. Henry was born there in 1945 and Gaby in 1947.[11]

Highstrung, worried, intense, Sari at first refused to accept that Gaby had cerebral palsy. "I was the one who yelled, who cried, who didn't accept it. I looked for medicine, doctors, specialists, some kind of cure. I made the rounds of the hospitals, I can tell you that!" Her faith in medicine, her fren-zied chase of remedies, experts, and therapies, corresponds with what we know of her background. Unlike Miguel, who "accepted Gaby just the way she is," Sari hailed from an affluent stratum of the Viennese Jewish commu-nity, at a time before the Nazis "cleansed" the rosters, when Jews made up more than half the faculty of the College of Medicine. Thus she grew up in a community steeped in reverence for the advances of medical science.[12] More-over, Sari had lost a child who might have been saved had she not been on a remote ranch in Chile. Betty, the oldest Dlugacz sister, was a physician, and Ana, the youngest, had studied medicine for a year before becoming a social worker.[13] Coming from these roots, this milieu, Sari turned with great vigor to medical amelioration as the "solution" to Gaby's cerebral palsy.

By Mexican standards, the Brimmers would have been considered mid-dle class, not wealthy, despite the presence of several paid employees in the household. Yet unlike most middle-class Mexican (or Viennese, for that mat-ter) wives and mothers in the 1940s and 1950s, Sari worked outside the home, operating a business upon which the family's livelihood relied as surely as it depended on Miguel's income. Nonetheless, the Brimmers seem to have divided child-rearing responsibilities along traditional gender lines, with Sari coordinating day-to-day activities and making major decisions for the children. Miguel would arrive home at the end of a day's work, interact briefly and lovingly with Gaby, then repair to his study to read. That Sari was the one to call doctors, pound on doors, and scour the medical tomes, speaks not only to her particularized background and personality, but also to her ascribed gender role. Gaby paints her as a study in neurosis, as does Poniatowska, who casts the popularized psychoanalytic concept in ethnic terms, calling Sari "a typical Jewish mother, overprotective, anxious because she can't do more, worried about the future, about the high cost of living, about money, about everyday life, about the failure she thinks her life amounts to." Perhaps that was so. Nevertheless, by the standards of her normative role at that time, in that place, she was also performing the work of a "good mother."

Sari advocated with equal force for her daughter's right to an education. Gaby attended the primary grades at a school for "handicapped" children, some of whom had intellectual disabilities. When she reached seventh grade, or *secundaria*, she wanted to attend a "normal" public school. None would accept her. At that point, and spurred by Gaby herself, Sari mobilized. "I closed the store and went knocking on doors," she said. Shunted from one department of the Ministry of Public Education to the next, she persisted until Gaby was allowed to enter Secundaria No. 68 in Tlacopac, San Angel, followed by *preparatoria*, or high school, and then the UNAM.

If Sari fought for Gaby's admission into the public schools, Gaby's "second mother," Florencia Morales, actually accompanied her to each educational setting, often lugging the wheelchair up flights of stairs and explaining to reluctant teachers that although she wrote down the words Gaby spelled out on the keyboard, Gaby herself performed the intellectual labor needed to complete the schoolwork. Even in the UNAM, Florencia had to implore professors to allow Gaby to remain in their courses; some simply expelled the pair from class, saying that Gaby made them feel uncomfortable.

Florencia had essentially consecrated her life to Gaby since 1949, when she began working for the Brimmers as a maid and laundress. She had left her impoverished family, campesinos in the tiny village of Maquixco el Alto in the state of Mexico, to work in Mexico City at the age of thirteen, as had her older siblings before her. Landing in the Brimmer household when Gaby was two years old, Florencia took a special interest in the little girl who did not talk or use her hands, but who obviously communicated with sounds and played using her left foot. Sari and Miguel welcomed Florencia's ability to communicate with Gaby and soon shifted her responsibilities from those of a maid to those of a personal assistant, or "nurse," for Gaby. While Florencia never cut off contact with her family of origin, she became an integral part of the Brimmer household, and a constant companion to Gaby.

After her initial visit to the Brimmer household, Poniatowska returned again and again over a six-month period, conducting interviews with Gaby, Sari, and Florencia. Sometimes she sat with Gaby alone. Other times, one or both of the older women joined them. Between visits, she began to receive letters and poems from Gaby, who ranged widely through her life experiences, touching on topics of family, friendship, love, lust, disability, politics, religion, mothering, and more. From these materials Elena crafted first an article and then a book.[14]

The article, which appeared in *Novedades* in three installments in May 1977, intersperses journalistic prose with photographs and sprinklings of Gaby's poetry. Poniatowska speaks in her own voice, quoting Gaby, Sari, and Florencia sparingly, as she describes how Gaby works, thinks, and lives. She conveys Gaby's acute interest in people and ideas, and her fierce reaction to social injustice. Cautioning readers against easy judgment or dismissal, she writes, "Seeing Gaby Brimmer shakes many convictions; many certainties prove to be wrong." ("Ante Gaby Brimmer, muchas convicciones se tambalean; muchas certidumbres resultan equivocados.")[15]

Then she moved on to other projects. Friends discouraged her from writing more about Gaby, chiding, "Why are you letting yourself get involved again in something that has nothing to do with literature or with the creative act of writing?" She had put the project aside when she received a plaintive call from Sari in December 1978: "It has been nearly two years . . . and no book. Gaby is going to be thirty-two years old. This is not possible, it is not fair." Galvanized, Poniatowska completed the manuscript within months.

The well-respected publishing house Editorial Grijalbo brought out the volume in December 1979: *Gaby Brimmer*, by Gabriela Brimmer and Elena Poniatowska. A long introduction by Poniatowska opens the book. The text then presents the braided voices of Gaby, Sari, and Florencia, speaking in monologue yet often arranged as if in candid response to each other. Structured as a loose chronology of Gaby's life, the timeline begins with her birth in 1947 and ends with the adoption of her daughter, Alma Florencia Brimmer, in 1977.

The book changed Gaby's life, as Avital Bloch recounts in the afterword to this volume. "Perhaps the publication of the book *Gaby Brimmer* will give [Gaby] the presence of potential readers, friends willing to visit her," Poniatowska writes. "Perhaps also *Gaby Brimmer* will open the eyes of the able-bodied to the thousands of handicapped people we shunt aside because we think they don't know what is going on around them." These predictions proved correct: *Gaby Brimmer* sold briskly in its Spanish-language edition, and Gaby Brimmer became known.

Who, then, is the author of *Gaby Brimmer*? Several critics, counting the book among Poniatowska's "testimonial" works, note that in *Gaby*, as in other works in this common Latin American literary genre, the authorship is contested.[16] Typically, in testimonial literature, a literate person, a person almost by definition of a more privileged social class, records the words of a nonliterate person, or a person who would not otherwise have the ability to reach a broad public. The editor becomes a joint author of sorts, a conveyor of the subject's words. An ostensibly silent partner, the editor of a testimonial work can be seen as facilitating the empowerment of a previously silenced person; viewed with a more jaundiced eye, the editor becomes an appropriator of the subject's story, a privileged party who wrests control of another person's power of self-definition.[17]

In *Gaby*, these tensions manifest themselves in a complicated fashion. Gaby, if not a class equal of Poniatowska, is hardly illiterate. She is highly articulate; in fact, she generates her contributions to the book quite literally in written form. Yet because she lives in a society that ascribes a "subaltern" status to people with disabilities, she does depend on Poniatowska's ability and willingness to bring her voice into public discourse.[18] This dependence would be true for any "unknown" riding on the coattails of a famous writer. For Gaby, a further irony ensues, in that her written contributions to *Gaby* appear as spoken words, in their placement alongside the transcribed speech of Sari and Florencia. Poniatowska, as editor, molds and organizes the text; in doing so, she both preserves and alters Gaby's self-presentation or "authorship."[19]

Gaby Brimmer thus occupies an unstable position among the genres of testimonial and epistolary literature, biography, and autobiography.[20] Although Gaby's name appears as coauthor of the book, she actually performs several roles: writer, biographical subject, witness, or "testimonial voice." In a similar way, Poniatowska shifts repeatedly among the roles of author, editor, and "testimonial recorder."

There can be no doubt that Poniatowska constructed the book's original introduction. She writes in the first person, expressing her own views of disability alongside a précis of Gaby's life. In her characteristic style, she brings others' voices into play right away, quoting Gaby at length and scattering bits of Gaby's poetry throughout the opening text. The narrative pulse of the essay nonetheless comes as much from Poniatowska's story as from Gaby's: Elena answered a call from Alejandro, she tells us, as plainly as she responded to the Brimmers' entreaties.

Many readers today will find Poniatowska's language, her discussion of disability, troubling. Much has occurred in the thirty years since the book's original publication, not least a sea change in the words and attitudes surrounding disability. Poniatowska writes of Sari's "torture" as the mother of a child with a disability. Pages of the introduction read like excerpts from medical texts, as if disability were rooted in individual bodies, "damaged" bodies. People with cerebral palsy appear as if in the throes of "illness," rather than in contention with barriers to their full participation in society:

> Few illnesses are as terrible, as denigrating as cerebral palsy; few have more power against the human spirit, because so often the body becomes a prison: a bundle of limbs and nerves, of cells and muddled tissues that do not respond. The brain gives orders, but the hand does not obey, and if it does, its movements are so pathetic and out of control that it would be better off not having moved at all. That is why people with cerebral palsy find it so easy to let themselves be defeated, to spend their time in a state of light sleep, unnoticed. To let themselves go, to float. Their bodies can't react? Well, as individuals they aren't going to do anything either. If what happened to them is against nature, why must they force themselves if even their strongest effort is only a ripple in the water? Besides, what connection is there between a brain that sends messages to which no one or nothing responds, and a sprawled-out body that looks like a rag, a piece of clothing drifting along?

Disability rights activists have fought hard to eradicate the understanding of disability that such images of catastrophe and self-defeat evoke. For three decades now, they have struggled against the depiction and treatment of people with disabilities as afflicted individuals in need of the medical treatment or pity or control of various experts. Like other "minorities," disabled people in unprecedented numbers have begun to view themselves as a distinct, even somewhat cohesive, group, and in a concerted way have begun to fight the multifaceted discrimination that restricts their lives. This perspective removes "disability" from the individual and from the realm of medicine, placing it instead in a social and political context. People with disabilities are not "ill." Rather, they face obstacles and prejudice — in the built environment as well as in the cultural, legal, economic, and social realms — that prevent them from exercising the civil and human rights due to any person in a just society.[21]

But in Mexico in 1979, this view of disability scarcely existed. As Poniatowska explains, in Mexico City, only one organization addressed the needs of people with cerebral palsy directly, and only a handful of groups in all of Mexico had begun to agitate for what could loosely be called "disability rights." "The Greeks used to throw cripples from the Tarpeian Rock and never worry about them again," a friend told Elena, to dissuade her from taking the time to write *Gaby*. "Don't have anything to do with sick people. Don't you see they wear you down?" From the cultural realm to the educational, the legal to the economic, "disability" in Mexico remained largely unexamined, unpoliticized — just as a disability rights revolution was erupting in the United States.

Taken in the context of its time and place, Poniatowska's introduction does make a modest approach toward the "modern." The now-outmoded language (which Trudy Balch has translated meticulously, never bending to the temptation to tilt the original toward current sensibilities) suggests otherwise. Yet Poniatowska cedes narrative space to others quickly in the introduction, foreshadowing the Rashomon-like effect that emerges abundantly in the body of the book: tales have more than one telling, more than one teller, more than one meaning.[22] To Poniatowska, the Asociación pro Parálisis Cerebral (APAC), directed by Carmelina Ortiz Monasterio de Molina, mother of a daughter with cerebral palsy, is a model institution, suffused with "an atmosphere of love and complete acceptance." To Gaby, the APAC and its director reek of an old-fashioned attitude that views people with disabilities as objects of pity, whose purpose in living is to secure the redemption of those who take care of them. By juxtaposing conflicting viewpoints, Poniatowska invites readers to question her definitions and interpretations, to interrogate her "ownership" of Gaby's story. And from the interstices of this textual construction, which is Poniatowska's calling card and genius, Gaby's voice emerges authoritatively, enriched not only with the legitimacy of felt experience but also with a complex and evolving analysis of disability.

Poniatowska's audible presence subsides in the body of the book, which openly contains only the triad of Gaby, Sari, and Florencia. Her silence is illusory, of course: as editor, she shapes, orders, juxtaposes, accents, and pares the others' voices.[23] *Gaby* is not a literal transcription of voices in conversation, nor does it pretend to be. It is, instead, a conversation constructed after the fact, and for effect. The effect, as in the book's introduction, is that Gaby articulates a more "modern" sensibility vis-à-vis disability than that expressed by Elena, Sari, or Florencia.

There is little indication that Gaby was familiar with the nascent international movement for disability rights, or with such fruits of its labors as the 1975 United Nations' *Declaration of the Rights of Disabled Persons*.[24] She did, however, have substantial knowledge by the mid-1970s of the modern disability rights and Independent Living movements in the United States. Her brother, Henry, had written to her about the emerging disability activism in the San Francisco area. With family there, she traveled fairly often to California, where her cousin Dinah Hills Stroe, a graduate of the University of California, Berkeley, brought her to visit the Center for Independent Living.[25] Founded in 1972 as a community organization led by and for people with disabilities, the CIL occupied the epicenter of Berkeley's disability activism. Ed Roberts and other disabled student activists who in 1970 had formed the Rolling Quads organization to demand access both to the university's physical structures and to the services that would allow them to live independently now brought their demands into the wider community through the CIL, where people with disabilities gathered and fought for their rights as full and independent members of the community.[26]

From even one visit to the CIL, Gaby would have recognized the outlines of a movement unlike anything she had seen in Mexico. Whereas in Mexico, most organizations that addressed the needs of people with disabilities did so from a medical, rehabilitative, or worse, a "warehousing" perspective, their counterparts in the United States took self-help, self-determination, as a guiding principle. The deep roots of the movement reached back into U.S. history to the self-advocacy of various disability-specific groups, most notably blind people and deaf people. Disabled veterans and workers had created cross-disability alliances, as when the League of the Physically Handicapped protested discrimination against disabled workers by the Depression-era Works Progress Administration. In the post–World War II years, the parents of disabled children had formed national organizations to address the medical, rehabilitative, educational, residential, and employment needs of their children; they had lobbied the federal government, which slowly responded.[27]

By the time Gaby became aware of it in the 1970s, disability rights activism in the United States had diverged in substance, form, and scale from its earlier variants. Spurred by the example of the progressive movements of the 1960s, buoyed by recent judicial and legislative gains, imbued with a sense of immediacy, and swollen in ranks by baby boomers coming of age, disability activists now took to the streets in "direct action." Gaby might not have known the specifics of the Rehabilitation Act of 1973, but she was surely aware of the demonstrations across the United States in 1977 demanding that the federal government develop regulations to implement Section 504 of that act, which prohibited agencies or programs that receive federal funds from discriminating against people with disabilities.[28] She did not meet Judith Heumann, founder of Disabled in Action, until the 1980s, but she probably heard of the group's protests in the mid-1970s against the demeaning United Cerebral Palsy telethon, which depicted people with disabilities as deserving of pity and charity rather than civil and human rights.[29] With curb cuts, ramps, and a panoply of assistive devices coming into more frequent use, the United States struck Gaby as a place where disability activism had made a tangible difference in people's lives. "I hope the Handicapped Rights movement in San Francisco gets somewhere, because if they succeed in the United States, we'll follow the example here in Mexico. And this is one case where it's good for us to be copycats."

"I have a cause, and maybe that's why I write," Gaby declared. "I want to tell the world that I'm fighting for myself and my people — for the handicapped — for them to be recognized as thinking, creative beings. As human beings. . . . I want us to have equal opportunities to live, to fight, and to be ourselves." She vowed to establish a disability rights organization in Mexico, based on three principles:

1 We shouldn't be isolated or marginalized from the "normal" world.
2 Sources of work should be opened up for us so we can be financially independent, at least partly.
3 The issue of cerebral palsy should be publicized, so we can demand our rights from the authorities, like any other citizen can.

In *Gaby Brimmer*, Gaby touches on virtually every major concern that disability rights activists in the United States, Mexico, and around the world would tackle over the next several decades. She writes about her life as she lived it, incorporating ideas and analyses that she has gleaned from various sources, and along the way claiming for herself and "her people" a full slate of human rights.

Gaby wanted what any young person might want: to live independently, with the assurance that she would not be confined in an institution; to perform meaningful work; to control her own finances, medical care, and other major life decisions. She wanted to satisfy her immense craving for knowledge through a challenging education. She wanted access to transportation and to the buildings and technology that surrounded her. As a woman with a disability, she fought for the right to love and make love; to form a family and household of her own choosing; to bear or adopt and rear children.[30] She wanted to be seen for who she was — no more, no less — and to be free of the stigma, prejudice, and discrimination that dogged her; she wanted no part of the sentimentalized pity or overblown adulation of people who expected too little of her. Gaby understood that people with disabilities needed to wage their own battles. Well-intentioned service providers, anxious parents, and kindly allies exacted a price, however unintended, for their support. There could be no substitutes in this revolution, only freedom fighters, and Gaby strained to enter the fray.

Gaby Brimmer captures the liminal moment between Gaby's ripening disability consciousness and her emergence as an activist in her own right. It also records a pivotal period in disability history, when the disability rights and Independent Living movements gained momentum around the world, and international alliances began to take shape. Gaby died in January 2000. For the last two decades of her life, she was in the thick of the fight and loving it.

NOTES

1 Elena Poniatowska, telephone interview by Lauri Umansky, January 31, 2008.

2 Ibid.

3 Beth E. Jörgensen, *The Writing of Elena Poniatowska* (Austin: University of Texas Press, 1994), xii–xix; Michael K. Schuessler, *Elena Poniatowska: An Intimate Biography* (Tucson: University of Arizona Press, 2007), passim.

4 Jörgensen, *The Writing of Elena Poniatowska*, xxi.

5 Elena Poniatowska, *Massacre in Mexico*, trans. Helen R. Lane (New York: Viking, 1975); Schuessler, *Elena Poniatowska*, 158–173.

6 Gaby Brimmer, "Argumento de la película 'Gaby Brimmer,'" November 26, 1980, p. 58, Gaby Brimmer Manuscripts, Brimmer Family, Mexico City.

7 Ibid., introduction.

8 Ibid., 58–60.

9 Ibid.

10 While in *Gaby* (p. 73), Sari says that she was born in Vienna, her niece, Dinah Stroe, reported to Avital Bloch that the Dlugacz sisters had all been born in Poland, before the family emigrated to Austria. Dinah Stroe, interview by Avital Bloch, Mexico City, April 3, 2008.

11 Dinah Stroe, interview by Avital Bloch, Mexico City, April 3, 2008; Stroe's time line and events comport with those recorded in *Gaby,* apart from the discrepancy mentioned in note 10 above.

12 Edzard Ernst, "A Leading Medical School Seriously Damaged," *Annals of Internal Medicine* 122, no. 10 (May 15, 1995): 789–792; Tudor P. Toma, "University of Vienna Apologises for Dismissing Jewish Doctors," *British Medical Journal* 317, no. 7161 (September 19, 1998): 770.

13 Dinah Stroe, interview by Avital Bloch, Mexico City, April 3, 2008; Ana Dlugacz, Dinah's mother, eventually moved to San Francisco, near her sister Betty.

14 Elena Poniatowska, telephone interview by Lauri Umansky, January 31, 2008; her article about Gaby appeared in *Novedades* in three parts, on May 9, 10, and 11, 1977.

15 Elena Poniatowska, "Gaby Brimmer, la Niña que es un Ejemplo para la Humanidad," *Novedades*, May 11, 1977.

16 Jörgensen, *The Writing of Elena Poniatowska*, 53–54, 67–68, 79–80, and passim; Amy K. Kaminsky, *Reading the Body Politic: Feminist Criticism and Latin American Women Writers* (Minneapolis: University of Minnesota Press, 1993), 60–76; and Claudia Schaefer, *Textured Lives: Women, Art, and Representation in Modern Mexico* (Tucson: University of Arizona Press, 1992), 61–87.

17 Ibid.; see also Gayatri Chakravorty Spivak, "Can the Subaltern Speak?" in *Marxism*

and the Interpretation of Culture, ed. Cary Nelson and Lawrence Grossberg (Champaign: University of Illinois Press, 1988), 271–313.

18 Kaminsky, *Reading the Body Politic*, 61–62.

19 Ibid., 73; Schaefer, *Textured Lives*, 61–87.

20 Kaminsky, *Reading the Body Politic*, 60–61.

21 The literature on the Disability Rights Movement and the ideas that propel it is voluminous; see especially James I. Charlton, *Nothing About Us Without Us: Disability Oppression and Empowerment* (Berkeley and Los Angeles: University of California Press, 1998); Doris Zames Fleischer and Frieda Zames, *The Disability Rights Movement: From Charity to Confrontation* (Philadelphia: Temple University Press, 2001); Paul K. Longmore, *Why I Burned My Book and Other Essays on Disability* (Philadelphia: Temple University Press, 2003); and Joseph P. Shapiro, *No Pity: People with Disabilities Forging a New Civil Rights Movement* (New York: Times Books, 1993).

22 In the 1950 film *Rashomon*, directed by Akira Kurosawa, four people give entirely different descriptions of a crime that all of them witnessed.

23 Jörgensen, *The Writing of Elena Poniatowska*, 79–88; Kaminsky, *Reading the Body Politic*, 61, 72; and Schaefer, *Textured Lives*, 65.

24 United Nations, General Assembly, *Declaration on the Rights of Disabled Persons*, General Assembly resolution 3447, December 9, 1975, http://www.unhchr.ch/html/menu3/b/72.htm; for a summary of U.N. activities regarding disability, see United Nations, Secretariat for the Convention on the Rights of Persons with Disabilities, "The UN and Persons with Disabilities," http://www.un.org/esa/socdev/enable/disun.htm.

25 Dinah Stroe, interview by Avital Bloch, Mexico City, April 3, 2008.

26 Many sources discuss the Center for Independent Living. See, for example, Fleischer and Zames, *The Disability Rights Movement*, 33–47; or Steven E. Brown, "Zona and Ed Roberts: Twentieth-Century Pioneers," *Disability Studies Quarterly* 20, no. 1 (Winter 2000): 26–42.

27 On the history of disability rights activism in the United States, see especially Fleischer and Zames, *The Disability Rights Movement*; Paul K. Longmore and Lauri Umansky, eds., *The New Disability History: American Perspectives* (New York: New York University Press, 2001); and Shapiro, *No Pity*. The definitive source on the League of the Physically Handicapped is Paul K. Longmore and David Goldberger, "The League of the Physically Handicapped and the Great Depression: A Case Study in the New Disability History," *Journal of American History* 87, no. 3 (December 2000): 888–922.

28 For an excellent discussion of the 504 protests, see Longmore, *Why I Burned My Book*, 102–111.

29 Fleischer and Zames, *The Disability Rights Movement*, 74; on telethons and their cultural meanings, see Paul K. Longmore, "Conspicuous Contribution and American Cultural Dilemmas: Telethon Rituals of Cleansing and Renewal," in *The Body and Physical Difference: Discourses of Disability*, ed. David T. Mitchell and Sharon L. Snyder (Ann Arbor: University of Michigan Press, 1997), 134–158.

30 An extensive literature now exists on disabled women's right to be mothers. For compelling stories about mothers with cerebral palsy in particular, see Denise Sherer Jacobson, *The Question Of David: A Disabled Mother's Journey Through Adoption, Family, and Life* (Berkeley, Calif.: Creative Arts, 1999) and Jay Mathews, *A Mother's Touch: The Tiffany Callo Story* (New York: Henry Holt, 1992).

: *Trudy Balch*

TRANSLATOR'S NOTE

The unique collage of voices called out to me the moment I opened this book. I could hear Gaby, Sari, and Florencia speaking, and it was a translator's dream! Vivid language, an engrossing, riveting story, three "characters" each with a different voice, and expressive, original poetry. I couldn't wait to get started.

The two major challenges awaiting me, I decided, were to maintain the conversational quality of the prose, and then to move to the realm of poetry in order to translate Gaby's poems, which are interspersed throughout the text. True, much of the poetry has a conversational tone, but each poem was still a separate entity, more like a monologue, often philosophical, and offering a deeper exploration of a particular theme. Some of them rhymed or had a regular meter, while others were freer. Close attention to all these qualities was required.

Overall, for the translation to be as riveting as the original, the three women's voices had to be as distinctive in English as they were in Spanish. Gaby is articulate, sharp, often slangy, and definitely not above profanity. Sari sounds more formal but is sometimes very colloquial — all at once. I tried to reflect the formal air by using fewer contractions in her dialogue and maintaining a weightier rhythm. Florencia has a warm and down-to-earth quality, but can also sound practical and coolly straightforward.

I eventually found it easier to work on the poems separately, crafting each English version, putting it aside for a while, and then coming back to it. Once I arrived at a final version (if any translation can be considered "final"), I put it back into the prose text and read everything together.

Slang was another major challenge. The story is being told in the late 1970s, looking back through the years to the 1940s and occasionally (when Sari discusses her life in Europe) to the 1920s and 1930s. I wondered: How careful should I be, in the translation, to keep the slang in the period during which the book was written? Very careful, I decided. This is a book very much of its time, and to use slang and vocabulary that smacked of later periods would yank readers out of the era in which these women were living when they were telling their story.

I also devoted considerable thought to the translation of vocabulary that describes what is now called "disability" in the English-speaking world. "Lisiado" (crippled) and "inválido" and "minusválido" (both on the order of "handicapped," as well as "invalid" in some contexts) are being edged out of use — particularly in the Spanish-speaking disability community — much as their equivalents are in English. Should I translate such terms as "disabled," in keeping with contemporary language? No, I decided; once again, it would take the book out of its time. The newer Spanish terms of "discapacitado" and "personas con discapacidad" (people with disabilities) had not yet made their way into these speakers' language — not even Gaby's. Thirty years ago and more, "lisiado," "retrasado mental" (mentally retarded) and similar words were typical and acceptable ways of referring to people with disabilities, just as their equivalents had been in English-speaking countries (and still are, among many people). In order for the English text to strike readers in the same way as the Spanish text does, the equivalents needed to be preserved.

I faced a similar issue with Sari's and Gaby's habit — in the text — of referring to people with cerebral palsy as "espásticos" (spastics). There were also instances in the text where Sari and Gaby used "spastic" to describe people with other types of physical disabilities; this tendency was verified by Florencia. Again, I decided that it was paramount to preserve the original expression, rather than making it fit sensibilities that have become more common thirty years later.

At the same time, I decided to leave certain words in Spanish, such as the terms for the different levels of school in the Mexican educational system. Though *primaria*, *secundaria*, and *preparatoria* do have rough equivalents in English (in the United States, generally "grade school," "primary school," or "elementary school"; "junior high"; and "senior high," corresponding to grades 1–6, 7–9, and 10–12, respectively), I felt that preserving the Spanish would also help preserve the Mexican flavor of the text. In a similar vein, I chose to preserve "Señor" and "Señora" Brimmer rather than translating them as "Mr." and "Mrs." Other such choices were "Mamá" instead of "Mom" (and often instead of "Mother"), "Papá" instead of "Dad," "Padre" instead of "Father" (when referring to a priest), and "Calle" (street) with certain specific street names.

In other words, while I wanted the text to read smoothly and conversationally (or poetically, as the case may be), I also wanted to get across its Mexican flavor, so clear and vibrant in the original. Keeping certain words and terms in Spanish, especially when the context makes their meaning clear, was one way to accomplish this goal.

The original text also has a flavor of Jewish culture, especially when Gaby recounts her experiences at the Marxist Zionist summer camp she attended when she was younger. Here my personal background became useful: the Hebrew words Gaby uses were familiar to me from my own synagogue and Jewish camp experiences; in addition, because of my experience living in Mexico and participating in Jewish communities there, I easily recognized Hebrew transliterations in Spanish orthography.

Readers will also notice that some of the people mentioned in this book — such as Gaby's caregiver, Florencia Morales Sánchez — have two surnames. This follows the custom throughout the Spanish-speaking world of preserving both the father's (Morales, in this example) and mother's (Sánchez, in this example) surnames for each individual, although in many instances people choose to use only the first (father's) surname. And, while I generally avoid footnotes, I did add several in order to provide a quick explanation of certain geographical and cultural details, as well as Mexican government agencies and the educational system.

I wish to thank the Hadassah-Brandeis Institute for the Research Award that helped support this volume, as well as the many people who read and commented on the translation or parts of it, responded to queries, or in other ways helped bring this project to fruition: Gaby's daughter, Alma Brimmer, and Gaby's longtime caregiver, Florencia Morales Sánchez; Angélica Herrera Mena, director of the ADEPAM; my colleagues from Espalista (the e-mail list of the American Translators Association Spanish Division), the PCM Translation Resources e-mail list, and the University of Guadalajara; Aura Estrada Curiel, whose untimely death sadly prevented her from seeing this book in print; Margaret Sayers "Petch" Peden, whose generosity, encouragement, and artistry have spurred generations of translators; Ruth Monroy; Elena Poniatowska; Daniel Sherr; Robert Wechsler; and Rivka Widerman.

As I translated this book, Gaby, Sari, Florencia, and their braided stories sprang from the page to life and stayed there. I hope their voices will ring in your heads as they have rung in mine.

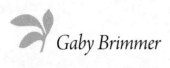
Gaby Brimmer

INTRODUCTION

 I follow the tracks that the wheelchair makes on the floor: they go from the living room to the library and stop in front of the picture window overlooking the garden. There is little furniture to stand in the way, which may be why Gaby's living room and library are round — homemade "stadiums" that she circles every day, around the ring, around the world, around the hours, around the day in just one world. And every day, two women thread a path behind these tracks: Florencia, the Nana, who is forever pushing; and Sari, the mother, whose angst too is spherical, a jail in the round, like the circle in which her daughter is turning.

All three women's heads are round because they wear their hair in the same caplike cut, a simple turn and turn of the scissors, in a spiral of black hair. Sari's spiral of angst gets darker at night, hanging over her always, stopping only at moments when Gaby holds her head erect and gives her a serious look with her green eyes, pointing with her foot at the letters on the writing board: "Oh, mother," she chides Sari, "snap out of it, don't keep torturing yourself this way!"

Sari's torture began thirty-two years ago, on September 12, 1947, when she gave birth to a six-pound, thirteen-ounce baby girl with blond hair. When the little girl was three days old, the nurse came into Sari's room and told her, "The baby's sick!" and began to cry. Frantic, Sari clutched her head between her hands, and her screams could be heard in the hallway of the "El Angel" Hospital: "Run, get the doctor, run!" But since the nurse continued to cry while standing "professionally" in front of her, Sari rose from her bed, her stomach wrapped in bandages, and said, "If you don't go downstairs, I'm going down to the 'foyer' just like this, so I can ask the first person I see walking down the Paseo de la Reforma for help. I want my husband! Call the doctors!" Everyone came running and saw that Gaby was very yellow. At that point Sari thought it wasn't so serious, but when she left the hospital with her daughter in her arms, she and Miguel went to a laboratory instead of going straight home. There a blood sample and some spinal fluid were drawn from Gaby, and a blood sample from the two parents as well. The result: Rh-negative for Sari, Rh-positive for Miguel. Sari and Miguel had had one perfectly healthy son named David, who was two and a half. When they brought Gaby home, David stood on tiptoe next to the crib to see what they had brought him, to see what kind of surprise lay behind the tulle veiling. When he moved it aside, the baby girl arched up from her head to the tips of her toes, and then Sari, standing next to her healthy son, discovered something completely unknown to either of them: spasms.

As a small child, when Gaby wanted to get from one place to another and there was no one nearby, she would drag herself on the floor until she got blisters. Then came Florencia Morales Sánchez, and from the age of five, Gaby took cover behind Florencia, her Nana, who protected her from the curious stares by wrapping her up in her embrace. With Florencia's strong arms around her, who could hurt Gaby more than her illness? Few illnesses are as terrible, as denigrating as cerebral palsy; few have more power against the human spirit, because so often the body becomes a prison: a bundle of limbs and nerves, of cells and muddled tissues that do not respond. The brain gives orders, but the hand does not obey, and if it does, its movements are so pathetic and out of control that it would be better off not having moved at all. That is why people with cerebral palsy find it so easy to let themselves be defeated, to spend their time in a state of light sleep, unnoticed. To let themselves go, to float. Their bodies can't react? Well, as individuals they aren't going to do anything either. If what has happened to them is against nature, why must they force themselves if even their strongest effort is only a ripple in the water? Besides, what connection is there between a brain that sends messages to which no one or nothing responds, and a sprawled-out body that looks like a rag, a piece of cloth drifting along? The human brain is still the most mysterious and least understood of all our organs, the most complex machine in the universe. In *Das Unwahrscheinliche Leben* [The unlikely life], Heinz Woltereck suggests that the brain continues to function up to seven minutes after the heart has stopped, and he asks, Is it the brain that keeps us alive, or the heart? Located in the lower rear section of the brain, the cerebellum, which we lyrically call "the tree of life," refines the position and balance of the head, as well as muscle position and voluntary movements of the body. The more developed the cerebellum, the more precise and exact a person's gestures and movements. In Gaby's case, the damage occurred in the cerebellum as well as in the cerebral hemispheres, and her locomotor centers were the most injured of all. For other people with cerebral palsy, such as Beati Molina, for example, the worst damage occurred in the left cerebral hemisphere, where the capability for speech is located. Yet with Gaby, nothing is less palsied than her brain, and nothing more astonishing, for example, than her memory! The top layers of Gaby's brain must be intact if she can receive such clear images from outside, if she can speculate about the universe and about herself, if she tries to communicate ideas to us by writing, if she stores and synthesizes information, if she sends messages to the outside world that are not only coherent but lucid and polished, the product of intelligent reflection, if she poses questions not only of a social nature but also related to matters of science — because had she been able to, Gaby would have been a biologist. For a time she was drawn to biochemistry and neurology; she studied the anatomy of the brain (she has always been impressed that a three-pound mass could be capable of explaining the universe), and developed a theory about how to assist people with cerebral palsy that even included the talking electronic machine now sold in the United States.

Gaby Brimmer did not learn what her illness was until she was admitted to the hospital in Baltimore, where she underwent a course of rehabilitative therapy. She began to suffer only when she became aware that she was receiving treatment; and in Baltimore, Gaby suffered. It was not physical pain, but becoming conscious of her abnormality. (Gaby thinks WELL and her brain transmits orders WELL, but her dead cells do not permit those orders to be carried out. The orders do not reach the cells that carry them out — "the effectors," in medical terms — because the systems are damaged.) In Baltimore, Gaby was able to perceive her condition intellectually, but she also began to fear that her family would reject her; she began to fear Sari's perpetual wavering, which continues to this day, because Sari has always tormented herself about her daughter's future: a residence? a nursing home? an institution in the United States? At that point Gaby was torn between her intellectual efforts — the certainties that coursed through her — and her uncontrollable muscular reflexes: her spasms and lifeless limbs. One morning her eyes returned to the only thing that obeyed her: her left leg and the big toe on her left foot. When she was a child, she thought it was normal that her left foot worked for everything, such as playing with her doll or tossing a ball. Now Gaby became aware of something else. Something that in the beginning was only a sensation: the awareness of effort. For Gaby, effort was the antidote to pain. She made an effort to focus her attention, and she made an effort with her muscles; she did her exercises, she concentrated on doing them well, and when she did, she fought against other reflexes of avoidance and self-destructiveness. The big toe of her left foot took on tremendous importance, because by using it Gaby could write: she could communicate. The effort of writing with the electric typewriter is and has been enormous, but Gaby has two vast capacities for concentration. One is interior, while the other is exterior; she reflects and observes and has time to do both. She says so herself: "My life really began to mean something when I was eight years old and learned how to write on an electric typewriter . . . with the big toe of my left foot and Nana's help, I've been able to go to school. I went to *primaria* at the Centro de Rehabilitación on Calle Mariano Escobedo, and even then I liked to write short compositions. After that I went to a public *secundaria* — No. 68 in Tlacopac, San Ángel — and I got my high school diploma at Preparatoria No. 6 in Coyoacán.* I had to make a huge effort to get into a public *secundaria* — they didn't want to let me in because of my physical limitations. I write poems without paying attention to rules or to rhyme. I get my anger out in my poems and vent my rebelliousness. Being rebellious is not at all easy when — as in my case — you depend on other people for almost everything, but I still come out and say I'm a rebel. I feel rebellious toward all injustice, toward systems and people who exploit others, toward world poverty, and above all toward myself when I don't want to or can't achieve a goal. Finally, I feel an immense rebelliousness toward people who want to make me look useless."

Gaby's mother made the rounds of hospitals, institutes, residences; she sought treatments and bought ultramodern equipment that perhaps would enable her daughter to take a few steps. One of her great worries — which became more evident in 1967 when her husband, Miguel, died of a heart attack — has always been "Where will Gaby live when I die?" There isn't a single place in Mexico for people with cerebral palsy except for the APAC (Asociación pro Personas con Parálisis Cerebral, or Cerebral Palsy Association), which offers classes until five o'clock in the evening; the DIF** has a rehabili-

---

* San Ángel and Coyoacán are both districts of southern Mexico City, and Tlacopac is a neighborhood in San Ángel.
** Desarrollo Integral de la Familia (Family Development Agency), a government-run social services and public assistance agency.

tation center, and there are associations for the handicapped in Cuernavaca and Guadalajara, but who will take responsibility for someone who represents a physical and financial burden if much of the time the parents won't even do so? Sari's sister and brother-in-law, Betty (a doctor) and Otto Modley, offered to support Gaby if she moved to San Francisco, California, where there are more possibilities for handicapped people. Gaby did not accept, but in 1973 she did have to yield to the combined pressure from her family to build her a small apartment at the Jewish Home for the Aged in Cuernavaca. There she would live out her days with Sari and Florencia. Gaby puts it this way: "I finally had to agree to go to Cuernavaca out of fear that my family wouldn't understand me. I thought they'd get more offended, and that we'd lose contact with Papá Otto and Mamá Betty, although I knew well that the one who would suffer most from that kind of rift would be my mother, who depends on them a lot — and I didn't want to cause her any more suffering. I caused them plenty of suffering by being born this way and by being a rebel in spite of it all. Although of course it was no one's fault that I was born this way:

Mamá, papá,
why was I born?
Because we were egotists
and wanted to fill vacuums,
and besides — and here's
the big contradiction —
you were born of the love
between the two of us.

"I wrote this same poem in a different way, in order to keep my parents from having to answer directly and not hold them responsible.

Mamá, papá,
why was I born?
Because we were egotists
and wanted to fill vacuums.

I was the big contradiction
born of the love between
two people.

"Typographically, this poem is an arrowhead."
Cerebral palsy is an irreversible injury within the central nervous system

that can occur during pregnancy, due to infections such as measles or German measles, the blood's Rh factor, diabetes, ingestion of chrome, exposure to X-rays, poor nutrition, the use of forceps during delivery, respiratory obstruction, asphyxia, inadequate anesthesia, and placenta previa (particularly in premature births). A child with cerebral palsy generally cannot walk or does not walk well, and in most cases cannot take care of itself; that is, a child with cerebral palsy cannot feed or dress itself or go to the bathroom on its own, and what is worse, it cannot communicate. Cerebral palsy is not progressive or hereditary, nor is it a defect to be ashamed of. It is not contagious; however, of every thousand babies born in Mexico, four are born with cerebral palsy, and despite this terrifying bit of information, only 250,000 cases in the entire country have been recognized and reported, which means that many families are hiding their handicapped children. Carmelina Ortiz Monasterio de Molina, who has a daughter with cerebral palsy (eighteen-year-old Beati, the seventh of nine children, the rest of whom are perfectly healthy), directs the only center in Mexico City that offers education programs for people with cerebral palsy, from kindergarten through high school, as well as rehabilitative therapy, outings, parties, and dances, all in an atmosphere of love and complete acceptance. Other rehabilitation centers mix hydrocephalics, mongoloids, and the mentally retarded — and cerebral palsy is not mental retardation. But doctors tend to make incorrect judgments and are often harsh with parents of children who have cerebral palsy. "Forget that you and your husband had this baby," a famous neurologist in Houston told Carmelina. "Put her in an institution, she's like a vegetable." This proves how ignorant the "supposed experts" are about cerebral palsy and the absence of human qualities.

Carmelina, her husband, and their six older children all agreed that they could assimilate the problem sadly and happily (even though it sounds contradictory), and live a normal family life, in which each member of the family — including the household help — gave and continues to give something special to Beati, and Beati in turn contributes to and enriches the life of each one. Beati's cerebral palsy moved Carmelina to agree to continue the work of the APAC, which had been founded eight years before by a group of mothers whose children had cerebral palsy. Currently, 125 people attend APAC programs and receive services there, from children to young adults, ranging in age from four months to thirty years. The expenses for each person total three thousand pesos a month, and the therapists and equipment are very expensive. However, treatment and education are provided to everyone with the same degree of care, and financial or social position play no part at all. APAC's doctors, psychologists, and teachers try to integrate children with cerebral palsy into normal schools and show that they can do different types of work, even though they do it slowly. But however slowly they work, they approach all their tasks more responsibly than so-called normal people do. (At the APAC, for example, the students make thousands of children's toys, and none has turned out to be defective.)

The reason that cerebral palsy is an irreversible injury to the brain's motor centers is because brain cells never regenerate, which is why Carmelina Ortiz Monasterio places so much emphasis on prevention during pregnancy. In the United States, analysis of amniotic fluid prior to birth has succeeded in reducing the number of babies born with cerebral palsy by 40 percent. But Mexican doctors do not tend to pay attention to this risk. When a famous gynecologist was asked to join APAC's medical board, he answered, "I can't, I don't know anything about cerebral palsy." No gynecologist has the right not to know if four out of every thousand children in our country are born with it. In Mexico, as in the United States, congenital cerebral palsy could be eliminated by a mass publicity campaign about the kind of care the mother should have during pregnancy, which would leave only the risk to which all of us are exposed: that of becoming handicapped by cerebral palsy due to an accident. The accident can be a very high, prolonged fever, meningitis, or a blow to the head. The degree of cerebral palsy depends on what part of the brain is injured. However, it is not at all related to mental retardation, which Carmelina repeats over and over again, because many people with cerebral palsy have superior intelligence.

The first time I saw Gaby, I didn't even dare to look at her. I was disconcerted by her spasms, by the fact that she would arch up in her chair or throw her head all the way back, as though her entire body were coming apart. But the way she looked at me so trustingly, so warmly, and above all so joyfully made me seek out her eyes, made me draw strength from them. I always found her eyes to be receptive, loving, without the slightest bit of suspicion. And — which I thought was wonderful — without the slightest hint of bitterness. After the interview I went to visit her again, and she began writing to me: letters, poems, whatever had happened that week. For Gaby, writing on her

"Che" — as she christened her typewriter — is what gives her life meaning. "What would I do without you, Che?" That's how this book began, and that's how I hope others will follow. Needless to say, writing is a tremendous effort for Gaby, and at the age of ten she soon faced a crisis of conscience, when she discovered the world of study. "I had to choose," she told me, "between studying and continuing to rehabilitate my body, because I'm not strong enough to do both. During the years when I was in physical therapy, Nana and I would be so tired when we got done that we couldn't study. One day I wrote to Aunt Betty asking her what would happen if I didn't do anything about my scoliosis. Would my body look more ugly? And even more important, would I be running the risk of more pain?" Gaby is constantly racked by convulsive movements that force her up in her chair; even if they don't hurt, the constant pain in her neck certainly does. She wears a kind of wide orthopedic collar around her neck that helps her keep her head up. But of course, the collar prevents her from seeing what she's writing. "I told Betty," Gaby continues, "about one of my friends, Arturo Gómez, who had to choose between physical therapy and his studies, and he decided he'd rather study. Not long after that, a doctor told him he should have an operation, and I was afraid he wouldn't be able to take it physically or psychologically, not to mention having to be in bed for eight months, in a cast. I'm afraid something just like that could happen to me. I talked with Arturo about whether we had the right to ask our parents to always be doing things for us, and he said, 'Gaby, I know perfectly well that I'm gradually wearing my parents out, but . . . what else can we do if we depend on them even to go to the bathroom? Besides, we have to live our life now, because eventually there won't be anyone — no Mamá or Papá — who'll take care of us because they love us.' Finally, I decided to study because what books would be able to give me, nobody else could. Betty backed me up, although every so often she'd get after me to exercise. I definitely knew that studying came easier to me than exercising — people almost always do what comes easier to them, even if later they realize they've made a mistake.

"In *secundaria*, I began to write about myself more. The typewriter Uncle Otto gave me broke, and I started using a brand-new one that I named 'Che' in honor of Comandante Ernesto 'Che' Guevara. On the wall across from where I write, I have a poster of Che, and his eyes look at me and say, 'Enough of writing stupid things about yourself! Do something for the lives of everyone else.' I know perfectly well that Che's dead. That's why I've made a commitment to him, and I repeat it over and over, 'Wherever death happens to find us, it's welcome.' What is death? If I know about Che's thoughts from reading his books, and his black eyes are looking out at me from that photo, then I know he's not dead. That's why I want to leave something of myself in a book too, so that when I die, I'm not completely gone. My mother has warned me, 'Don't forget that for many people he and his followers were just a bunch of thugs.' I smile and think, 'And the people who killed him — what are they?'

"It's been twelve years since Che was murdered. Others have come after him, and now Facundo Cabral and his song 'América del Sur' remind me of him more and more.

"'You look at me and I see you, Che Guevara.'"

Gaby can write for three or even four hours straight. Florencia puts the typewriter on the floor for her, next to the window overlooking the garden. Gaby types five or six pages, letter by letter, with the big toe of her left foot. When I express my admiration, she says, "I'm no hero — it's life that's pushing me." She writes almost every day because she keeps a diary and corresponds with friends and family, some of whom are crippled. Her foot is small and delicate, and she moves it very skillfully. One day she got the idea of starting a conversation in writing with her "Che," and that's how she began a dialogue with herself, a kind of psychoanalysis. As she sits in front of the typewriter, Gaby tries to face her problems without fear. She has the strength of will to criticize herself and enough knowledge of psychology to analyze herself systematically. Now Gaby wants to try to study for a degree in literature at the Open University.* For a while she thought about studying psychology, but just recently she declared, "I don't think everything has to be analyzed. You lose the mystery of life and of what it means to be human." Whether she gets her literature degree will depend on the publication of this book, on Florencia's health, and on the way Alma develops, as she'll be starting kindergarten in two years. For now, Gaby has started an exercise-based physical therapy program again. She made the decision barely six months ago, when her spasms got so violent that she was incapacitated for a month and could only make it through the day — the long journey from morning until night — on Valium. But the Valium would make

*A division of the Universidad Nacional Autónoma de México (National Autonomous University of Mexico, or UNAM) that offers coursework and degrees through individualized tutorials and — in the Internet age — online programs.

her depressed, even in tiny doses, like 2.5 milligrams. Then she would try to escape everything by going to sleep, but when she woke up she didn't feel well, and she'd complain to Florencia, "Why did you let me go to sleep? Why?"

Here is an example of how Gaby writes in complete freedom and vents her feelings to the point of swearing when she talks with her Che: "Alone with my Che, I ask him, 'What do you want to talk about?' About what kinds of sons of bitches we all are, every last one of us? About the little wooden bird that makes such a dumb-looking decoration on the table where I have my plants? About how gloomy it is to have a day without a tiny ray of sunshine that would bring a little comfort to our souls? Or about the bitter expression on Mamá's face when she has to take care of me because Nana took a well-deserved chance to go out? A mother who, although she understands her daughter and supports her in everything, doesn't know that she hurts me with her passionate, temperamental personality, because in order not to make her suffer more, I have to squelch many nearly uncontainable feelings of aggression, rebelliousness, and rage, and hide my tears of anger? My brother doesn't want to cut the umbilical cord with my mother, and this ties him down more every day. Right this very minute she's thinking about a trip to San Francisco to see her little boy. Let her go, but let her stop being such a pain in the ass with her long faces and her sad stare, because I hide my bitter expressions whenever I can!"

> Father, come quickly, for my love is running out
> it wears away like life
> hurry, my father, because life is ebbing out of me,
> it spills harshly
> in the corners,
> it gets stuck on any nail,
> the maid sweeps it away
> the first time she cleans in the morning.
>
> Come father, come.
> Not coming would mean
> letting a sun burn out,
> my sun that was shining
> and giving off its light
> only
> because of you.

"Days ago I woke up happy because there was a possibility I could start writing for a small newspaper in Cuernavaca that Esperanza Figueroa, my geography teacher in *preparatoria*, had recommended me to. She has never turned her back on me. As soon as I gave this good news to Sara, my mother, the first words out of her mouth were: 'If you send them your poems, they'll steal them.' How am I ever going to feel secure about anything if my own mother doesn't make me feel secure? Hmm? And then, Che, they don't want me to boast about it, because if I'm very happy, my morale could go down in less than the blink of an eye? Why doesn't she keep her damn deep-down pessimism to herself?

"What's serious is that I blow up at her too. I get angry, I hurt her, and I vent my bitterness and my resentment of life on her. Then I'd like to heal her devastated face, make the wounded look in her eyes and the trembling in her lips disappear, but she goes off to do all the things she has to do, and when she comes back we start a new conversation. I wish my father had never died his stupid death! He was the one who really made me feel secure, and whenever I saw him I would feel like other people couldn't be bad. But what else could I ask of my poor mother—who tries to support me in everything—and of Nanita, who lives for me?

"Besides, when I see wars, the political situation in Latin America, the fall and death of Allende, betrayal, Guatemala, Argentina, Brazil, Uruguay, Nicaragua with that pig Somoza, Vietnam craftily invaded by China, it makes me feel like turning off the TV and sitting in the dark, going back to being a fetus in order to take refuge in my mother's warm womb . . ."

Naturally what Gaby reads is connected with the National University and the university atmosphere. That is the source of her fixation on student heroes like Che Guevara, Camilo Torres, and Genaro Vásquez Rojas, of her knowledge of Tlatelolco and all those events that were so important to Mexico, of her participation in the 1968 student movement. Her attitude toward life is the result of two major influences: one, the fact that Florencia Morales Sánchez, her Nana, has devoted her life to her; and two, her father's Marxism. For that very reason she feels much more accepted among the poor, who have no expectations, than when she ventures to the entertainment spots, cinemas, and theaters frequented by Mexico's middle class. There the rejection is patent. And forget about going to a restaurant. Everyone ends up looking at her as though she were from another planet—whenever they don't have their noses stuck in their plates, with an unhappy expression on their faces.

What is wonderful about her mother, Sari Brimmer, is her total acceptance not necessarily of Gaby herself but of Gaby's criticisms of her character and her attitudes, of her intolerable (according to Gaby) pessimism, and of her being so neurotic. Sari's unconscious motto seems to be "I suffer, therefore I am." If she's not suffering, she doesn't feel she's alive. Her masochism is the breath of life. Yet Sari is the head of the household, the one who takes responsibility. I have seen her care for Gaby, hanging on her every word, taking her on her own to hear a concert at the Sala Nezahualcóyotl,* without the help of Nana Florencia. I have seen them argue, mother and daughter, and seen the laughter dancing in their eyes. Gaby laughs with her and her sweet face laughs too, the laughter makes her entire body shake, laughter all day, everywhere, laughter bringing her to life, because laughter is a part of life and Gaby has chosen it and Gaby wants to smile at you, she wants to smile through her spasms, through the pain in her neck, in her throat. Yet in her eyes, curiously enough, there is humor. That is when I can easily imagine her playing with David under the covers, when he used to call her "Miss Gabardina," and their parents tried to get them both to listen to classical music. I imagine her with her nose that turns up at the end, wrinkling when she laughs, and her round, mischievous little face, a little imp who loves to tease, ready to play joke after joke for the pure joy of being able to burst out laughing.

Music is as much a part of Gaby as it was of Christy Brown, the author of the two books *Down All the Days* and *My Left Foot*. *My Left Foot* has particular meaning for Gaby because it is Brown's autobiography, the story of an Irish boy who is now more than forty years old, from a very large family (he was one of twenty-two, of whom thirteen lived past infancy) and poor; his father was a bricklayer and his mother an admirable woman who — between loads of laundry, cooking, taking care of her family, and her husband's heavy drinking — devoted herself to integrating Christy, her only sick child, into life. Very well, he was not like her other children, but he was HER child, HER baby, she gave birth to him, the doctors have told her that he is a hopeless case, that he will never be able to live on his own. Some say his defect is hereditary and that he will be that way until his dying day. His mother took these blows and remained absolutely certain that her child was not mentally retarded. Despite all the evidence and with no basis whatsoever for her opinion, Christy Brown's

*A concert hall on the campus of the UNAM.

mother was convinced that the life of this little boy — whose head rolled back uncontrollably, whose limbs seemed like frayed cables shot through every so often by a horrible electrical charge — had meaning. She KNEW, that's all. That is how Christy Brown, who could only make guttural sounds, who drooled, and who had no way of moving around except for dragging himself on the floor, was initiated into life. His brothers and sisters — showing how wise children can be — took him everywhere in a homemade wagon, which is how he participated in the children's games in his neighborhood: going fishing in the river, playing ball, running races in the street, stealing apples from the trees and then running away. Christy Brown, lying in his wagon, is an important figure. He guards the treasures. They hide the stolen fruit under his shoulders, they put the ball there. Even though he can't run with the rest of them, Christy has fun with everything, he feels good, until one day he notices the first sympathetic gaze and asks himself, "What's the matter with me?" Until one day the wagon breaks too, and Christy Brown asks himself over and over, "What's wrong with me? Why aren't I like everyone else?" A lot of time goes by until his parents can buy him a wheelchair; Christy's personality changes, and when the longed-for chair arrives, Christy doesn't want to go out with his brothers and sisters any more. He can't stand people seeing him. He would rather be alone than arouse the compassion of others. Besides, he has discovered something he hadn't known about until now: music. Sitting next to the radio, Christy decides that the music he likes best is what his family hates, which is "classical" music. Even his mother grumbles "You and your mad music" when she sees him. But Christy drags himself on the floor to be near the radio, and there he listens, almost in a trance, to the slow, majestic, noble sound that to his ears is almost unbearable because it is so beautiful. The music sinks into the handicapped boy and strikes a chord deep within him, making him tremble in a sort of ecstasy. Music opens the doors to a new, undreamed-of world, an infinite world, as though a fountain of unknown water were welling up within him. Music brings tears to his eyes, music makes him change. After the last notes have died down, they still resonate in the air for Christy Brown. He stays there for a long time, next to the radio (now turned off), and only gradually does he find his way back to the everyday world. For the first time, Christy Brown knows that there is something that can pull him out of himself, make him forget his crooked face, hands, and arms, and his useless legs.

Little by little Christy Brown's brothers and sisters (twelve, remember?) grow up, put on suits and dresses, fall in love, go out with their first boyfriends or girlfriends. Christy watches all of them from his chair; attentive to family life, he is the first to find out what time they got back from the dance that night, who they are in love with, why the blue outfit and not the everyday one, why the long sessions in front of the mirror to slick back their hair. He was to collect all of this in his book *Down All the Days*; but to give you an idea, he paints with his left foot, gives his paintings away, draws pictures and then colors them in, and does it with such skill that he wins a contest in the *Independent* newspaper. For the first time, a member of the Brown family was in the paper, and all of them were proud.

The reason I'm talking so much about Christy Brown is because there is a parallel between him and Gaby. The only part of his body that responds to the orders emanating from his brain is his left foot; they both paint, they both knit, they both write, they have both struggled like wild beasts to get people to notice them. Gaby, of course, has had to face greater obstacles, because being a woman is not the same as being a man; maleness fosters creativity, femaleness hinders it; being a writer in Ireland is not the same as being a writer in Mexico. Christy Brown has married; Gaby, as a woman, awaits the arrival of her period every month, which depresses her and makes her lose three to five days of stability and work. Yet getting her period makes her like other women on earth, which not only makes Gaby very proud but makes her mother proud as well, and she takes things a step further: "If Gaby wanted to have a child of her own, I would help her. I would be with her during that time, no matter what happened, because if my daughter gets her period, she can conceive." In the days before she gets her period, Gaby gets very nervous, very touchy, everything irritates her — but that is what most of us women are like, isn't it? More sensitive. Apart from that, Gaby has always wanted to have a child, and in 1977 she was at last able to adopt a little girl — Alma Florencia — six hours after she was born. This does not keep her from continuing to read and write, although it would help her considerably to find someone to read to her. "I have never read Marx," Sari tells me, "but Gaby, on the other hand, knows his work." When she was seventeen, Gaby announced, "I think that studying is the only possible occupation for me, and I'm never going to stop." Sari proudly brandishes before my eyes the philosophy of Spinoza, which is what Gaby is reading these days, while on the bookshelf flash the titles of the books that Gaby always comes back to: Tolstoy, Dostoyevsky, García Márquez, Mao, Octavio Paz, Rosario Castellanos, Bertrand Russell, Father Camilo Torres, Jung, Max Weber's "Politics as a Vocation" and "Science as a Vocation," Freud, Carlos Fuentes's *Aura*, García Lorca, Kafka's *The Metamorphosis*, Pablo González Casanova's *Democracy in Mexico*, Jorge L. Tamayo's *Geografía económica y política* [Political and economic geography], *Redil de ovejas* [A flock of sheep], by Vicente Leñero, and *Pedro Páramo*, by Juan Rulfo. Einstein, his hair white and wild, smiles down from the wall. In addition to what she reads for her classes at the university, other books have had an impact on Gaby, such as the biography of Helen Keller — though much less than one might think. Gaby never slips into the swamp of self-pity. I would never have dared, for example, to bring up Dalton Trumbo's film *Johnny Got His Gun* with her. But one day she mentioned it, quite naturally, stopping at the part that had impressed her the most: when Johnny beats his head on the pillow in Morse code, repeating "Kill me, kill me, kill me!" and she told me, "This film has helped all handicapped people in the world be treated better. Besides, there is no antiwar testimony more convincing than *Johnny Got His Gun*."

Gaby's thoughts are powerful, although the most vulnerable part of her body — the part that is most exposed because it is so visible, because it makes her lack of control so obvious — are her hands. Christy Brown also complained about his hands; he would look at his brother Peter's hands, dark, strong, meaty, with fingers that could grab whatever they wanted, and then he would compare them to his own, which seemed odd and gnarled, with constantly twisting fingers that made them look like two snakes. Gaby tightens her hands into a fist, they are small and soft. Everything about Gaby is delicate and refined, but even better is that small foot that obeys her commands and has a tendency to jump mischievously onto my skirt so that I can caress it and she in turn can caress me. That is also the way she caresses her daughter, Alma Florencia: "and you saw how she lets me caress her with my foot when she needs to feel love, because she's the one who makes the rules about when she wants to receive or give affection; when she doesn't, she takes off in her baby walker, and then I know she doesn't want me to touch her at all." One thing that particularly struck me — perhaps because if I have it, I don't put it to use — is Gaby's inner freedom. Even though her condition makes her very dependent, Gaby does not grab onto anything, any support, to go on living, except perhaps her love for her two mothers, Sari and Florencia, from whom she also draws the strength to rebel: "The two of them forget that I have *my* life too." Sari is a typical Jewish mother, overprotective, anxious because she can't do more, worried about the future, about the high cost of living, about money, about everyday life, about the failure she thinks her life amounts to. Florencia thinks she always knows what is best for Gaby. Gaby has stayed admirably independent, and what largely saves her is her sense of humor, the product of a clear, sharp intelligence:

"Good heavens! Did you see what your mamá hung up where you have the little cross from Arturo?"

"Yes, I realized it this morning when I woke up. She put a Star of David there.

"Tomorrow is Sunday and maybe I'll go to church, but not to pay attention to the sermon, which always goes in one ear and out the other. I'll go to feel tremendously small, to be able to be with my creator, to argue with him and with myself, to look around me, to compare lives, and to leave there more calm and rebellious than I was when I came. I go to a church when I feel like . . .

"Shut up your big trap," Gaby writes in English, "don't write what you are thinking, you have to go on living."

Yes, Gaby has wanted to die, to not wake up, especially when she takes an antihistamine for a sore throat and it makes her depressed. Once she wrote this to me on the alphabet board, but not without deliberately making a joking little face to go along with it: "But you see, Elena, there's no way I could even kill myself. Whose hands would I use?" And then she added, "Don't worry, I love life very much, life has given me a lot. But you know, the only perfect crime is suicide, and [she smiles from ear to ear] sometimes I'd like to commit a perfect crime. . . . You could be the detective.

"In the end, I pray: 'Thy will be done,' so tough luck, I'll live until He says. But when I want to be as sincere as I can, I feel the genuine need to say 'My will be done,' even if it's only for a few hours. On the other hand, it's never happened, and I'm not always willing to play dumb. Of course I know that I'm responsible for myself before Him, and that I don't have to answer to anybody but Him.

"How far will my awareness and I get? Why the hell do I think I'm going to fail before I even get started? That's enough, I'll start studying, writing a poem — I don't want to be a parasite. It's been an hour since I've given or gotten anything.

> I am seeking God, but
> I cannot find Him
> perhaps He is in the sun
> perhaps in a flower
> or in a kiss
> in this fly sitting
> on the wall,
> in the well,
> near the wool.
> Where is He?
> In a person,
> in a note,
> in a cry,
> in love,
> in an embrace
> in our conscience
> in a planet far away
> beyond my window,
> in the light
> in the air
> where is He?
> Why doesn't He answer?
> Mother
> bring me the flyswatter.

"Ever since I was a little girl, I've gone to church truly believing in Him, but I didn't say so because I was afraid my parents would criticize me, since they brought us up outside of any kind of religion. I memorized the prayers I heard Nana saying, and I would feel as though a little of Christ were penetrating into me. Whenever I went into a church, I'd want to make myself invisible in order to feel more alone and be able to pray better. The first thing I would ask Christ to do was free me from the wheelchair that ties me down so much. I grew up, Christ was eternally crucified, and I understood that he was not God, but a man on earth, and that in his name millions of lives were destroyed; men, women, and children have been killed in his name in religious wars. People still kill in Christ's name today, and I didn't want anything more to do with him. But oh God! How difficult it is to live without something to comfort you and without a support that is stronger than you are! Without my realizing it, a tiny bit of faith in God stayed within me. I demonstrated my faith by constantly wanting to be close to nature and to be alone with it, quiet, meditating in order to feel the communication with Him. What was I thinking within that voluntary solitude as I faced the Creator, underneath a tree or looking out to sea? I simply let my imagination loose, let it run immensely free, like a seagull, which despite its rules of group living, can cross the sea and get to land. Alone."

> God
> where are You,
> that I do not feel You
> in my being?

> God
> I cry out to you,
> I want to take refuge in your arms.

> God
> I seek you everywhere
> in a young man's arms and caresses
> in a child's tenderness
> in the power of one of Violeta Parra's protest songs
> in "the glory of your Son."

> And you, God
> Why do you not come to greet me?
> Where are you?
> I have been seeking you for a long time, my Love.

"Last night I announced, 'If I were a man, I would have become a rabbi.' I don't know why I said that if I feel cut off from Judaism — maybe it was so I wouldn't get into another argument with Mamá. I've noticed that if I talk about Christ with love and respect, she immediately counters with 'Jehovah, the God of Gods.' I've explained to the old lady that if you don't love and respect Jehovah, you won't love and respect Christ either. So to keep her from bringing up more questions, I talk about being a rabbi, but actually it doesn't matter to me, and neither does the priesthood or any of those damn things. I sincerely believe that all pathways lead to God. Cut off from Judaism? Well, I can't say I'm not because I don't know what it is. My mother's connected to Israel and other weird stuff, she goes on and on about Israel, my cousins Dinah and Miriam have also gotten involved in Judaism, and now she'd like me to get involved too. But if it was so important to her, why didn't she give me an education that emphasized Judaism more? Maybe because my father was a Marxist, but for all his Marxism, he wasn't a bad Jew. I, on the other hand, am not a good Jew. I've never gone to my father's grave, which is in the Jewish cemetery, and I don't even feel like going. I'd rather have an image of him alive than see a depressing grave where his wonderful brain is rotting."

As far as Catholicism goes, Gaby does not accept the communion of saints, the power of suffering, the redemption of humanity through pain, the glory achieved after crossing this vale of tears, or bearing our daily cross on each and every one of our shoulders. She doesn't agree, for example, with Carmelina Ortiz Monasterio de Molina: "When Carmelina says that that we handicapped people were put here so all of you could be cleansed and who knows what other kinds of crap, she's making God into a being that sacrifices thousands of His children so that a few can achieve 'glory.' This concept doesn't fit with the image I have of God or with what I've learned in the Bible — but I'm wrong about that, because in the Bible, Yahweh is a god of anger, not of goodness." Nor does Gaby agree with Carmelina when she tells the story of how her eighteen-year-old daughter Beati, who has cerebral palsy, was with a group of young people talking about abortion one day, and during the most intense part of the conversation, Beati got her alphabet board and wrote, "I am thankful that I was born." One of her friends replied, his eyes filled with tears, "Beati, I swear to you that I will never say anything in favor of abortion again." Gaby says that Beati's case (as does her own) represents a privileged example among thousands of people who have been relegated to the last room in the house, the pigsty that is farthest away, without the slightest possibility of a life that is human, let alone normal. Gaby does not accept the notion that handicapped people have been entrusted with a mission to make the world a balanced place, to humanize it. She gets angry: "That's nonsense!"

She rejects Carmelina's dictum that, "There is no pain in the world nor any tear cried that does not create beauty and goodness." Gaby does not want to be one of those who suffers and weeps so that others can be saved and go to heaven by taking care of them. She pushes her little foot furiously in all directions: "What ought to be prevented is that an illness as terrible as cerebral palsy happens at all."

If Gaby Brimmer does not cling to Judaism or Catholicism — though she may invoke God fairly frequently — what does she cling to? Her mother, Sari, and her Nana Florencia, but she does not cling to them the way misfortune clings to the world. Rather, she keeps a critical distance, allowing herself to pronounce judgment on one or the other. Every so often she rants and raves at her two mothers, and what she says about the one who gave birth to her can seem especially harsh. Yet — amazingly enough — both Sari and Florencia accept Gaby's opinion. They do not try to influence her; neither one feels like a heroine, and nobody plays at sacrifice. The absolute mental clarity of these three women prevents them from playing any role. No one tries to be worthy of admiration; there is no St. Teresa of the Child Jesus here, although Florencia's humanity and sweetness, her absolute devotion, may border on sainthood. Nor is there any Joan of Arc fitting herself out: Sari comes and goes; she does not hear voices, she does not think about consecrating herself to anything, no celestial music resounds in her ears. As both of them put it, no concessions. As Florencia says, they do what life has in store for them, and that's all there is to it. Gaby's first audience may be me, after José Falconi's interview in the March 20, 1965, issue of the magazine *Mañana*. Gaby rails against her mother, but her mother doesn't just stand there either, and she often replies to one of Gaby's sharp remarks by saying, "Wait a minute, Gaby, just because you're outspoken does not necessarily mean that you're being fair." Sari argues and she defends herself, though sometimes she also acts like a little girl and ends up sticking out her tongue or making a face — a healthy, healthy, healthy gesture. Here every problem gets aired, nothing is held back for the confidante alias confessor. Sari has never subordinated herself to Gaby. Psychoanalysis takes place every day between the library, living room, and dining room, in the sunlight that comes in so beautifully through the picture windows.

Obviously Gaby is the center of the household, the embers in the hearth, the flame in the votive lamp. This is because Sari — like Christy Brown's mother — integrated Gaby into family life from the beginning. What's more, she made her the center of the family. Of course, Sari had more financial resources than Christy Brown's mother, and this enabled her to visit hospitals and seek treatment in the United States, where her two sisters, Betty and Ana, live. Without his mother, Christy Brown was in danger of becoming something to be fed and cleaned once in a while, and then hidden away again. Sari Brimmer's decision never to shunt her daughter aside was essential in Gaby's life. From Sari on down, everyone had to respect Gaby and come to terms with her. Once a visitor spoke only to Sari, believing that Gaby could not understand. Sari immediately stared hard at her daughter and asked her a question, and the confused visitor saw how Gaby would use the alphabet board to participate in the conversation, express her opinion, and give orders. Then Sari sat back in her easy chair, happy to have shown that although her daughter's body was lifeless, her mind was untouched. And it was of superior quality.

Six years ago, on April 22, 1973, Easter Sunday, my only sister Kitzia's son Alejandro was in a car accident near the El Dorado ranch, in Culiacán, Sinaloa. A minibus collided with the Volkswagen he was traveling in, and to get Alejandro out, they had to take off the door on the passenger side. Alejandro was seventeen years old. He was a tall, strong boy, and until then the most inquiring and intelligent of his five siblings. Now he is twenty-three. After the accident and the trepanation and tracheotomy that immediately followed, my sister began to make the rounds of hospitals with her injured son: first the Clínica Londres, then the Centro Médico, and finally the Institute for Social Security and Services for Public Employees Hospital for Incurables, in Tlalpan, at the southern edge of Mexico City. In every single one of them, they told her there was no hope; Dr. Guzmán West, the neurologist, said categorically, "He'd be better off dead." Another young doctor said that in the Hospital General they let accident victims like Alejandro die. "They die from stress ulcers or from one of countless internal hemorrhages. Besides, since there's no one to feed them, it's the best thing that could happen to them." Not a single doctor was optimistic; one advised Kitzia to put Alejandro in another institution for incurables where he could spend the rest of his life until "beneficent" death arrived. "He won't even realize it, he's lost a lot of awareness." How could they be so cruelly sure? My sister fought like a lioness. She never waited submissively in the hallway. All that stood between Alejandro and the doctors' death sentence was his mother. At the Centro Médico, Kitzia managed to get into the intensive care unit, which does not usually allow family members inside. She was there day and night, helping not only Alejandro but the other patients. One night at the Clínica Londres, during the first week, he had a hemorrhage. Kitzia called the blood bank, alerted the nurses on duty, and ordered a transfusion, and I watched her clean the black blood that kept coming out of Alejandro as though she were cleaning a newborn, with the steadiest and most loving expression on her face that I have ever seen. It has been one of the most important lessons of my life. She was so convinced that her son had to live that she inspired other people to feel an emotion that swung between respect and dismay. One fine day, she decided to take out all of Alejandro's catheters, and took sole responsibility for it. A month later, during the afternoons, next to Alejandro in the Hospital for Incurables (a gloomy hospital that was painted green, where there were more elderly people than young ones), I saw Kitzia write and write, quickly and feverishly. She was also reading poetry—Neruda, I think. It was her way of venting her emotions. Then I gave her a small paperback called *The Family of Man*, which depicts—step by step—all the expressions that make us precisely that: human beings. Laughter, tears, the birth of a child, the harvest season, death; a little book that includes a photograph showing portraits of two elderly couples on a wall, and below them, all lined up, are their children and their grandchildren, and their great-grandchildren and their great-great-grandchildren: "You are my descendants." The book begins with the last fragment of Molly Bloom's soliloquy, from the end of Joyce's *Ulysses*: ". . . and then I asked him with my eyes to ask again yes and then he asked me would I yes . . . and first I put my arms around him yes and drew him down to me so he could feel my breasts all perfume yes and his heart was going like mad and yes I said yes I will Yes." Kitzia paged and paged through the book for days, until she left it a rag.

One day, at that same moldering, depressing hospital, I asked a doctor who was tying a kind of plaster and iron cast that could hold a body—legs, torso, arms, and neck—to a post, "My goodness, doctor, what is that?"

"We're going to have the patient in Bed 10 stand up today, and we're going to leave him standing for a few minutes."

"And Alejandro?"

"I'm afraid we won't get to that point with Alejandro."

A week later, my sister got a taxi and, without anyone helping her, took her son out of that place where people were waiting to die. She carried him in her arms as he lay across her lap like a Pietà, but she was not resigned, not one bit. No; her struggle was to begin at home, a struggle that is still going on, against doctors, nurses, clergy who speak to her of Christian acceptance. She turned Alejandro's bedroom into the main meeting place, the center of the house. She would come home from the store and empty her bags onto his hospital bed so he could see what she had bought; she put on music for him, turned on the television, put out stuffed toys, put up flowered curtains; every time the phone rang, she would say, "It must be for you" and bring the receiver close to him. She talked to him about everything, her comings and goings, her argument with some policeman, and — more than anything — jokes; joke after joke. She made his bedroom the most important room in the house, a haven: the first room you walked into, the only one with a real purpose, the center of the universe. Alejandro began to smile. All he could do was move the two big fingers of his right hand. Kitzia drew an alphabet board for him, and today Alejandro uses his fingers to show what he would like and what he wants very badly. He lives in Houston now, and I haven't seen him for two years. Perhaps this is why I went to see Gaby and wanted to meet her when she sent for me. I could not ignore an indirect call — or maybe a very direct call — from Alejandro.

We are so accustomed to having human communication proceed according to established norms, along paths already taken, that we do not explore any alternatives. With Alejandro and Gaby, I discovered that there were alternatives, and that they are powerful and leave a profound impression. I remember certain times at the hospital, when I stayed very quietly next to Alejandro, silent and not moving. All we did was look at each other, and we knew we loved each other infinitely. I had the impression that Alejandro was more attentive than other people, people who were always in a rush, scattered, longing to go out to their different activities or diversions. Being confined makes people with cerebral palsy expectant and receptive. They have a superior capacity for concentration, like Gaby, who has hours and hours to reflect, hours of solitude next to the window, staring at the glass overlooking the garden, the way a technician keeps staring at the Moviola in order to back the film up, stop it on a certain image, run it again, run it at top speed in order to incite laughter. Gaby has a tremendous need to feel that she is being looked at by other eyes; the river of her childhood winds along, sometimes bringing back her father, other times her brother, her Aunt Betty and Uncle Otto, or Luis del Toro. Whole days go by in which Gaby does not ask for the alphabet board because she is recharging, like a battery; during these days of solitude, she is always remembering; it is her way of staying alive, but also her way of making decisions for the future. So too in the Alejandro I saw there was something thoughtful and immanent that made him seem more present, more essential, more attentive to daily life and to the life of the person talking with him than everyone else who was supposedly safe and sound.

In my encounter with Gaby, Florencia, and Sari, I perceived something of the burning bush; the accumulation of energy was too great, I could not allow them to envelop me. When I published my interview, I thought: "Well, that's that, the interview came out, I have my burden to carry too, Gaby's situation has no relation to mine." I went home wanting to put my children back into my womb, in order to inoculate them. But Gaby's face pursued me, and her letters started coming. I told some friends about my experience with Gaby, and later about the commitment I'd taken on: the book. "But what does this have to do with literature? Do you think you can make things any better for her? If not, why are you getting involved? Start writing, work on your own things, why are you being a good Samaritan? You're only doing it so you don't have to confront your own life, your novel, your writing — not other people's." Or more radical conclusions: "The Greeks used to throw cripples from the Tarpeian Rock and never worry about them again." "Don't have anything to do with sick people. Don't you see they wear you down?" or "Why are you letting yourself get involved again in something that has nothing to do with literature or with the creative act of writing?" I listened to the voices and obeyed the order, but Gaby's face would keep appearing to me in the front seat, the passenger's seat, and I would remember Alejandro's accident. One day, in December 1978, Sari called in despair: "It has been nearly two years," and her voice was breaking, "and no book. Gaby is going to be thirty-two years old. This is not possible, it is not fair." I felt bad. Sari was right.

Today, Gaby only finds people to read to her once in a while. With the adoption of Alma Florencia, Nana is busier. Perhaps the publication of the book *Gaby Brimmer* will give the seagull (as I usually call her) the presence of potential readers, friends willing to visit her, because as Sari says, "They come once, but they do not come back." Perhaps also *Gaby Brimmer* will open the eyes of the able-bodied to the thousands of handicapped people we shunt aside because we think they don't know what is going on around them. I know that people who are untouched by prejudice will come to see Gaby, people who are not deterred by her convulsive movements. Beyond the spasms, the useless arms, the wheelchair, is a strong and intelligent young woman, a terrific person who's really with it, truly beautiful, beautiful of body and soul — do you see her? With an impish little face, just like when she was a little girl; a girl who knows how to give life a good fight from her wheelchair, a girl whose green eyes say everything she does not put into words, a girl who knows that life is a risk and has wanted to take that chance, a girl who holds out her hands and head to you, a head full of flowers.

PART I

There's a person sitting across from me. I can see her in the windowpane; I know who she is, even though I don't always recognize her. She's slender and short; her eyes, which tell you everything about her soul, are amber or green, depending on what she's wearing. She's got a very nice figure, and all she needs is to be able to show it off. One hundred percent woman. The last detail of her physical appearance is a braid she's just had cut off. Oh, and I forgot to tell you she's in a wheelchair. (I forget this insignificant little detail because she herself forgets it at times.)

Who am I?
I'm a product of my time,
I'm a slave to the motor,
the motor in a car, in a blender,
in my T V set,
I like getting on airplanes
and listening to the sound a tractor makes
listening to the music right here
and I'm thinking of
putting a motor
in my chair.

Because of the Rh factor in my parents' blood, I was born with cerebral palsy. When they realized what had happened, they rushed me into physical rehabilitation to see what my uncontrollable body was actually capable of.

SARI (the mother)
David was born very healthy, but when Gaby was born her body arched up like a bow. Never in my life had I seen a spasm or seen someone's body fold over in two. When I was pregnant, the doctor didn't do blood tests on Miguel

(my husband) or me, which might have saved Gaby because then she could just have been given a blood transfusion when she was born. Some doctors are like that. It's a matter of chance. I'd had a healthy son, so I never thought I would have another child who wasn't. Very soon, Miguel and I realized Gaby wasn't mentally retarded because she wanted to imitate everything her brother David did — controlling her sphincter muscles, asking for the potty — and, with great hope, we tried to help her. For me, the first sign that she was normal was the smile of satisfaction on her face when she finished her bottle, a smile just like any other baby's.

FLORENCIA *(the nana)*

She was a beautiful little girl, her hair pure gold, such a perfect little face, green eyes, with a nose that turned up at the end. But her hair — how I remember her hair! I started working for the Brimmers as a maid in 1949. Back then there was a nurse taking care of Gaby, and the other maids told me she'd gotten jaundice a week after she was born, she turned yellow, she was yellow all over, she would arch up, and she began to move every which way. Her parents took her to the doctor and he said: cerebral palsy.

Señora Brimmer always remembers that when I came here, I would only answer yes or no, and I didn't talk with them at all. She figured I wouldn't last too long because of that. The way I looked at it was that my work was my work, and that's what I was there to do. And that's all there was to it. I'm from Maquixco el Alto, a village in the state of Mexico. I came to Mexico City because people were so poor back home. All there is to live on is what you can harvest during the growing season. When it rains, the crops grow, there's corn and beans, and when it doesn't rain, there's nothing. We were very poor and there were so many of us, nine children altogether. My mother took us to Mexico City one by one so we could earn a living and not be such a burden to her. I went to work as a maid and laundress for Señora Brimmer, but when the nurse would go out, I'd stay with Gaby, and we started getting attached to each other. I was thirty years old then.

GABY

It was because of Florencia that they realized I could communicate what I was thinking by using my left foot, because I kicked the ball back when I was playing with her.

FLORENCIA
We'd sit Gaby down on a sheet on the floor and put sandbags around her so she wouldn't fall over. I'd throw the ball and she'd kick it back with her foot. That meant she could think! Right? She had a doll. She would take its clothes off with her left foot and try to put it in the water. A child who didn't have a brain wouldn't do that, would she?

SARI
Miguel accepted Gaby just the way she is. I was the one who was always exasperated. I never resigned myself to seeing her that way. She realized this right from the start, because very early on she would head for her father, who would pick her up and play with her like nothing was wrong. I was the one who yelled, who cried, who didn't accept it. I looked for medicine, doctors, specialists, some kind of cure. I made the rounds of the hospitals, I can tell you that! But Miguel simply loved her. I never had that capacity for acceptance; I thought something had to be done, that my daughter couldn't stay that way.

FLORENCIA
I liked to carry her because then no one realized what she had. I'd wrap her up partway in a blanket and take her outside. She'd stay perfectly straight, as straight as can be, and she liked to see everything. She had blue eyes, later they turned green. I'd get her dressed, I'd give her a bath, I'd put her in her little dresses, get her ready, sometimes I'd braid her hair. She was very pretty and very mischievous too. She was always mischievous, just like her brother.

SARI
I don't think I've ever forgotten, not even for an instant, that my daughter has cerebral palsy. That thought is with me all the time, like a knife through my heart.

FLORENCIA
I saw that she was a child who couldn't do anything without help from somebody, and it seemed natural to take her to the bathroom, take her out in the sun, feed her. I even began to talk with her, me, who's so shy, because with her I wasn't embarrassed to talk about what I was thinking. We'd chat, and I'd feel like she understood me.

SARI

The minute I realized Gaby was dressing and undressing her doll and could hit the ball back to me, that she wanted to be with her brother, that she was trying to take part in conversations, I picked up the telephone and called my sister Betty and brother-in-law Otto Modley, who live in San Francisco. They had read and studied thousands of pages about spastics. Since Betty is a doctor, she'd get tons of medical literature, all those scientific journals coming to her office. That's how they found out about a woman who was spastic (that is, who had cerebral palsy) who painted with her left foot. I remember that phone conversation with my sister as though it were yesterday. Betty and Otto both asked me to send Gaby to the United States because it would be easier to help her there.

GABY

Nobody asked for my opinion.

SARI

In the United States, I thought, maybe they'll teach her to eat with her hand. Here we used to tie a wooden-handled spoon to her little hand and make her lift it to her mouth. We did this with her left foot too, because she was very limber, and we worked with her for months and months, but we never got her to eat on her own. I said, "At least let her be able to feed herself on her own, at least let her be able to do that," and I took her to the United States with great hope.

GABY

My mother's two sisters live in San Francisco, California. Betty, the older one, is a doctor and lives with her husband, Otto, just the two of them, because their only son died twenty-four years ago. He was nine years old, very smart from what they tell me, and he got cancer just like that. Aunt Betty closed her office and did nothing but take care of him. She spent every minute with him until the inevitable happened. He died on October 2, 1953, and since that day Betty and Otto have devoted themselves to their nieces and nephews: my mother's children, David and me, and Aunt Ana's children, Miriam and Dinah. Before the tragedy, when I was eight months old, my mother took me to the United States for thousands of physical, neurological, and psychological tests to see what my chances for rehab were. We stayed with Betty, Otto, and my little cousin, Tommy. Then we went back to Mexico, my mother bursting with hope because now she knew her daughter was mentally healthy. Life went on as usual, and a year before Tommy got sick I went back to San Francisco to a school for handicapped children in Redwood City. I spent a year there, and every weekend my aunt and uncle and Tommy would pick me up and take me to their house. We'd go out somewhere, and then on Sunday afternoon they'd bring me back. Besides that, Betty would come to see me one day a week at the school, which was kind of far from town. From what they tell me, we had a farm with lots of animals, and I would almost always go around the court-yards and patios in my walker, watching how the baby chicks lived with the hens, the kittens with the mother cats. When I saw them all cuddled up under their mothers, I missed my own mother very much.

FLORENCIA

While Gaby was gone, I kept helping Señora Brimmer around the house, but of course I always missed her. When she came back from the United States, she was wearing braces from her hips to her feet. She could stand up with them on, and we would do walking exercises in the garden. She'd manage to take a few steps by herself, with Señora Brimmer or me helping her. We were always hoping she'd be able to walk.

SARI

Yes, both of us — Nani and me — had Gaby by the arm, one hand under each armpit, and there was a time, a very short time, when she walked. Nani and I would stand with our arms out so she wouldn't fall down, and she could go the whole way between my arms and Nani's. We did thousands of things that have simply been erased from my memory because of all the problems we had to solve every day.

FLORENCIA

Gaby eats everything, and she has ever since she was a child. Even chili pep-pers — she loves spicy food. The only things she doesn't like are eggplant and Jewish food, except for chicken soup with matzo balls, which is traditionally Jewish. Gaby's grandmother used to make delicious chicken soup with matzo balls for her, and she says she's never tasted any other soup like it. She loves food with chili even though it makes her cough, and she loves all kinds of Mexican food, like *mole*, and also tacos, tamales, and all those other *antojitos*.

SARI

I found out about the Cerebral Palsy Institute in Baltimore, and once again I was filled with hope. Betty and Otto offered to adopt Gaby so she could have all the advantages of a U.S. citizen, but I said, "What? If she was born to Miguel and me, it's the mother's and father's job and no one else's to take care of her. Everything plays a part: love, a little reasoning, who knows what else . . . still, when I found out about the Cerebral Palsy Institute in Baltimore, I took Gaby so they could show her how to use the new braces they had there, braces that every U.S. citizen has a right to. Since Betty and Otto live in the United States, they took responsibility for Gaby, to see if she would learn to walk, to manage on her own even if it was just a little, to at least lift a spoon to her mouth.

GABY

In the Cerebral Palsy Institute in Baltimore they put us to bed at six o'clock in the evening and got us up at seven in the morning. A lot of the kids couldn't sleep at all, and they got frustrated. And besides that, the night nurses would get us up and take us to the bathroom, and leave us there for hours, all by ourselves. I didn't make friends with any of the nurses or doctors, or with any of the other patients because I didn't speak English and there were hundreds of spastics there from all over the world, children of ambassadors, businessmen, and people like that. What I learned in Baltimore is that nobody should be marginalized.

SARI

In the hospital I saw Gaby walk for the first time, leaning on crutches. They made some very modern braces fitted especially for her, with a mechanism that worked subtly and smoothly. I saw her walk with them. A famous therapist, a speech therapist, got her to start making sounds. The Institute accepted her as a permanent resident, but I just couldn't get used to seeing her so alone, so very alone, even with all those technological advances. I went back to Mexico and cried day and night. Then I decided to go get her, and Nani went with me. Gaby was seven years old.

GABY

That's where I first learned the meaning of loneliness, the kind of loneliness
that erodes the soul, eating away at it, destroying it at the same time as it annihilates you, what you have, and what you've achieved. You don't believe in
love or in being productive, or in God or even in yourself, and you begin to
doubt everything. When they put you in therapy, the doctors and nurses don't
remember that you think or feel, and since you can't talk, well, they don't talk
to you, and then they go away and leave you with people who — like you —
can't talk to each other either. It's a good thing I was only there a few months. I
wanted to see how much I could tolerate without starting to cry, without saying anything to anybody. I would do my exercises because I knew that some
day I was going to get out of there anyway, that there were sick people who
had it worse. When I got home from the Institute, I hugged my aunt with my
feet. I didn't want to let go of her because I didn't want her to let me go back
to a place like that. By hugging my Aunt Betty with all my strength, as hard as
I could, I forgot how miserable I'd been. What did it matter any more if I was
with them? Thank God I could get out of there to the warmth and love of my
parents, to the protection and patience of my aunts and uncles. That night,
back home, I went to bed telling myself that life was beautiful, with all its big
problems and its little ones too.

> I don't know how to walk
> but I do know how to fly.
> I don't know how to talk
> but I do know how to listen
> to the music
> and lyrics
> of Joan Manuel Serrat.*
> I may not know how to go up,
> but I do know how to climb,
> and I may not know how to stroll
> but I do know how to sit
> and gaze at

*Barcelona-born Joan Manuel Serrat (1943–) composes, writes, and sings many
songs focusing on social issues, as well as songs whose lyrics are taken from contemporary poetry.

the sun setting
over the mountain
and the sea.
I may not know how to stare
but I do know how to look at
my dog's
sweet eyes
that speak volumes.

If I had Aunt Betty in front of me right now, I'd tell her: "Señora Modley, I love you very much, and I love your husband, and I know you both love me, too." To be honest with you, I don't know if they'd understand, but Betty is like a second mother to me. And not just because she taught me how to read. She and Otto were the first people who had faith in me. The two most important sentences I remember Betty saying are "Be realistic" and "Señorita Impaciente." Little Miss Impatient! Betty opened my eyes to what I could do and to what I should stop doing, and she taught me to remember the word "patience" in connection with everything I might want to do. She used to sit down to read out loud to me in English because that's what the language teacher said to do. I went back to Mexico after that year, but my Aunt Betty and Uncle Otto kept tabs on my progress, and whenever they could, they'd invite me to visit for a month or two or even six, in their house, where Nani and I felt comfortable. Aunt Betty put a lot of effort into teaching me to read. Whenever I'd get frustrated and upset, she'd say: "Señorita Impaciente." I saw what Salvador Allende got by being a pacifist. He would have been better off being impatient. I'm not here for the fun of it, I'm here because I have no other choice.

FLORENCIA
Both of them, Gaby's aunt and uncle, are very good people.

SARI
Betty is very sensible and very calm. I'm very nervous, and I'm tense and excitable. Betty and Otto are the personification of responsibility and doing one's duty. They love David very much, but Gaby means more than anything to them, not because of her illness, but because they admire her personality.

FLORENCIA

I was scared when I got on the plane, because I'd never flown before. The Modleys picked me up in San Francisco, and I waited three days for Gaby to get there from the Cerebral Palsy Institute. When they brought her back from Baltimore, she didn't recognize me and wouldn't let me come near her. All she wanted to do was hug her Aunt Betty with her hands and feet. She seemed very frightened, like she didn't want to come near a soul. What could they have done to her to make her act this way? I wondered. Like a dog that runs away the second it lays eyes on a human being, Gaby would drag herself toward the farthest corner of the room. It hurt to see that she was rejecting me, but her aunt and uncle explained that she would get used to things again slowly. In the hospital they gave her physical therapy, they made her walk, they put braces on her and made her do exercises, with her hands, with her legs, over and over again. To relax her spasms and make her nerves loosen up, they'd put ice on her legs, they'd put her hands in ice-cold water and then rub them with ice. Her aunt and uncle were very good to us, and as soon as Gaby got there I started getting used to San Francisco. They'd take us out places in the car and I'd have Gaby on my lap, they'd take us to the park and we'd have a good time. I even got to like the food.

GABY

San Francisco
I miss your streets so high
uphill slowly and down so fast
San Francisco
I miss your ambience
of crazy youth
and exacting grandparents
young people going up
and grandparents coming down
like the streets.

FLORENCIA

San Francisco's nice. It's good to see so many different kinds of people running around on the streets.

GABY

I've always thought Aunt Betty was the epitome of objectivity. We write to each other all the time, and she knows all about my life from my letters. She knows every step I take, all my feelings and my problems. She's even my doctor — she's the one who increases or decreases how much Valium I take. I know I can count on her, and that a lot of times she's even ignored whatever Uncle Otto says to come be with me.

> The presence of solitude, I would like
> solitude that is nothingness,
> nothingness that is death
> and from death, I am born once again!

> I want your presence too much.
> The presence of your body and your soul,
> The presence of your entire being,
> close to me in the window
> even if all we do
> is watch the rain fall together.

Uncle Otto was the one who realized that even if I couldn't do anything with my hands, I could use my foot. You know, I don't feel like I'm handicapped, because I've learned that all human beings have limitations, problems with themselves and with society, with nature and with God. There's a reason why I'm saying all this. My friends can do whatever they want with their lives, but they run into obstacles too. So why should I feel like I'm so handicapped just because I can't do the things I want to do? That's why I have a normal life that's happy, sad, aggressive, exhausting, and sometimes depressing. Yes, they're right, the conflict between what I'd like to do and my physical limitations will never end. My mind is in such good shape that I forget about the rest of my body, and I make very normal plans that sometimes shake everybody else up and me too when I actually try to do them. But that's still not such a big problem, because I know how to come down from the clouds. It's all right. I've got my frustrations, a lot of them, and I admit it. I soothe my pain by putting my sensitivity to work and — more than anything — my thirst to live my own life.

Sometimes my feelings are very complex. I don't open up that easily, but when I do, I like to do it completely, even though that's not always possible because of the natural limitations that every human being has. That's when I get overwhelmed by fears and insecurity, and to make them go away I turn to the typewriter and write. I pull out everything that's happening to me and put it down on paper, trying to get back to "normal." I love my typewriter because I use it to communicate with everyone else, with all of you, and I can more or less control what's going on with me. Exactly twenty-five years ago, when my Uncle Otto Modley saw that my left foot worked very well for when I wanted to play, he figured I could communicate if I had a typewriter in front of me, and that's what happened. Besides typing, I knit and paint with my left foot, which is why I call it my "foot-mouth."

I knit and sigh
but oh what a sigh!
this soul breathes out.

(I remember a day
when my left foot
was knitting
until it could go on no longer,
knitting a long white scarf
for my love.)

I knit and think
that every life
is, if I may say so,
like this knitting of mine
that with great care and heed
I will now finish.

I knit and see that each row
I complete
is a time
to remember.

I knit and listen
I hear the song of the soul
that shouts out to me,
"Go on knitting,
and live."

I knit and smell
the wonderful
and exciting aroma
of the pure and intense
flower
of work.

I knit and feel
I touch the fabric
I have knitted
so soft
when it could have been
rough
and without form.

I knit, and in knitting
I use the five senses
my God gave to me
because there is no greater pleasure
nor sharper pain
than what all of us call
dedication.

Years ago I drew a face on the side of a box, and above it I wrote: "You're somebody, help yourself. Are you suffering? Help yourself," and below the face I put: "Do you love someone? Keep on loving, because it's the only thing that matters." This is reason enough to start walking in the ways of the Lord, isn't it? Alone, without anyone to stop you, exercising your legs, your body, and your soul. And as you run, your blood flows faster and you think more clearly, though sometimes not, but you keep on running until you fall down on the ground, dizzy, tired, gulping down air. That's why it feels so good to stretch out on the rain-dampened ground and fall into a sensual slumber or maybe get up to go on walking and walking. Well, you might wonder, if she's never walked, how does she know what it's like to run? Do you really think you can feel something only if you've actually done it? In any case, I remember that when I was little, I could walk alone in our backyard, and the sensations on the soles of my feet when I stepped on the wet grass — or when it was dry or dewy — are etched in my memory. I remember how much it scared me to walk on the tile floor and go up the stairs with Nana always behind me, watching out so I wouldn't fall, and yet still encouraging me to wander around the house and around the yard.

FLORENCIA
Uncle Otto said she should get therapy to be able to use her toe to write on an electric typewriter. When we got back from Baltimore we went to the English Hospital, where they gave her occupational therapy, to teach her how to use her leg, her foot, her toe to write, since she was never going to be able to do anything with her hands.

GABY
A young woman put the typewriter on the floor in front of my wheelchair, put my left foot on the keyboard and turned on the typewriter. I heard the hum of the motor, and she said to me in English: "And now we are going to learn to write."

FLORENCIA
When she finished the program at the English Hospital, we started going to a special elementary school for sick people. It wasn't anything new for me to be with sick people. It was natural, it didn't depress me to see them. I'd already been living with Gaby, so it was all normal for me. I'd help out with whatever was needed with the other children, because not all of them brought some- one to take care of them. So, one of them wanted to go to the bathroom? I'd take one of them and then another. Gaby got kind of jealous because she wanted me to be with her and nobody else. I was with Gaby all day, at school in the morning and at home in the afternoon. At night I'd sleep in her room, I've always slept with her.

GABY
I have to admit that I was never happy in the "special" school, the Centro de Rehabilitación on Calle Mariano Escobedo. Nana and I would go in a van that came to pick us up, and that's when I started getting jealous of her helping the other children who came by themselves, all the rest of them, the other kids in the class who didn't have anyone to help them go to the bathroom, or blow their noses, or sit down. Now that some time has gone by I'm grateful to her for looking after them, and I laugh at how jealous I was. But back then seeing

her help the other kids and watching her carry them and hug them made me feel very envious, because I was so insecure. I thought she might end up loving one of them more than me.

The second reason I didn't like it there is that I never felt like I was handicapped. I've always felt out of place in the environment I come from — I mean, with handicapped people — because I can see that they don't understand anything either, the same way "normal" people don't. I think handicapped people are exactly like "normal" people, not a single bit better. It wasn't just the parents who insinuated that Nana was the one who did everything, but the kids did too, and the worst part is that they believed it. That's what they always said, and they repeated it over and over, that without her I'd never have gotten as far as I did. That's partly true, because I did like to play more than I liked to study — like any normal kid — and she'd chase after me until I'd sit down at the desk. But this idea that I didn't study or do homework or think on my own, that Nana was the one who did the work, that she wrote everything — that absolutely burns me up. They're just like "normal people" — they only see what they want to see, they don't think and don't even bother to use their heads, which are empty to begin with. I challenged them, I said each one of them had something to give, and that they should contribute. But what happened? They would pretend they didn't understand. They'd rather stare off into space and daydream, repeating whatever they heard their parents say. And that's as far as they'd go! Why doesn't God give all of us the same weapons to fight with?

And the third reason I was unhappy there is because I always felt depressed when I couldn't "talk" like usual, when I saw how nobody did anything to help themselves, and how the "help" people did get was dry, cold, and inhuman.

FLORENCIA

She went to *primaria* like a normal little girl. Sometimes she'd be lazy and wouldn't want to do her homework, and we'd get into an argument because I'd make her study when she wanted to play. "First your homework," I'd tell her, "and then we'll go play." We argued about that all the time. I'd get after her and her father would scold her, "Gaby, do your homework first and then you can play." They gave her a lot of homework at school. I'd ask for it in class, and if she had to do arithmetic problems, I'd put down the numbers for her and she'd give me the answers with her foot.

GABY

I remember two things from when I was very little. One is that some nights my father would have my brother and me listen to classical music. We'd wrap ourselves up in the down quilt and then — after all, we were just kids — we'd start playing with our feet under the quilt instead of staying still and listening to the music. David called me "Miss Gabardina" and I called him "Daví," and that's the way we fought and played. My other memory is of my grandmother. I don't know whether she was dumb or a conformist, but she was definitely a typical storybook grandmother. She kept wanting to give everyone something to eat all the time, and she spoiled all of us too much. She'd sit down to read any kind of book for hours, and we wouldn't know when she was in the house or not. Her favorite dish, which she ate every day, was enchiladas with fresh white cheese, and she never told my mother that I did anything bad. Grandmothers play a very important role in a child's life, because elderly people reflect an image of goodness that makes you trust them. A lot of love, a lot of stories, that's what she gave me. It's nice to remember our grandmothers, isn't it?

FLORENCIA

David was a very good-looking little boy, very strong but a little devil. He'd throw his toys out the window of his room onto the street, and I'd keep having to go down and get them, who knows how many times. He was three when I started working for the Brimmers. I'd carry him to kindergarten and go pick him up. In the street people would say, "Oh, what a pretty little girl," because with his curly hair he looked like a little girl. He would pull all kinds of pranks. He'd turn on all the water faucets, lock the doors, he wouldn't want to eat, and I'd have to run after him to get him to eat; there I'd be behind him, the spoon in my hand. His parents went to work early in the morning and didn't come home till it was dark. This didn't seem so strange to me because I'd already worked in houses where the mother and father went out and the children stayed home.

GABY

We really were a handful when we were kids. We had a good time, we'd get into fights and Daví didn't have an easy time letting go of me. We'd play soccer or baseball in the backyard with his friends or mine, or we'd run races in the wheelchair. When we played soccer, I'd sit on the grass and be the goalie. I got hit in the face with the ball every time, and I fell out of the wheelchair so many times that I don't know how I stayed in one piece.

Do you remember, Daví?

FLORENCIA

David didn't spend much time with Gaby. He'd rather go running around with his friends, and Señora Brimmer used to indulge his every whim. When he got a little bigger, she'd take him all over the place in the car, to his music lessons, painting lessons, swimming, tennis. David didn't like to stay in the house; he'd even rather go sleep over at his friends', and he invited friends to stay over too. They'd spend a little time with Gaby and then get bored and go out to play in the street. Or they'd play soccer in the garden; they'd let Gaby play for a little while and then they'd ask me to take her inside. David was always very fast in sports, and in school he always did well in physical education.

SARI

I wanted to keep up a normal life. I would invite friends over so the children could see that their father and I had friends. Xavier Guerrero, the artist, and his wife, Clarita Porcett, came over for dinner many times. The drawings I have hanging in the living room are by Xavier Guerrero. We had a very active social life, at least while Miguel was alive. Now I only invite people over for tea, and if I get invited somewhere I don't go. At night I'm always tired; the older I get the less energy I have. What I like to do is go to matinee concerts at the Sala Nezahualcóyotl.

GABY

There used to be people in the house, lots of activity. Now nobody even shows up by mistake.

SARI

Every time David wanted to invite his friends to the house, I would give him permission. They would sleep over, they would yell, they'd run around, have pillow fights during the night, they would sleep in the beds and in sleeping bags. All of it was fine with me because I was integrating Gaby into the lives of "normal people," because she participated — even if it was just a little — in the pillow fights and the races up and down the stairs. One way or another, they had to accept her, get used to her, treat her naturally, while she got to spend time with children her own age. Of course, they used to invite David to sleep over too, and I would give permission.

FLORENCIA

I never saw those kids include Gaby in their games. Children are very self-centered, and whatever bores them, they just drop. They didn't even used to spend half an hour with her. That's another reason I think she got so interested in books.

GABY

So, with a board painted with the alphabet that Nana and Sari put on the bottom part of my wheelchair, I use one of the toes on my left foot to answer questions, and Nana repeats my answers out loud. Nana is with me for everything, I depend on her physically but not mentally, get it? Sometimes I feel like I won't be able to go on, but thank God I have Nana with me, and she doesn't let me sink too low. She's the one who keeps me from being taken away to an institution for the handicapped, she's the one who said, "But if I'm taking care of you, why do they want to take you away?"

FLORENCIA

I never thought, "Well, I'm going to dedicate my life to Gaby." It just worked out that way. I didn't think anything, I'm just here.

SARI

For me, Nana is the soul of nobility and she doesn't even know it. She nourishes in every sense of the word, she gives and gives and gives with no regrets. She's not even aware of how devoted she is. Gaby's physical and emotional stability is the work of Nani, Nana Florencia Morales.

GABY

I'd like to tell you about everyone in my family, but I already mentioned Nana, and I'm going to talk about her first. The most important person in my life is perhaps my Nana Florencia, who shares my struggles and has been at my side every inch of the way. She goes everywhere with me, and I love her deeply. Nana came to my house in 1949 as a maid, back when I had a nurse. Florencia says she began to feel very attached to me, and I felt the same way.

SARI

Back then, Nani did the cleaning and washed Gaby's diapers, and sometimes she'd go over to her. I think Gaby was about two then, and I didn't realize that this woman was observing everything, without opening her mouth or saying a word. She was very, very quiet. I thought the English had a reputation for being closed and cold, but after I met Nani, I thought, "She's got the English beat hands down."

FLORENCIA

I started working when I was thirteen, for some poor people who sold things from a stand in the street. My mother left me with them because it just happened that when we were getting off the bus from the village, a lady told her she was looking for someone to take care of her baby. My mother hit it off with her and said yes, but then some of my aunts here in Mexico City came to see me and said I couldn't keep working for them. I was sleeping on the floor, taking care of the baby, washing the dishes, running errands — you know, whatever they asked me — things that were easy to do, of course, but they had me running around all day, and even though they treated me very well, like one of the family, they were very, very poor, too poor. That's why my aunt took me out of there and said, "I'm going to take you to where the rich people live." And she took me to another house — and this time the owners were definitely rich — where a cousin of mine was working. It was an old house on Calle Jesús María, near the church of La Soledad, near La Merced market, and it felt like being in the lap of luxury, but there was also a lot of inequality. The family lived upstairs and the servants lived down below in some filthy, disgusting basements. They gave us cots whose mattresses were crawling with bedbugs; we didn't have a bathroom or running water, and the toilet was an awful hole in the ground with a cut-out board over it, just horrible, filthy dirty, and very dark. But upstairs everything was beautiful, fit for a king, the floors shined because we waxed them so much. Those people were so rich that they even owned horses, but that meant the basements were full of rats and cockroaches and other bugs. They paid me well — eighteen pesos a month. The *señora* never said a word to me; there was another maid who used to tell me what to do. But my mother got me out of there, thank goodness, and I managed to go home for a year and get my strength back, because I'd gotten awfully thin and run-down. Then I went back to work in Las Lomas, in Mexico City, this time for a dentist, and after that for a lot of different people until my cousin Petra told me that the owner of the store where she worked was looking for a maid for her house: that was Señora Brimmer. I started out by cleaning the bedrooms, doing the laundry, and ironing, but I also took care of Gaby on her nurse's days off.

SARI

I had a leather goods store at Amberes 58, in a very elegant area, and I called it GABY. Half of Mexico City knows me. I sold leather items. People would stand in the doorway and say in English, "That must be a Viennese shop, it has all the charm of a European shop." A lot of foreigners would come in, a lot of people from the United States and high-society Mexicans too, because all the leather was imported. I bought it myself in leatherworking shops, I'd look for the best in all the factories. Miguel had a sweater and wool goods factory. We both worked a lot when we came to Mexico, a lot, even Saturdays and Sundays.

FLORENCIA

Señora Brimmer would go off to work, so would Señor Brimmer, and I'd stay home with Gaby. Señora Brimmer was always full of energy, very emotional, and she always talked in a loud voice. Señor Brimmer was quiet, a very good person. He'd get home at night and go give Gaby a hug; she'd take David to his afternoon lessons on the days when he had them. That's what most ladies do with their children: take them to different lessons.

SARI

Gaby changed my life. Still, I did have a life that could be called normal. Besides, I don't know how other people live, because even though I know they go to cocktail parties or take trips, I also know that behind all of that, there are things about themselves that they never really tell. So it looks as though they have easy lives, and I suppose my life looks easy to them too. I say hello and give them a hug, they say hello and give me a hug, and whatever is behind the façade we don't discuss, at least not at the cocktail party. Apparently Miguel Brimmer and I did normal things, we supported our household, were punctual, went to work, stayed honest, didn't deceive anyone. I think we were honest with everyone and every situation, we tried, we tried. I talked about everything very openly in front of the children: the threat of war, not having what we needed, how things had gone for me in the store that day, the customers who'd come in, my nerves, my worries. Miguel was terribly introverted; I wouldn't be able to tell you what he thought because he never told me. He gave and that was it. And he kept quiet. I never really knew what he thought about Gaby's problem because he never showed his feelings. I yelled and cried and looked for doctors, I tore my hair out, and he kept quiet. Being at home and seeing that my daughter couldn't move used to drive me mad, it made me terribly, terribly anxious. Miguel never said anything. Most of the time he would take a book and settle into an armchair to read, and I'd have to calm myself down alone.

GABY

We grew up, and because of that we had more needs. I needed special attention, and fortunately I got it from Nana, Florencia, my Nanita. Mamá worked, Papá worked, and probably the only thing we missed out on was having Mamá take care of us herself. She used to give David a ride to and from his tennis lessons, but that wasn't taking care of him, it was being his chauffeur. Papá was more accessible. I remember how I'd climb up on top of him when he'd sit down to watch TV, and I remember how he'd scold me when I acted up or started fooling around. I thought he was perfect, even though I'd get pretty mad when he wouldn't let me watch *El Cuento* with Cachirulo the clown on TV or when he'd give me a kiss even though I didn't want him to. Lots of times people need to be scolded a lot before they'll do anything—I've already told you how lazy I was about doing my homework when I was little. Nana tried to talk sense into me, and if she couldn't she'd tell my father. He always asked how the children had behaved when he got home.

FLORENCIA

Señor Brimmer was a very good person, he always listened, he was a good man. He used to take us out to the country; he'd carry Gaby on his shoulders and we'd go walking along. He'd look for pine forests because they reminded

him of where he came from. He liked to breathe the air there, and he'd tell
Gaby to fill her lungs with the good pine air. We got to see many places all
over Mexico; he would drive, he loved to take us on trips. Sometimes Señora
Brimmer would come with us, sometimes she had to stay in Mexico City
because of her work in the store.

GABY

> I'd like to know, father,
> if you took something of mine with you
> when you died.
> I'd like to know, father,
> why, with each passing year,
> I feel closer to you.

SARI

As Gaby says, he gave. He treated her like an absolutely normal daughter. I was
the one who was infuriated. Doctor after doctor, treatment after treatment. I
couldn't stand the idea of Gaby going through life as a spastic — my daughter
had to live. Gaby has been in a wheelchair for thirty-one years now, and she
will be for who knows how many more. That was something I simply couldn't
digest, it was intolerable for me. There is no name for that pain, there simply
isn't, there isn't, there is no way to describe it. I can't even begin to try.

GABY

Mamá would get frustrated because she couldn't understand me when I
talked, and her eternal impatience toward me made me feel anxious. I always
told myself, "You're not going to be insecure or a conformist. No. That's not
the role you're going to play, you've got a part that's much more beautiful
and interesting. You're not going to play the role that society and your family
expect, you're not going to marginalize yourself."

> I'm afraid
> afraid to touch
> and be touched.
> Afraid to hurt
> and be hurt

terribly afraid
of being alone and being with others.

I'm afraid
afraid to stand up for
what's considered mine,
afraid to
get back
what is already lost
afraid to say I want
and I need.

I'm afraid
afraid of friend and foe
of known and unknown
of the ignorant and the wise
of conservative and liberal
of ancient and modern.
And perhaps what I fear most
is myself.

From all of my fear
I draw enormous strength
to go on living.

Sometimes Mamá would sweep into the house like a hurricane, saying she'd read in a magazine that in the United States this or that medicine gave absolutely miraculous results. Or she'd talk about a home for people who had the same illness I did, how people had told her wonderful things about it. That used to upset me a lot. She was only expressing what my whole family was worried about: What would happen to me when they died? They looked for day-care programs, institutes, residences, without ever finding the right place.

SARI
If the parents don't give up their baby during its first few days, they'll never do it. If a couple with a several-week-old baby diagnosed with cerebral palsy came to me today and asked, "What do you think?" I'd say, "Get that baby out of there, take her to some kind of residence!" That's what my life with Gaby has

taught me. I don't think I did right by her, but she says I did, that what I did was best. She wanted to stay at home, but to me, maternal bonding and everything involved with being a mother is always open to debate. Besides, how would I know if someone else might have been able to take better care of her if I was never in that kind of situation? I visited many residences, many institutions for the sick, and I wasn't satisfied with any of them. I went to the United States, to Europe. I left her; I cried all the time, and I missed her. If someone had told me, "Give her up before it's too late," I would have done it. But you can only do that when the baby is a few days old, maybe a few weeks, because after that you form ties (at least that's what happened to me) that are stronger than anything in the world. Giving her up once I knew her, shared her spasms, her eyes, her crooked movements, her smile, her glance, was impossible. It was impossible for me, impossible for any normal mother. We stayed together. If there is any strength, it comes from Gaby, not from me. So you have to assume she would have made progress anywhere she went, anyplace she was. That is why I think giving up the baby is the right thing to do, but it has to be done in the first few days, when the baby is unaware of what is going on around it, and before you yourself realize what you're doing. No, I don't feel I sacrificed myself. Maybe it's difficult to understand. I never felt guilty about Gaby being born this way. I felt guilty about the way I brought her up, because I never brought her up, I just loved her, and that is a mistake because you have to bring children up. I never felt like I wanted to hide her; on the contrary, I used to take her out to the street, and when I would hear people saying "Poor little thing" behind my back, I'd tell Gaby, "They're saying how much they love you."

FLORENCIA

I never use the ABC when I'm alone with Gaby. I don't even put it on the footrest of her wheelchair, because I understand everything she says. She talks to me in sounds, and I know when she wants to go to the bathroom, when she wants me to read to her, when she has a headache and wants an aspirin, when she's cold, sleepy, everything.

GABY

I can speak with my mouth. I did when I was a kid, and I do now, too. But Mamá wants me to write because she's impatient. I communicate with my Nana with my mouth, with her I hardly use the ABC at all.

SARI

I know, I know, Gaby gets fed up with the ABC. For years now, Nani has been scolding me, "The reason Gaby doesn't talk is the ABC." I invented it out of frustration. I couldn't understand my own daughter, and I couldn't sleep and couldn't sleep until I made this writing board. Then I found out that all families with children like Gaby put writing boards on the footrests of their wheelchairs or on the arm or wherever they can. Nani, quite justifiably, with all her integrity — which I always make a point of — with her sense of ethics, could not grasp that I was frustrated. If she had been Gaby's real mother (she is), but if she had given birth to Gaby, she never would have gotten frustrated, she would have kept struggling and struggling and struggling, and maybe today Gaby would be able to talk. I had to devote myself to both of my children and to a husband with a weak heart. I'm not looking for excuses. I was impatient, I was neurotic, call it whatever you like. I admit everything, but I didn't understand her, I didn't understand my own daughter, and for me, that was almost like being dead. Some young people understand her, and that's great! If they lived with her, they would probably learn more quickly than I. The emotions I felt toward her and with her were always so vast, so intense, that I stopped doing what I was supposed to do, and I couldn't find another way. Nani claims that Gaby could have talked, but I don't know, I don't know, I don't know. I only know that it made me want to run away out of frustration because I did not understand my own daughter.

GABY

Mamá still thinks that whatever comes from Europe is the best. She takes tea at five o'clock, like the English do. She was a rich girl who married a poor boy who was too tolerant or indifferent (here I go questioning the strength of Miguel Brimmer's character), and besides that his view of what women were supposed to do was different from what every other man thought. He gave my mother complete freedom; never an obstacle, never a negative. He listened to her with the greatest respect. It's possible he could have been influenced by her character in the thirty-two years they were married, because my brother's personality is a reflection of the way she brought him up, not the way he did. From what I remember, she was always the big boss, and he never exercised the father-figure role that was his responsibility with a boy — that is, my brother. Mamá always let David do whatever he wanted, and when my father raised the slightest objection, she'd say he was too little, that the responsibilities would come later. Not too long ago I found out why my mother decided not to scold my brother for his actions. She was afraid he'd run away from us if she got strict with him. I don't know, that seems like a dumb, illogical excuse to me, because David ran away from home pretty soon anyway. He rebelled and went his own way, good or bad, but it was his own way. He dragged the family and the person who to this day is his biggest defender — Mamá — with him.

> You were there
> like those idols
> who wait patiently
> for something to happen.
>
> Walking, always walking
> together and apart
> little by very little
> and in no hurry at all.
>
> But if some day
> we feel
> that the road
> is too long,
> let's put aside our canes
> and walk together.

SARI

David rebelled when I began to teach him German and English regularly. He wanted to go outside, he wanted to play tennis with the kids or ride his bicycle. Of course a ten- or twelve-year-old child rebels against everything. I never "brought up" my children. I always loved them, but a mother and father have an obligation to bring children up, and I didn't know how. David took guitar, piano, and violin lessons, and I would take him there and bring him home. I was the chauffeur. His friends used to stay overnight because I wanted to balance the situation by having healthy children around Gaby. That was normal. In the house, I wanted David's friends to play with Gaby, and there were always children in the garden or the bedrooms. That was how I tried to integrate Gaby into normal life. But David preferred to go out with his friends rather than bringing them home. David and Gaby are very different, but then all of us are innately different. David was born healthy, people say, and Gaby was born sick, so I tried to be fair with his life and hers too.

GABY

My father never exerted any control over my mother at all. He was incapable of asserting his authority, so of course she always got her way, at least as far as bringing up David was concerned.

SARI

Miguel was a fount of wisdom. When he got home from work, he would shut himself up and read. He had a phenomenal memory, which Gaby clearly inherited, because I've never been able to remember things the way he could. I think he realized early on that all that could be done for Gaby was to accept her and love her. But I wasn't like that; I have never been passive, I've never just accepted things. He decided back then that he would not discuss Gaby's illness with me. Gaby soon leaned toward an intellectual life, imitating the one her father had, the way he would read, write, and study, especially philosophy. She loved to listen to what he had to say and ask him questions. She was interested in international politics, and he would explain everything to her in great detail.

FLORENCIA

I loved him very much, and sometimes I dream about him and I think he's still with us. He never had a bad word for anybody. David's almost two years older than Gaby, and Señor Brimmer kept wanting him to do things with her, but he'd just go ask the *señora* if he could go out, and she would say yes to everything. Señor Brimmer didn't talk about himself very much — he was very controlled, but she wasn't. Before he had his first heart attack, we used to go for walks all the time, and he'd carry Gaby on his shoulders.

SARI

He had heart problems for seventeen years, from when he was forty-three until he was sixty, when he died. He died on August 22, 1967. He would carry his nitroglycerine in the pocket of his trousers, in his jacket pocket, in the trunk of the car. He always had it with him, he took it everywhere in case he had another attack. Because of his heart problems, he usually stayed home and read.

GABY

Last night I was talking about my father. I should have a picture of him along with my ID card and the picture of Enrique. Oh my God, if he could just be with us now! I adored him, and I loved his gray–light brown eyes that reflected warmth and love. He had very long eyelashes, but you couldn't see them because of his glasses. Overweight, very proud. A real sage! No one will be able to take his place. Everything fell apart once he was gone, at least for me. He adored me, but when I'd throw one of my tantrums, the harsh words he'd use to scold me hurt more than if he'd hit me. Throughout my life, whenever I've felt like goofing off, I remember what he used to say, and I make an effort and sit down to write or I ask Nani to read to me, if she has time.

If life is a dream
Let me not be awake.
Death is
"an eternal dream."
Sometimes I dream
of beautiful love stories
that really come true.
I dream I'm with you, my father
that I'm in the sea
I dream that the rain
will sing me to sleep.

I also dream I'm a bird,
that I fly beneath the sun
and feel the way it spreads warmth
with all its love.
I usually dream of violence
and the hunger to be free
that is held back by death.
Alas! To dream is to live
between sadness and happiness
with anguish and hope.

If life is a dream
Let me not be awake.
Death is
"an eternal dream."

FLORENCIA

When Gaby finished *primaria*, her parents and I figured that she'd gone as far as she could with school. Gaby was the one who insisted she was going to go on, and she wouldn't let anybody stop her. She wouldn't take no for an answer: "I want to keep going to school." Her father took her side, and then Señora Brimmer looked for a place that would take her, a public *secundaria*. Gaby did the first year in a private school called the Instituto Canadiense, but at the end of the year they told us that she wouldn't get any credit for it at all, not even from the Ministry of Public Education, because the Instituto had taken her as a favor, as an auditor, that's all. They let her in because they felt sorry for her. They just thought Gaby was there to hang around for a while, to kill time. That made her really angry, and she was the one who insisted that her mother find a public school with normal students.

GABY

Lord, my God,
now it's your turn to feel my fury
the fury of centuries
stored away in my mind
the fury buried
within me.

Lord, my God,
I demand the peace of the soul
that you do not give me,
I demand health
for a beloved friend
but you do not listen,
I pray for a better world
and you seem deaf.
I am faithful to you
but you don't care.

Lord, my God
I am only a human being,
passionate
and insecure.
Take me
lead me to the stream
where the shepherd saw you
and let me drink your body too.

Lord, my God,
listen to me just this once.
Guide me, protect me
on the steep pathways
I now begin to travel.

For thirty-two years, I've gone down roads that most people have probably never heard of, and I'm exhausted. So, every so often, I resort to silence. My exhaustion isn't just physical, it's psychological too. I've been using the ABC for years, and to be honest, it wasn't just that the people I met got tired of seeing it, but using it was making my scoliosis worse. That's why I've learned over the years and through my own experiences that you can only get somewhere in society and with your family by being a rebel, because I'll always be dependent on other people, because nobody can feel my feelings for me and do what I'd like to do for myself, because there'll always be someone in the middle. Legally I don't exist, at the bank they have me down as "incapacitated," and even though this lousy money is supposedly mine, I can't take out a cent without somebody else's signature. So I don't have anything of my own. The only thing that's really mine is my rebelliousness.

Lord, challenge me too.
Life, challenge me.
Give me struggles that are difficult
because without them I don't exist.

Challenge me and test me, Lord,
every day, every hour, every minute
challenge me body and soul
because without this struggle, I am nothing.

> Come, I challenge you
> Be honest, be yourself.

I'd like to go into some more detail about the constant dependence of someone who's crippled. I think people who are born with physical defects accept their dependence more easily than people who for some reason end up crippled as adults. Those of us who are born like this, whether it's severe or not so severe, have the "advantage" of not knowing physical independence, and this helps us see the help we get from other people as natural. But people who know what it's like to be free have to go through the trauma of the accident, and then they suffer an even worse trauma when they realize that they can't do things for themselves any more, or even go out whenever they feel like it. Maybe their friends gradually distance themselves; maybe they go through hours of time alone. Of course they despair, the same way any of us would if we suddenly found ourselves locked up. But you can get used to anything except not having enough to eat. How do you get used to being dependent? Every cripple will give you a formula, ranging from self-pity to facing life, taking it by the horns and getting it under control. I feel sorry for the ones who fall into self-pity, not for the ones who rebel.

> I'd like all of you to understand
> that I'm like everyone else,
> a magma of loves, passions, angers, desires,
> defects and qualities
> longing to find peace.

> I'm not angling for praise
> nor do I claim to be better than the rest,
> all I want is for people to listen
> to what I can give
> and after that to go away
> to the beach, to the sea
> and the mindless, faithful shade
> of my solitude.

SARI

What did I do? If I did anything at all, it was because Gaby was there constantly, pushing me. In all honesty, and not to sell myself short, but that's the truth. "Mother," she said, "I'm asking for your help. Go out and start knocking on doors. One of them will have to open, and then I'll get into a public school. Because the way I am, I need to be with normal people, do things with normal people. Go to the Ministry of Public Education, go downtown — go, go, go." First, my eyes widened with surprise, because I could not believe my daughter would want to go on with her studies, especially that way, in the unprotected and competitive world of public school, where if you feel like it, you study, and if you don't, you flunk and get left behind. But I did what she said. I closed the store and went knocking on doors, and the first one that opened belonged to Susana Vigil. Susana took me to see Lucha Rodríguez, who was a miner's daughter. Lucha works at the daily paper *Novedades* and at the Ministry of Public Education. She's a wonderful woman who's taught me a ton of things. She understood the problem, and thanks to her, they let Gaby take the examination. Still, I needed help in the Ministry every step of the way. They sent me from one department to another, and there were so many procedures to follow, so much paperwork. At every window I had to give the same explanation, official documents came and went, waiting rooms and lines, photographs, fingerprints, medical certificates. With a barrage of requirements like that, I wondered how I would have gotten anything done if I hadn't met Lucha Rodríguez. She was the one who got them to speed everything up. Of course, Gaby and Nani had to appear before the authorities so they could confirm that I was telling the truth. They notified us that the examiners from the Ministry would come to our house. You should have seen the excitement on the faces of the teachers who asked Gaby her one hundred questions! Did they admire her! Well, I lived on Valium the entire week.

GABY

Don't think it was easy. I had to work my head off for them to let me in. They didn't want to give me the final exams even though I'd done all the work in *primaria* just like everybody else, because they couldn't be sure it was really me giving the answers. They had Florencia lugging my wheelchair up and down the stairs. We went all the way to the Ministry of Public Education to ask, to beg them to send an examiner to my house to give me the exams, and it was always the same story. We had to explain the way I worked, that they could ask me the question and I'd answer with the help of the electric typewriter. That's what finally happened: the examiner came to our house to give me the exams, he asked the questions, and I answered using the typewriter. I passed, and got into seventh grade at Secundaria No. 68 in Tlacopac, near where we lived.

FLORENCIA

They used to give Gaby her tests at school. I'd bring her writing board, put it on the footrest of her wheelchair, and she'd "dictate" the answers to me while I wrote them down. If it was a long test, they'd give her a little longer than the other students, because sometimes she'd have a teacher who was nice, and I could ask for some more time. Then I'd look for a classroom or else they'd leave us alone in a classroom, and Gaby would give me the answers by pointing to the letters on the writing board. What Gaby has is a terrific memory, because you know, when I'm in a rush, I forget about everything. Not Gaby. All I did was write down what she told me letter by letter, and I did it as well as I could. Gaby always studied that way. If they put the questions or the assignments on the blackboard, I'd copy them down. Then we'd go off someplace by ourselves, so we wouldn't bother the other kids or distract them, because I had to read louder so she could hear everything. She'd answer, and I'd write down what she told me. That's how we did *primaria, secundaria,* and then — starting in tenth grade — *preparatoria,* but it was *secundaria* and *preparatoria* that were really tough on me, because of what we had to study and also because of what it felt like there — the way they left us so completely and absolutely alone.

SARI

I was going to drive them, but now I had something else to worry about: Miguel's health, because he insisted on continuing to work, in spite of his fatigue.

FLORENCIA

Once in a while another girl would come up to us on our way out of *secundaria.* We would tell her how Gabriela used the writing board to talk to other people, and she would hang around for a little while and say, "Oh, that's neat, oh, that's so interesting!" But the next time, she would walk right by, and we would wave at each other from far away. Everybody was in a hurry; none of our conversations lasted very long.

GABY

I'd have liked to stick around a little after classes to see what was going on, but Nani would immediately start pushing the wheelchair toward home.

FLORENCIA

They'd stare at us and walk right on by.

GABY

I had a hard time making friends. To be honest, I hardly made any — communication has always been pretty complicated for me. First of all, when I was little, I was kept away from other people, but I actually liked being alone. Then I grew up and began to need people, and I would try — although at times it was terrifying — to approach other people. But Nana never did anything to make it easier for people to start a relationship with me.

> I'd like to be silent just for a while
> so the silence
> could show what I feel inside.
> Talking — what good does it do to talk
> if a sea of words
> might have nothing to say?

FLORENCIA

A lot of people in the *secundaria* and *preparatoria* would ask me, "And can she hear? And understand?" Well, it made me upset when people asked those kinds of questions, because if she was there, it was because she understood everything. I don't see the point of asking a question like that. At the university it wasn't just the students who asked me; the teachers did too: "Could she read, could she pay attention?" This is the kind of thing an uneducated person, like me, might say, but with a teacher, I don't think there's any reason for it. Then I'd hand the teacher a letter from Gaby explaining things. I'd have several copies of it, one for every new teacher who would get flustered the moment he walked into the classroom and saw us. There was one who came up to me and whispered, "Well, you two can't be in my class because I don't have any experience with this kind of thing." Others just flat-out rejected us because they said we were a distraction to everybody else. But I always handed them the letter that said this:

Dear Professor:

I want to go to school in order to broaden my knowledge and my experiences. To me, love is a very complex emotion that is impossible to make sense of, but it's something you can feel. I oppose the death penalty, and I don't think anyone has the right to deprive a human being of life because of any evil that person might have done. I don't support it. I don't believe in life imprisonment either. I'd like to be out in the country right now, with my father, my mother, and my Aunt Betty and Uncle Otto — but I also want to go to school, and so I'm taking this opportunity to introduce myself: I'm Gabriela Brimmer, I was born this way, but I've liked to study since I was a child. I'm a matriculated student, and as you know, some people doubt my ability. The person with me only helps me take notes, but I do the rest. I answer the questions on the tests with my writing board, which has the alphabet printed on it, because it's not so easy to understand me. But my helper understands me quickly. At home I write on an IBM electric typewriter with the big toe of my left foot. I also use my big toe to point to letters on the alphabet board.

Please forgive me if I've written too much, but I wanted to explain to you how I work.

Sincerely yours,

There were some teachers who were more understanding: Esperanza Figueroa, one of the *preparatoria* teachers, was wonderful. She gave Gaby lots of chances to participate. The teachers were usually more welcoming than the students, who seemed to think she shouldn't be there at all. It was like they were rejecting her. They would never help me with the wheelchair. That's how we did *secundaria* and *preparatoria*. Gaby took exams and passed everything; I couldn't follow what she was studying any more because I don't have her brains or her memory. A lot of what she explained to me on the alphabet board I didn't even understand. In *preparatoria*, she made friends with someone who still comes to see her: Deborah, who comes over once in a while. But most people didn't want to make Gaby a part of their group.

GABY

I have a lot of Otto in me. I like to give as much as I can, as much as I possibly can, and whenever that gets hard, I start drifting, and I can't stand it. I get furious with myself. When you feel furious with yourself, then you've really had it. That's the reason I fought to get out of there, to get accepted into a school for "normal people." They didn't want to take me; nobody did. They'd ask Nana if I could hear, if I could see okay, if I could understand, and I'd listen to her curt, irritated answers, about how did I write, what did I write with, what did I have, what, what, what, and I'd sense Nana was humiliated at being exposed to everybody's curiosity. But we didn't let them get to us. She went up and down stairs, carrying me from here to there. I would write stupid letters to the *secundaria* teachers so they'd see I could think and communicate, so they wouldn't get scared when they saw us there and wouldn't be afraid of us.

SARI
People aren't bad; they just don't think.

GABY
I wasn't the only one who had problems back in *secundaria*. Nana was pretty weighed down, too. It wasn't just that she was physically exhausted from carrying me around with all my stuff and the wheelchair, plus the bookbag and everything. She'd get depressed, and on top of that she had to deal with my mother's depressions and, of course, mine. Anyway, both of them are my mothers, and each one does it her own way. They suddenly forget I have my own life, even though I have my physical limitations, and they go overboard trying to protect me. That's when I yell: "Lord, let me live my own life a little." And it's then — and only then — that I'd like to run.

Lord, let me suffer in my own way,
let me.
Let me love who I want,
let me.

Whether you're in love or in pain
forbidding brings no gain.
Let me weep for the dead
and laugh and weep for the living
but let me.

Let me see a rose, a flower,
human suffering, hear the wind,

the music, feel the warmth of the sun,
the cold of a lonely night, breathe
the healthy, fresh scent of the land,
and feel a flower in my hands.

Let me live, laugh, weep and die
with the joy of a youth fulfilled.

Let me create a god of my own
and pray for a world
without class, without weapons, without wars
a world where god is a human being,
a human being who loves all human beings
and lets them love and suffer
weep and rejoice
all in their own way.

FLORENCIA

The Brimmers were always saying they'd give me driving lessons so we could get to school, so Gaby would even be able to go to college. They kept telling me, but it never came time to do it. How? What was going to happen? I don't know, Señor Brimmer pushed me to learn to drive so I could take Gaby to school and back. I ended up having to take twice as many, three times as many lessons as most people. They paid for twenty lessons in three weeks, that's how nervous I was. It was hard, very hard, and I lost weight because I was so scared. I even used to dream about the car at night, and I'd break out in a cold sweat. I lost so much weight the month I was learning, and afterwards I still kept getting thinner. I thought I was going to crash, I felt like driving was something beyond me. At first I was absolutely miserable when I took the car out. I really had to work at it. Now I've gotten used to it, but I still feel like I could get into a crash, and I still turn into a bundle of nerves. After I park, I have to take out the wheelchair that I put in the back, open it up, and then get Gaby out of the car and into the chair. Then I take the bookbag or whatever it is we have to carry, and finally I lock the car.

GABY

Secundaria and *preparatoria* were when Nana stood in my way the most. She wouldn't let me make any friends, and she was always leaving the ABC at home "by accident." That was when I fought back by not letting her read my father's books at night. Nana took it like I wasn't letting her read because I was jealous, and she was right. Still, what hurt most of all was the way she left me so alone, but she wouldn't let me twist her arm, and she didn't do anything to help me out of my loneliness. I even got to the point of hating her because of this. I felt like I was too tied to her, and the more I clung, the happier she looked. In me she found a substitute for her life without friends, where her only interest was devoting herself to me and making herself indispensable in my life.

FLORENCIA

Didn't I ever want to get married or anything? Maybe, I don't know. No, come on, I wasn't cut out for that. I'm a real crybaby, crying helps me let off steam. I never had any time to think about what I was going to do. I'm just here, that's all. Gaby has been my life since 1953. I've been with her for twenty-six years. I remember 1953 very well, because that's the year my mother died. I've been with Gaby for a long time.

SARI

Nani doesn't let anyone help her because she has a sense of refinement. She can always handle things herself, she never even asks anyone to help her with the wheelchair. But I also think she keeps people away from Gaby. She used to be harsh so people wouldn't come up to Gaby in the street, she wanted to ward off the morbid fascination Gaby would arouse in a group of apparently normal students. She wanted people to come up to Gaby because something inside them said they should, which hardly ever happens anywhere. I think that what Gaby and people like her — spastics — have to do is help others understand what it's like. But how do you do that? Put a sign on yourself? Yell through a bullhorn: "Come closer, I understand everything, I can love you, I want all of you to love me"? I thought about hanging a poster like that on Gaby once, but then I gave up on the idea. How do you build a real relationship between normal people and "abnormal" people? Gaby wrote a number of letters to her teachers to explain to them: "This is what I'm like, and I know how to behave, I do everything for myself, my brain can function, no one else helps me with these kinds of things." I pushed her to write those letters, which is how she made friends with some of her teachers. But then they lost touch, because that's what relationships are like; people lose touch, and others come along or don't come along, and life goes on.

GABY

How did I start feeling insecure? I think it was when I got into my teens, when girls start to flirt with boys. I started developing very late. I didn't get my period until I was sixteen, and before that, I felt bad when I saw that other girls were developing. I felt like I was worth less than them, even though at home everybody said not to worry, that it would happen in good time, and it did. But I realized that even though I was a woman now, no normal guy would come near me. I got more and more insecure, and I threw myself into studying to help make up for how great it would have been to have somebody to talk with, to go out with. I almost always got good grades, which made my father proud of me and my mother, too. But I didn't have the stimulation of a man-woman relationship, even though people do get hurt in relationships. Then came the problem of having to pick a major at the university. I'd told my family I'd study biology, even if I didn't get my degree. The only major that really appealed to me was what I'd never get a job in: biology. Why bother trying to explain it? Labs, having to use your hands to do certain experiments, being able to move around easily, and so forth. Then came my family's objections, this one's "ahs" and that one's "ohs!" and I started bouncing from one humanities major to another. What would it be? Literature? Political science? Sociology? Sociology sounded good. I registered in the Faculty of Political Science and Sociology, and enrolled in the journalism program.

FLORENCIA

At first we didn't understand anything about the university. We'd go to first-year courses where the teachers would stop dead in their tracks and say, Well, no, they'd just as soon not have us in their class, they didn't feel competent to teach Gaby. Then I'd tell Gaby what happened, and when she got home she'd start typing the teacher a letter, and the next day I'd deliver it personally. I'd keep saying: "Gaby works like this and studies like that." We'd explain everything, how we worked and how much she hoped the way we did things would be all right, or anyway that the teacher would understand. Sometimes he'd end up saying, "No problem whatsoever, of course, that's what we're here for." Other times the teachers would let us in, but you could tell they didn't really want to, and I resented that. And sometimes they flat-out rejected us because "it wasn't good for the rest of the group."

GABY
I was happy, but Nana wasn't.

FLORENCIA
Gaby says she didn't have enough contact with young people at the university. I really saw it as a waste of time, I had the feeling they weren't going to have much to do with us anyway. That's why I didn't go over to them. Some of them came up to us because they had some kind of sick curiosity, morbid curiosity. They'd ask if Gaby could swallow food, if she slept sitting up, if her eyes rolled back in her head. They'd see her foot moving on the ABC and say, "Wow, that's cool, really cool, that's something else, we're gonna come over to your house and talk with you" — and that was it, because they never showed their faces again. They'd call once, but afterward you could tell they didn't care. We used to give a lot of them our address and phone number and everything, but then they never came. We weren't going to go looking for them and say, "You said you were going to come over and see Gaby on such-and-such a day, didn't you?"

GABY
If you asked me what I'd do with my life if I were "normal," I'd say: I'd be a pilot, a mountain climber, a doctor — but a pediatrician or child psychologist, because adults bore me — I'd play the guitar, I'd have a harem so men wouldn't get bored with me and I wouldn't get bored with them, I'd adopt five children, I'd be scared of being just another face in the crowd, scared of any type of human alienation, and scared of what kind of future we'll have if we keep doing as bad a job with "progress" as we're doing now. What a combination! Pilot, mountain climber, and doctor. With either of the first two I'd be in contact with nature. Being a doctor would be even nicer, because if you do your job with love, you can help and not destroy. But since that wasn't my fate, I'll keep on being me. And what's "being me"? That question has yet to be answered.

SARI
I never tried to tie my children to my apron strings. The very first thing I ever did was to put a distance between myself and David. I was the one who

wanted to cut the strong ties people say children have with their mothers. Cut the umbilical cord. But I couldn't put any distance between myself and Gaby at all. If she had been able to run with her own feet, I'd have said, "Run, my dear!" But since she couldn't and still can't . . . I don't tie her down even now.

FLORENCIA
At the university, we had to climb up two stories from the parking lot to the Faculty of Political Science and Sociology. I think that if the kids saw I was alone with Gaby, trying to get her out of the car, trying to get the wheelchair up the stairs, well, they might come over and offer to help. But they'd only help if I asked. Otherwise, they didn't even lift a finger. They'd stay sitting on the railing while I was struggling. In the middle of all that, I'd forget about the ABC and leave it in the car.

GABY
I used to tell Nana that the way she was acting made me feel insecure, that it made me feel bad. This insecurity turned into unexpressed aggression, which is where my inner loneliness came from. Since I didn't want to blow up at the woman who was always there for me — and is still there for me — everything would make me feel depressed, and I couldn't even tell anyone, "I feel bad, I need to feel your arms around me." It also made me feel bad to tell my mother about everything that was happening to me, because she had her own problems, and besides, what could she do for me? She's the kind of person whose temperament and personality used to make life complicated before and still does now, and I don't want to make life more complicated than it already is.

SARI
Adolescence and puberty are difficult times in the life of any young person. Just imagine the kind of crisis they cause in a spastic who realizes that life isn't going to be able to give her everything she wants to take from it.

GABY
I think that for other people to love you, you need to create friendship and a sense of togetherness. I'm not talking about a superficial kind of togetherness, but a really intimate togetherness, when sometimes you feel happy and sometimes you feel sad. I've been lucky enough to experience this kind of friend-

ship on a very profound level, and the strange thing is that my women friends feel more comfortable talking about their problems with me than with their mothers. This has been happening to me for years. But still, I'm just like every other human being: all I think about is my own damn self, because when I've got a man, I dump my girlfriends, and when I don't have anything better to do or don't have a male friend, I go back to my girlfriends, and that's the way it goes. You want to know more about what life is really like? I learned to be this way because a lot of my girlfriends did the same thing to me, and, hey, they're right! It's more fun to be with a guy, and you get more out of it than you do being with a girlfriend, no matter how much you like her. I'm not making excuses or anything. I'm just telling the truth. But the worst is that when you try to be interested in the people you think are your friends, when you try to help them, they begin to tell you they don't have time, that . . . and you see they don't have time and don't want to talk, don't want to read you a book or help you, and one day — without any warning — they say good-bye and never come back. At first you miss them, and then you wonder what will happen to them, and you wish with all your heart that they'll end up being fighters like you, that they won't let anything knock them down, and that they'll be okay. Stinking human race, you make me sick, and I'm including myself in that too.

I want to die on a winter day that's
nasty, gray, and cold
so I'm not tempted
to go on living.

That's the time of year I'll die
because all I've gotten from the world is cold.

I want to die in winter
so that children will make
little snowmen
on my grave.

FLORENCIA

Whenever Señor Brimmer saw Gaby looking unhappy, he'd take her for a ride in the car, he'd take her out for a drive. And if he didn't do that, he'd plan a trip for the weekend, and Gaby's face would light up. He could drive for hours without getting tired. We used to travel a lot. We'd go to so many places, like Chiapas, Guanajuato, and Acapulco. Señor Brimmer was very easy to get along with. He was a good person, he'd figure out when people were feeling bad or depressed, and he'd try to make them feel better. I can't drive for such long distances and go on the highway to take Gaby places any more.

GABY

Nana's a terror behind the wheel.

SARI

I don't do many things with Nani and Gaby because I think we should get a rest from each other sometimes.

GABY

I'm going to tell you about something that happened years ago, when my father and I went to Pie de la Cuesta, near Acapulco, and climbed some dunes to watch the sunset. We'd always, always watch the sun set together when we went on vacation. Papá would get very quiet and not take his eyes off the horizon. That afternoon he helped me out of the car and got me settled comfortably in a beach chair. I took off my huaraches the best I could and played with the sand, which by that time had cooled off. In the morning I'd burned my feet because it was so hot. I don't know how long we were in that beautiful place. When I saw that the sun was sinking toward the ocean, turning into a ball of fire suspended in the sky by unknown forces and that the sky was illuminated with an indescribable reddish hue and the clouds looked like the pink cotton candy for sale in Chapultepec Park, I felt tremendously alone before the enormous, rhythmically moving mass of water that was filling my ears with the wonderful noise of the sea; and when I saw that minute by minute this star we owe our lives to was slipping away, something happened to me that even I couldn't have predicted: tears came out of my eyes. My father had gone for a walk, and when he came back and saw me crying, I guess he thought I had gotten sick or something, because he picked me up right away and took me back to the car and the hotel.

Later I thought, "Papá, didn't you understand that in that moment I was really at one with the Creator and felt so united with all human beings, with the plants in the water and on land, with all the animals and, more than anything, with you, who out of true love brought me to this place?"

But I didn't tell him. All of a sudden the damn ABC made me sick.

SARI

Water is very good for spastics, and when Gaby was a little girl I always tried to get her out in the sun so her bones would solidify. We'd put her in a little swimming pool in the garden, and she'd play in the water, splash water on herself and everyone else, like all children do.

FLORENCIA

When she was little, a very little girl, Gaby loved bright-colored dresses with lace. Now she hardly ever wears dresses, because since she has to use her left foot and move her legs over the ABC, it's easier if she wears pants. Sometimes she'll put a dress on, but after a little while she'll want me to take it off.

GABY

It's not that I feel like I'm such an intellectual, but I'm not interested in putting a lot of stuff on my face. Of course I like to look good, but — for example — if I'm in a store, it bugs me so much to see all the dresses and accessories for making women "beautiful" that I don't let Nana buy anything in peace. I'm allergic to perfume and scented creams, so when someone puts cream on me — Mamá gets this idea every so often — I break out. Do you really have to wear eye makeup or lipstick to feel good? Bracelets and necklaces get in my way, and you can just forget about rings. I think store owners invented all this monstrous "feminine" baggage to make more money.

> Miss Mexico
> beautiful though you may be
> it's your beauty
> that shows you're a lie.

> Society acclaims you
> fortune awaits,
> as your image
> bursts onto the screen
> another image is struggling,

seeking its freedom
or a crust of bread.

Never will you go
to impoverished villages
but of course you'll say yes
to a trip to the United States.

But it's not your fault at all,
it's society that's done you wrong
doing your hair and your makeup,
applauding you on the runway
and hanging a medal around your neck
like a prize cow
(the one with the most milk,
that doesn't flick flies
away with its tail),
or the best-fattened pig
in the pen.

Miss Mexico
you're penned in.

SARI
When I was young I liked everything. Ball gowns, young men, waltzes — I'm
not from Vienna for nothing — pastries, lightheartedness, laughter. I loved
Persian lamb, soft furs, I frittered away everything on being happy. I loved to
ski — I think it is the most complete and beautiful of all sports — and when
I first came to Mexico I used to water-ski at Lake Tequesquitengo on Sundays with Miguel, and later with David, once he could stand up by himself in
the water.

GABY
Sari cuddles her neurosis close, there's no one who suffers like her. No one
else has endured the fate of having a son who's immature and a handicapped
daughter who will never be able to live on her own. Never on the face of the
earth lived a woman who ended up a widow with children like that, it just

never happened before in the entire world. My mother was rich, thrifty, she thought the only way to get ahead was by working hard. I never knew the young Sara, without any problems or major needs, full of joy and a passion for life. Then came World War II, and after that, life was a constant problem, just like it would have been for me if I'd had to flee to a foreign country that was different in every way from where I'd come from. First she lived in Chile, where her first baby died and she had one or two miscarriages. My father would go out to work on the ranches and leave her alone for days at a time; she must have felt lonely, I can imagine how bored she must have been. My grandparents lived in Mexico, and she was the one who decided to move, stripping my father of what he loved: nature and the countryside. Another change, another problem. David was born in Mexico, my father didn't find a good job and had to take whatever came along because there were three mouths to feed, three bodies to clothe. From the beginning David was a headache for them because he didn't want to eat. They had to run after him, tell him stories to keep him entertained, and then slip the spoon in his mouth without him realizing it. And on top of all that, I was born like this. There were doctors, hospital visits and hospital stays, equipment, trips, matters of conscience, my mother's eternal desperation, my father's death, David's running away. Then the money began to run out and Uncle Otto had to cough up money for everything.

SARI

I was born in Vienna, and I was always in love when I was young. Our last name was Dlugacz, and we weren't rich, but we lived comfortably. I studied to be a secretary. Later, I married Miguel Brimmer and we had to leave Vienna when the Nazis came. We went to Chile, where we lived out in the country for seven years because my husband was a self-taught farmer. That was how he earned a living. Since no children came along, I tried to adopt two Chilean children. I have always been impulsive and passionate, and when I get an idea or want something, I want to make it happen that very minute. Then I got pregnant, lost the baby, and got pregnant again. My parents lived in Mexico, and one day we went to see the Mexican consul, who received us respectfully (even affectionately, I would say), and told us: "Here is your visa for Mexico, because Jewish friends have done me many favors." The truth is that I wanted to leave Chile because I had lost a child out there in the country and I was pregnant with David, so I insisted on coming to Mexico to be near my parents. Besides, Miguel used to go away for days and days, and he liked living in the country, but I didn't.

In Mexico, Miguel had to go into business. He'd picked up Spanish well right away, and besides that, he spoke French and Italian. He learned Spanish during the three-week trip from La Rochelle, France, to Chile. In Chile we lived on the Hacienda de San Miguel, and Miguel worked for a man named Arturo Matte Larraín, who ran for president of Chile some years ago.

GABY

Ever since I was a little girl, I've traveled mentally and spiritually. To travel is to change, to revitalize yourself, see other things, be in touch with nature. I inherited my father's love of nature; I like to see plants grow and flower, I watch them from the window. I can look at the garden for hours. When we take trips, I like to go to the country to breathe the pure air and remember when I was in a scout troop with David. I feel like breaking the laws of nature and going back to being a girl of twelve, when David, who was fourteen then, and a group of scouts and I would go camping for a week or two near a lake or reservoir or a river where you could wash and get water for cooking. My mother pushed hard to get me into David's group, and thanks to the scoutmaster's wife, they took me in spite of my physical limitations. The group had both boys and girls, all Jewish, and everybody was somewhere between nine and twenty years old. It had a leftist orientation, with a very demanding way of looking at the world. Most of all, it was a Zionist group. That's where I learned a little bit about the state of Israel and its problems for the first time, but I admit I was too young to really take it all in. Besides, I had enough problems communicating without asking about all that.

When I first joined, my brother was already in charge of a group of younger kids. I ended up in his girlfriend's group—she was the leader or assistant leader. Nana and I went to three different camps. After we went to a few meetings, they let me go to a camp called "machaneh" or "moshavah" in Hebrew, depending on what its main focus was. We slept on cots in a bungalow, we did guard duty at night, and when we went out hiking, David carried me on his back or one of his friends did. I didn't weigh them down. They barely got tired because I've always been thin, on the skinny side, really, and from David's back I could see the waterfalls, the forests, the lakes, or the ocean. We climbed mountains and craggy hills, and I learned how to build campfires with every-body, I learned to smell the fields and the grass, and even to put up with the dust from the dirt roads. I also learned how to adapt to all kinds of situations when I was with them. I really liked being with the guys and girls there, because they all helped me feel like part of the group. When they couldn't take me along, Nana and I would explore the area around the camp. Whenever we sat down to eat, all hell would break loose. We'd yell, "We're hungry, we want rice, some meat, and a piece of cake!" And what they really gave us was beans, meat, and vegetables, and some fruit candy or a chocolate bar. At night all the groups would sit around a campfire and listen to a talk about history, or else we'd just sing. My brother had a reputation for winning contests, and when-ever he lost he'd be furious, especially if it happened in front of the girls. Since he was good-looking, the older girls would hang around me so they could snag him. That made me feel kind of insecure, because I didn't know if they were hanging around me because they wanted to be friends or because they were using me as a trampoline to get closer to my darling brother, who was so handsome that even I, his sister, was unconsciously in love with him. But he was forbidden fruit, so tough luck.

When it got to be a certain time of night, we would all go to our tents. There were usually four or five, with cots. Only two or three groups of two stayed to do guard duty in two-hour shifts, and then other people relieved them. At night there was always a campfire — called a *medurah* in Hebrew — that stayed lit to frighten away the animals and keep the people doing *shmirah* (guard duty) warm.

The next day, very early, the bugle would wake us, and then we'd get up and make our beds because if the inspector found anything not in its place we'd really get it! That meant having to help in the kitchen. Afterwards we'd go to the river and wash, and then we'd have eggs, beans, and coffee for breakfast. We'd really dig in after the fresh air and morning exercises among the differ-ent kinds of trees.

When we went to the second *moshavah*, we took a tent for Nana and me. I don't know why we got this privilege, but it was probably so Nana could be comfortable. This time the camp was on the banks of the lake at Necaxa, and we got to go swimming and have sports contests, races, and high jumping. What I remember most, besides the prizes my brother won, was a hailstorm that blanketed the entire area. It was very cold that night, and our cots got soaked, and so we decided not to sleep in the tents. We built a huge campfire even though we were afraid the wet wood wouldn't last through the night. We started singing and dancing, and Nana dressed me in the warmest outfit I'd brought, although that was damp too, and it felt freezing at first.

Yes, of course this was one of those military-type organizations. They trained young people who wanted to go to Israel, where unfortunately everyone has to serve in the army, even the girls. The kids who went to the camp weren't always from left-leaning families. Some of them were religious, even on the fanatic side, and some were problem kids. I'm not sure whether this switch from being religious to what we'd call Marxism or materialist philosophy (which to me are two different things) was good for them, because I don't know a single person in my group who stayed in Israel for good. They all went for a while, to try things out there, but they came back because they wanted the comforts and nonmilitarism of Mexico. I'm critical of Jews who clamor for Israel but when push comes to shove would rather have the peaceful life of the countries where they were born. The hard life in Israel, full of danger and death, wasn't for them. If God had made me physically healthy and my parents had inculcated Judaism in me, I'm sure I'd have gone to the land of my ancestors Moses and Abraham right from the start.

The third and last *machaneh* was in Valle de Bravo, near the lake, where even though nature was more beautiful than we could hope for, the mosquitoes ate us alive, not to mention what they did to our mood, and we couldn't enjoy the beauty of the place. But we tried to get to the Bridal Veil Falls, and we went out around the lake.

FLORENCIA
Ever since Gaby was little, what she liked to do most was go on a trip. She used to go on trips with Otto and Betty Modley in San Francisco, and because back then she could walk a little if someone had her by each arm, we'd take the opportunity to get some exercise.

GABY
I liked — loved — going to the country, ever since I was a kid. Whenever Nana and I had a chance to go somewhere, we'd take the maids and my dog, Connie. Nana would fill up a scout backpack with lots of things and put it on me, and we'd get on a bus going out of town.

FLORENCIA
Gaby can put up with a lot. She can be on a bus for hours without getting
tired.

GABY
I took a lot of trips, some for pleasure and others to see doctors and rehabilitation centers in the United States. I went to Europe, too. But there was nothing
like going places with my friends the Gómezes when Arturo was alive. Once
we took a trip along the Pacific coast, to Acapulco and Zihuatanejo, and into
Michoacán, to Uruapan and Pátzcuaro. I liked Acapulco when I used to go
with my father, but this time I couldn't stand it. The skyscrapers blocked the
view of the ocean, the ocean was disgusting, and the people who lived there
had been pushed up into the hills where there wasn't any drinking water or
electricity or any kind of services at all. What's going on? Why did they do
this to the bay? Since I didn't have the answer to these questions, my body
responded by getting weaker and weaker, while my brain wandered off into a
tremendously apathetic loneliness. I retreated into myself and wanted to get
out of there as fast as I could. I felt discouraged, but when we set off down
the highway to Zihuatanejo, the feeling of heaviness began to lighten once I
saw the vast expanses of mangroves and coconut groves that enrich your soul
and make you meditate. We went through the Costa Grande, moving away
from the ocean every so often only to have it come back into view in a different color: blue, light green, emerald green, violet. We stopped the car to
gaze at it in all its splendor. As we crossed the dry hills that had been burned
by the sun, a different feeling began to sink in: desolation, the poverty of the
land itself and of the villages settled there years ago. The transformation from
parched dryness to the luxuriance of mangroves and coconut groves seemed
surprising. We went through a lot of little villages and got stopped a number
of times by soldiers who wanted to see whether we had any drugs on us. They
searched the car, and while they were going through everything I thought of
the guerrillas in the sierras of the states of Guerrero and Morelos. I remembered José de Molina's songs about revolution, and I longed to see Genaro
Vázquez, whom I admired so much, even if it was only from far away:

Genaro and Che are two trees
walking with the forest

stretching out their green branches
they are mangroves and palm trees
lianas and coconut groves.
Genaro and Che are two trees
hidden in the sierra.

From their branches now dark
the brave ones inch down.
In the hollows of their trunks
they have hidden their weapons
and from the leafy heights
they descend at dawn.
They are mangroves too,
and they are also the forest
which is why, in the Costa Grande,
people say the forest walks,
full of trees moving forward,
full of men who are trees.

The campesinos are the land, they are fertilizer and seed.

But those who go up to the sierra
soaring up into the night
carrying their ancient rifles,
they are her only guardians
her true lovers.
They watch over her if she falls asleep
and awaken her
by calling her name:
"*Tierra mía,* my land, land of freedom."

Genaro and Che are two trees
in whose branches dwell
the most verdant hopes.

At sunset we got to Zihuatanejo, a village that is still untouched, and when
we couldn't find a place to stay we went into a lot where something was being
built and pitched our tent on one of the foundations. But the tent couldn't

hold all seven of us, so we put the seats in the car all the way back, which made two very comfortable beds for Nana and me. The night was clear and the sky was full of stars. We gazed up at the sky for a while, and after that we all went to sleep.

From my bed in the "José Camilo," which is what I'd named my car, I thought about everything I'd seen. I kept looking at the stars, the tallest palm trees, and then the stars again, and little by little I fell asleep.

The plants will sprout as you walk by
you will sow flowers of love with your hands
and they will name you Camilo Torres.

You existed, and I never knew it!
a man of great spirit
and I never knew you
soul of love
whom I discover now.

Glorious apparition
Glorious light of my being
Clean, transparent
who, when injustice looms,
raises his voice.

We crucify you
with every day of conformity,
with every day we do not struggle,
the misfortune of those
who do not want to understand
that every day is in need of redemption.

The fields will sprout
the songs will bloom
and a thousand and one Camilos
will bear fruit.

The next morning we put on our bathing suits and spent the whole day swimming in the ocean. We ate seafood; Nana fed me oysters, and they tasted heavenly. I got a lot of sun, because unlike those "healthy" spoiled brats I liked to feel the sun beating down on my body. At night we camped on another beach called "La Ropa," where several people had pitched tents, and they were very friendly and invited us in. We saw a beautiful sunset, and I fell asleep to the sound of the waves crashing rhythmically onto the beach.

> I am looking for a place
> but I don't know where to go
> nothing soothes me
> all that breaks out along my coastline
> are storms.
>
> When I loved
> I suffered
> when I played
> I got hurt
> if I hated
> I despised myself.
> I have studied.
> I have learned,
> but nothing
> has dispersed
> the hurricanes and storms
> along my coastline.
>
> I am looking for a place
> but I don't know where to go
> nothing soothes me
> all that breaks out along my coastline
> are storms
> destructive hurricanes
> that form from my ideas.
>
> When I loved
> I suffered
> when I played
> I got hurt
> if I hated
> I despised myself.

I have studied
and I have learned
but none of it
has dispersed
the hurricanes and storms
along my coastline.

David got off to a very sad start in life because my mother was so anxious to somehow get back her first child, the son she had in Chile who died — when he was only a few days old — from a brain tumor, according to her doctors. When my father saw how my mother despaired over losing her little boy, he made her another right away. Then she insisted on moving to Mexico because Chile was where she'd lost a baby, and all four of my grandparents were already here. Plus the Modleys had emigrated to San Francisco. My mother — pregnant with David — wanted to be closer to her family.

Then David was born, and all of my mother's hopes and desires centered on this small child, who was very weak. He didn't eat well, and he had stomach problems all the time, although today he's over six feet, wins tennis championships, and always has a good suntan. Then I was born with this problem we know only too well. David wasn't told about what was going on, because my mother wanted to spare him any problems, so she tried to keep him away from the conflict that I represented in her life, in my mother's life. I say my *mother* because I never felt like I represented conflict in my father's life. We grew older, and even though it looked like we were together, David spent all his time at friends' houses or in the street — but never with me. When my father realized what was going on, he tried to make things better by making David spend more time with me, but my mother kept saying he was very young to have responsibilities, that the responsibilities would come along when he got older. This may seem like it contradicts the letters where I talked about how David and I used to play with each other and go out together, but our opportunities for spending time together were few and far between, and we hardly had any at all once he was a teenager. At that point I did spend plenty of time home alone, always with Nana or with the maids, but never with my brother.

David is intelligent but spoiled; he's irresponsible, he's selfish. When Papá died, Mamá and the whole family demanded that he take care of us —

his sister and his mother—because he was the only man in the family. The poor guy couldn't manage to grasp this awful situation, and the only way out opened up: an airplane, get on a plane and get out of there. My poor, darling brother! not to mention: My poor mother! But in the end, we all shape our lives in our own way, and he had to do it by hurting himself and hurting us. At the time, I think I came to hate him, and I also hated my mother, who ran off to take care of him while forgetting that I existed. Nana and I ended up alone for months. Since then, what little communication there was between us has broken off. I don't deny that we love each other, but real communication? No. He communicates with Mamá, and is more in touch with my Cousin Dinah than with me. That's his choice.

FLORENCIA
David was free to do whatever he wanted ever since he was a boy.

GABY
I don't feel guilty about the way we are. David shook off the ties that could have brought us together, and besides, I didn't ask to be born this way. And if he left home so young, I can see why, because nobody could live with my mother and how neurotic she is.

SARI
I always tried to be with whoever needed me most during a time of crisis. David says I always favored Gaby, that I overprotected her, that he felt alone. Gaby says I always did whatever David wanted, and that was why I did not bring him up right. All I did was love them, that's all I can say. When I saw that David had taken his passport and the money for a ticket to the United States, I went after him because seventeen is too young to handle things on your own.

GABY
I've told Mamá over and over—and sharply—that he's better off without us. I don't like playing along with the "sick girl" game either, because I just suffer more. I know my mother very well. For her, being alone is death, but she's fine if other people are around. I can't help her, she never even instilled in me any feelings of wanting to be with her. In fact, I can feel her increasingly strong desires to be without us.

SARI

I went to see how David was doing, and of course Gaby was jealous. He had started his first year at the University of California at Berkeley, majoring in economics, and my sisters and I were pushing him, even though his real calling is painting. He is a very gifted boy and very sensitive, very intelligent, excellent at drawing. He won first prize in a contest at the university, and I took some of his drawings to José Luis Cuevas, who told me they were exceptional. But David's own instability and emotions took him to Zurich. He got married there, and I think he supported himself partly by doing illustrations and giving tennis lessons.

GABY

David is my only brother, and I love him very much. He lives in Germany, he's married, and he has a daughter named Yael. He's got problems like everybody else, and that's exactly what I've told him: that doesn't he realize that all of us have problems, that we all get depressed and our heads get messed up, and even our bodies get messed up if we let those problems get to us? "But David, listen to what I'm telling you. I've got plenty of reasons to be a lot more bitter than I am, and I don't get that depressed. You've got healthy hands and feet, you've got a talent for making people like you, you draw, you slide your pencils over the paper to make something good out of your ideas. You're healthy, you're lucky enough to have a wife and daughter, you know five languages and you can support yourself from that if you use them well. Your family loves you, you've got our support for whatever you end up deciding to do. You can open up a life ahead of you, you've got it in you to do it. A rough stretch? Come on, David! Lots of things could be worse, and I'm not telling you anything you don't already know! That it always happens to you? You're one more person on earth who needs to fight to survive. You've got problems with your wife and even with yourself? Every relationship has its problems, and you have to try to solve them as best you can, and be generous to yourself and everybody else. That's the goal any reasonable person should aspire to, and if you don't see it that way, David, you're an idiot and you're really messed up. If you want to receive, you have to give, that's the way it works in this lousy, wonderful life. Be happy every time you pick up a pen or pick up your daughter, be happy you can walk up a mountain and breathe the wonderful air from the celestial heights, and at your age don't start to be the picture of pessimism like Mamá. You walk, you see, you grab hold of things, you listen to music and the wind, you have a sense of touch, you have hands, you have everything you need to channel your situation toward a goal. Do it. And when the sun comes up every day, when you wake up, think about everything you've achieved, David, Brother."

SARI

David always told me: "Mother, stop worrying, I'm right here. I'm so sorry I can't show you, but what I'm thinking of doing for Gaby I'll do, and I'll do it after your death. It'll never be the way you do things, because I'm a different person, but I'll do it. Trust in life a little."

GABY

I haven't seen him for years, but he writes to me once in a while. I write to him a lot more often.

> An idiotic warmth
> rises in my spirit
> a crazy laugh
> bursts from my lips
> and a sad look
> comes to my eyes.
> I'm thinking of you,
> and to keep from crying
> I laugh,
> to keep from talking
> I stay quiet,
> to keep from exploding
> I stay calm,
> to keep from running
> I sit down,
> to keep from answering
> I don't ask questions,
> but to keep from thinking
> what do I do?

"Of course I'd like to come live with you for a while, with your wife and daughter, with Nana, in a little house in the United States, since you say you're going to move from Germany to San Francisco. But it's also true that Dagmar's family is trying everything they can to keep her there, which is understandable. We'll see."

SARI

I would like the family to be back together again, at least be on one continent, but that is a decision for my children to make.

GABY

David's situation has caused a lot of arguments between Mamá and me. What blows the lid off the little patience I've got is that she always falls for his little game. She sends him money right and left, she runs off to see him, she gets upset, she calls her sisters on the phone. Well, let them do whatever they want! Screw them! Let them torture each other, let them stomp all over each other, let them give in to her being a mother who gives till it hurts and his being a freeloader of a son! David's found his calling. He'll never stop asking for things and my mother will never stop giving, but as far as I'm concerned, helping David means screwing him over!

But I'm not a part of this mess, because the sad truth is that David and I don't have a brother-sister relationship or the kind of communication my mother has with her two sisters. So as far as him staying in Zurich (Dagmar is German) or going to live in San Francisco — he doesn't even take me into account, he doesn't even ask my opinion. Okay, we've grown far apart morally and physically, but I don't think I'm a complete stranger to him. His letters to Mamá are full of insecurities. He accepts the fact that he's done things that weren't fair, like leaving us when we needed him most. He's angry at his family, which doesn't want to help him this time around, but he promises not to leave his wife and daughter in the lurch. To me, it sounds like blackmail in order to tug on Mamá's heartstrings. I've told her that if she keeps on helping him, he'll never grow up. He keeps asking for money, for help, he thinks it's normal for Mamá to get on a plane and come get him out of a jam. It's time for him to grow up and fend for himself, because unfortunately the family's not always going to be around to help us and support us with everything. Let him grow up! is my cry, a cry that Mamá doesn't like because she's taken on the role of Mother Protector. The role of a mother has its limits too. LET HIM GROW UP, FOR GOD'S SAKE!

The solar mirror
of my painting
reflects the love
I feel for you.

I have painted, no doubt about it,
many landscapes
trees, flowers, rain
suns, skies, expanses of land,
springs
and winters.

I have painted
everything I can manage to see
through my window.

The solar mirror
has
fantasy,
reality,
happiness
and sorrow.

But what it most reflects
my brother
is the love
I feel
for you.

David's written me about the Handicapped Rights movement in San Francisco. We'd already heard about it, but not in much detail. They're fighting to make society pay attention to them, to give them mental and physical work that fits their abilities. For example, I could write for a newspaper, review books and even records because I listen to a lot of music, and do articles about literature. The *Rehabilitation Gazette* in San Francisco has published two of my poems translated into English. A magazine in Guadalajara for handicapped people has published my poems, too. But if I wrote for a normal paper or magazine, I could publish something every week. That's why it terrifies me — I mean, if I want to get ahead so badly and I'm constantly fighting for it — it really terrifies me to know that my brother, who has everything, gets depressed, feels anxious, and suffers from insomnia, when he could give so much to other people and to himself.

FLORENCIA

David has called me "Flor" ever since he was a little boy. I like him very much, and he's smart, always was. He didn't fail a single class in school, and he wasn't exactly killing himself studying either. He was always at the top, always ahead of the other kids in his class. He got "excellents" on everything without even trying. He's so sweet with me: Flor this and Flor that. He's Señora Brimmer's favorite, probably because she knows that with me around everything's taken care of with Gaby. So she can walk out the door calmly and do whatever she needs to do without worrying about having to get back because Gaby is home alone. Those two kids were very bright, right from the beginning. David was so smart that even his teachers ended up saying there wasn't anything else they could teach him, because he was such a good learner.

GABY

I hope the Handicapped Rights movement in San Francisco gets somewhere, because if they succeed in the United States, we'll follow the example here in Mexico. And this is one case where it's good for us to be copycats. I admit the United States is the most advanced country in the world. Personally I don't have anything against the people, just against their government. To be honest with you, I'm an anarchist. I don't like any government anywhere because all of them have gradually disillusioned me, which has been a very tough experience.

SARI

From time to time, I feel down, and then I run to San Francisco to take refuge in my sisters' arms.

GABY

Up to now, I've gotten a lot of love from my family and my friends. So I believe in love, but not as a movement that can change us as political beings. A political being is only interested in power, and doesn't love anybody. I believe in an individual kind of love that creates and destroys, in love of oneself, which produces beauty for the individual and for everyone else. I also think people need a cause to live for, and can't just be living for themselves. I have a cause, and maybe that's why I write. I want to tell the world that I'm fighting for myself and for my people — for the handicapped — for them to be recognized as thinking, creative beings. As human beings.

> And people do not change . . .
> solitude grows and grows
> and love that is not love
> becomes confused, blurred, cold and egotistical,
> and extols nothing.

I want us to have equal opportunities to live, to fight, and to be ourselves. One day I said to myself, "What cause do I live for? Why am I doing this?" Then came my answers: "For my family? Ha! They don't need me. For my friends? They need me even less. To fight for my people, the handicapped — that's what my cause could be." Even though I might not feel comfortable around them because they don't make an effort, and because they think the reason I've been able to get ahead is because of Florencia and not because of me. I get obsessed by that kind of thinking, and it destroys my good intentions.

FLORENCIA

What I see is that a lot of parents treat their sick children like complete infants. They don't motivate them or talk about what's going on in the world. If you don't stimulate someone's intelligence, it atrophies. The Brimmers always talked about books and what was going on in Mexico and around the world in front of Gaby, and in front of me, too. That exchange of ideas was very stimulating for Gaby. She'd listen to them without ever getting worn out, and she'd put in her two cents with the ABC. They would talk about literature, politics, the television news shows, even the comedies and tragedies on Channel 13. These conversations took Gaby out of her own world and made her a part of family life, and life all over Mexico, too.

GABY

Life's no fun if you live just for yourself, there's no point to it at all. That's why I decided I'd take on our cause, the cause of all handicapped people every-where. That I'd show them and the world what could be done. I think every-thing in life is like a game of chess: if you don't move your pieces, you don't risk anything, good or bad. The more experiences of any kind that you have, the more you know about it all. I don't know, maybe life is a never-ending adventure where a lot of the time life itself is at stake. But you've got to put up a fight, because if you go down fighting, it's an honor, but if you lose because you're lazy or you just don't feel like it, you sink a little lower every day. Yeah, there've been lots of times I've said to myself, "I'd like to see myself fight, to fight for something I really want." I want my stubbornness back, I don't want to let myself get the better of me. God, give me back my stubbornness. I've learned that you have to insist on what you want in life. I've finally realized that the fight to survive is what matters the most.

FLORENCIA

Gaby gets annoyed with people who have the same illness she does because she sees they don't try as hard as she does or make the same effort. I think what's happening is that they're not as smart as she is, even though a lot of them try to improve when they see her. They even try to sit up straight in their wheelchairs.

GABY

I'm listening to modern music on the radio right now, and I've got four books I'm planning on reading. They're on top of the TV, next to the pictures of two friends, a picture of my little niece, and one of my sister-in-law, Dagmar, when she was expecting. All that stuff up there is a mess, but I like it that way. It looks kind of disorganized, but that doesn't really matter. The feelings and ideas I have in my head dance around all disorganized too, but it's easy to get them organized when I want to. When I'm feeling bad or depressed — here's a prescription from me to you. When I feel lethargic and like going to sleep, even though it's not time to go to bed, I sit down in front of my typewriter and start a dialogue with my "Che." I tell him what I'm feeling, and he answers me. I'll give you an example:

"Praise be to God, Che, and to solitude."
"Hold on, what are you talking about? Have you lost it?"
"Let me recite one of my hymns for you, Che:
    Praise be unto You, Lord,
    for the life and solitude
    You have bestowed upon us with love

bestowed on this species of semi-gods
semi-vile people, semi-horrible beings
that we are, we humans.

Amen."

"Hey, what's the story! What's going on with you? You're running away from something. You're spending hours and hours knitting like crazy, but you can't fool me. Tell me what's bugging you."

"You know perfectly well what's bugging me, Che. I'm exhausted physically and mentally."

"Yeah? You don't say. All I can see is that you're laughing like some kind of idiot for no reason at all, so don't try to change the subject, kid. Tell me what you're running away from. Stop blabbing at me and communicate. I tell you, I liked you the way you were before, not the way you are now. You'd make crazy plans, and one way or another you made them happen. There was something gutsy about you, you really wanted to assert yourself."

"It's just that since Papá died, I've got . . . I don't know how to describe it to you. . . ."

"Listen to me for a second, you dope. Cool it. Don't be an idiot like your brother. You know what you've got inside. You've got a lot of talents, and the first is your writing. That's why I don't like to see you knitting all the time like some kind of dummy. . . ."

"The thing is that knitting relaxes me. Painting too. My paintings have sold in San Francisco, Che."

"Listen, this kind of escapism is fine for little old ladies. You can't waste your God-given talents, so start studying. Start reading, really start reading. What are you reading now?"

"Nothing in particular. The newspaper, the magazine *Punto Crítico*. I've got *Capital* here, Adolfo Gilly's *The Mexican Revolution*, but I can't concentrate on anything and I start daydreaming."

"Leave the dreams for someone else, dammit!"

"But I'm never going to have a real profession, Che."

"Listen, honey, you can study whatever you want. What you can't do is work at what you want to do. Get it?"

"Yeah, but . . ."

"But nothing, dummy. Don't give me any 'buts.' I don't know how you're going to do it, but I want to see you back the way you were before, asserting yourself with everyone and — this is what's most important — with yourself. There's something inside you that only you can and should do. So come on, start reading, start doing something worthwhile. But get a move on, the sooner the better. Ciao, ciao, *bambina*."

"Ciao, Che. All your talking has made me feel better."

"Give it a rest, all right?"

"Right."

FLORENCIA

When Gaby gets depressed, she doesn't want to do anything, not even watch TV. Nothing appeals to her, and she just goes to bed. Yes, that's right, when she's feeling down, she goes to sleep, but she wakes up very angry. Why did I let her go to sleep? she wants to know. And she ends up in a bad mood.

GABY

I'm alone, just like in the beginning, so what am I supposed to do? I'm tired of the contradictions, of struggling, of everything I know and don't know, tired of not being able to tell it like it is. Tired of how ridiculous life is all the time, and tired of death, which doesn't dare show its face here, no way. I'm healthy!

I don't think I ever wanted to die when I was in *preparatoria*, and I was never totally depressed. All in all, it was a good time for me. Okay, I had a lot of allergies — I sneezed, I had asthma, things made me itch. Maybe it had something to do with the change of seasons, plus all the smog made it worse. Then I'd take half an antihistamine pill and half a Valium, which would make me depressed and sleepy. It'd let the world go on without anything mattering to me. That would make me feel unhappy and dissatisfied with myself, and I'd fall into a vicious circle that didn't make any sense. But I managed to break out of it by studying and by using everything Nana read to me, until my allergies went away, and my *prepa* years along with them.

I don't know how to live
without giving love.

I don't know how to exist
without telling all of you that giving
is inherently more difficult, more beautiful.

I don't know how to exist
if I don't give
a flower
a note of music,
a smile,
or cry a tear good-bye.

I receive love,
I give love,
I receive hate
And it hurts so!
My soul is human
and it knows how to hate
so much, that sometimes
it wants to kill.
To murder? Yes,
don't be scared of this word,
because I did not invent it
it was taught to me by people
who say they have laws.

I do to them what they do to me
and so the game goes,
hate for hate
love for love
we'll go on living
with An Eye for an Eye.

The other day I went to see the Simmermans. They are such aristocrats
that I never feel comfortable there. Señora Simmerman couldn't manage to
keep her mouth shut, and she made a comment that made the bile rise in
my throat, something I've heard ever since my happy childhood from envious mothers and certain teachers who "specialize" in cerebral palsy. She said,
"If all of them had someone to help them, who'd go to school with them . . ."
It was obvious she was talking about me and Nana. What she said has two
meanings. First, there's what's on the surface: Yes, it's true that not everybody has someone to go to school with them. Then there's the deeper meaning, which is impossible to understand if you don't know what it's like at the

Centro de Rehabilitación: According to that, Nana does more than just go to school with me and help me take notes so I can study at home, and she does more than just make it possible for me to communicate. Oh no! What it means is that everything I do—like tests and homework—is really her creation, and it turns out that not even my thoughts belong to me. And that means I'm a fraud, hiding behind the intelligence of a capable woman: Nana, who accepts this supporting role for some strange reason nobody can figure out. To Señora Simmerman—who's of course a specialist in cerebral palsy, because she's visited institutions all over the world, because she supposedly knows a lot about it since her own son has cerebral palsy and she's "worked with" many of his sick friends—it's not just that I can't move or lift food to my mouth or go to the bathroom, it's that I can't even *think*. According to her, Nana does my thinking for me. I'm sick and tired of this, I'm fed up. Because if I get a 5 or a perfect 10 in school, it's my own mind that's to blame (if anything is to blame here). More than anything else, I'm fed up with people not believing in me. I feel like going to the Centro de Rehabilitación and handing them a copy of my autobiography, my experiences, and the poems I write, and then taking refuge at home with my peace. Let them read it all, let them read it. Believe me, I'm sure that woman doesn't have the inner peace that I've had since I decided to go to school. Sometimes I prefer the incredible silence of the house when it's almost empty. I think silence is your best friend whenever you want to get to know yourself better. And the way things are now, I can keep quiet for days at a time.

> Fire brigades, put out the blaze!
> this blaze I feel today
> burns in my soul and my body
> burning, searing
> all that is inside!

SARI
Gaby is so passionate that she is unfair at times. In the case of Fernando Simmerman's mother she is extremely so. Well, we've argued about it a lot.

GABY
I'm going to tell you about my friend Fernando Simmerman. He's got cerebral palsy like me, but he's in worse physical shape than I am. Fernando's very

good-looking, and extremely sensitive and intelligent. We went to the Centro de Rehabilitación on Calle Mariano Escobedo together, and he thought Nana was doing everything for me, just like a lot of the others did. The reason is because he saw the progress I was making, and because he didn't have a Nani in his life like I did. His birthday was May 1, so Nana, Mamá, and I went to see him, of course. I stayed a while with Fer and Nana. She acted as interpreter for me — there was no way I was going to send her off someplace else. Besides, Fer doesn't talk very well, and he's worse than me when he gets emotional. Yes, I know, that's a normal way to react, and I accept it. Whenever I see Quique, who I'll tell you about later, I can't say a word. I start trembling and I can't even manage to move my foot on the ABC. But dammit, everything that happens in Fer's house seems abnormal to me. In the first place, like I said, Fer doesn't have someone whose job it is to take care of him. Well, that's okay, not everyone has the luck and good fortune to be in Florencia's hands. But you try to talk with him and what happens? Why hasn't he been trained how to do this? My God, whose fault is it? He can do it, he could if somebody taught him how. Everything turns into a river of emotion and slobbering while his mother and my mother chat and have tea in the living room.

SARI

Gaby feels bad around people who are handicapped. You know why? She grew up with David and his friends. Now her childhood friends — the ones from the Centro de Rehabilitación, I mean — have disappeared, and so her world is made up of normal people. We only go to the Simmermans' once in a while for tea, but Gaby always returns in a state of fury that is hard to control. Their son, Fernando, also has cerebral palsy, and she loves him very much.

Saying good-bye to someone you love
rips you apart, breaks you,
hurts you,
tears your soul to pieces.

Are my lips smiling?
Let them smile!
Does my voice speak?
Let it speak too!
Where am I going?

I don't know!
I only know that I go
with faith and hope.

Now Fernando is going to *secundaria* at the APAC, I think. Actually, they put him back in sixth grade, but that's to be expected because he had been out of school a long time. I hope things go well for him, and that they're able to give him a lot of help. Fernando is a man who deserves to get ahead.

FLORENCIA
Handicapped people usually stick together because, of course, they have the same problems. The people who've gotten closest to Gaby have had some physical problem or some illness.

GABY
If I try to talk with him, Fernando loses all his energy. Can't he use an ABC by now? At times like this, believe me, you don't feel like being with him either. You can't stand to see him tie himself up in knots to get out one half-intelligible word. His mother? Instead of staying with us, she sits with other society ladies like her, and leaves Fernando — who's dying to be able to communicate, and for people to communicate with him — to sink or swim. God! I really resent Fer's mother; I feel absolutely infuriated with wealth, and I feel tremendous resentment toward those aristocratic Simmermans.

The tree that once bore your name
has dried up.
Blame the earth
where I planted it
Blame the heavens
Blame me,
who didn't water it.
Time blots out
your name, Fernando,
the beautiful memory
I left behind.
Blame the heavens
Blame anyone

stronger than you
and me.

I'm grateful to my mother, who even though she has her faults — a mother isn't a superior being, and she can't be perfect — made me what I am. Thank you, Florencia; Papá, if you can hear me, listen to this: Thank you because you never rejected me the way Fernando's father rejected him, from the day he was born and he saw that he wasn't well, that he was sick, through no fault of his own. I'm grateful to my aunt and uncle, Betty and Otto Modley, who did whatever they could to help me develop, and had faith in me. And why not? I'm grateful I'm the way I am. Why doesn't God give all human beings a way to defend themselves against nature's obstacles? It makes you angry that a guy as sensitive as Fernando can't express himself. I'm not saying he should get an education exactly like mine, because that has its problems too. But dammit! They could have given him enough independence to grow in his own way, and not put him inside a gilded cage so that nothing and nobody would be able to touch him. Life isn't something to be avoided; you have to let it kick you around, and no parents can predict the life their child will end up leading, so they can't cut that child's wings. That's what they've done to Fer. I rebel against that with every bit of strength in my body. It makes me sad and angry to see a human being with his wings cut off. That's what Fernando's parents are doing to him. Well, actually, his father just ignores him and spends all his time at work. But his mother clips back his wings every day. She doesn't let a single new feather grow.

> I was asking for them when I came in
> I was asking for them as I left
> What was I asking for?
> A ray of sunlight?
> A moonbeam?
> A ray of love?
>
> I was asking for them when I came in
> I was asking for them as I left
> but what was I asking for?
> The life not lived
> the love not dreamed

the rose that does not exist
the writing not written
the game not played.

I said Fer's mother kept him at a distance from me because he liked me. Fer and I loved each other in a way. "Marry me," he said. That's why I'm even more angry with Señora Simmerman. There wasn't anything wrong with what I wanted for him. I just longed to see him develop, to see him give what he has inside of him, like so many of us. It's incredible how a mother can be so wrong! When I see how handsome Fer is, how tall he is, with a soul so full of things that he can't communicate to anyone else, I get infuriated, and I'd like to scream at his mother, "You see what you've done to your son?" I don't say that out of spite or because I think I'm better than anyone else. I'm not the best kind of girl or the worst, but I was ready to give him some more lines of communication with the outside world. It's fine that his mother has kept him from ending up in a home or in some institution in the United States, but other than that, all she's done is get in his way. And let's not even talk about his father. He's a son of a bitch, and he's never accepted Fernando. Both his parents were constantly ashamed of him, but at least his mother — even with all her social engagements, her dinners and cocktail parties — didn't let anybody take him away. It's always the same story with rich people: they endure their sick child, their "abnormal" child, like some kind of fault they have to hide away. I had good times with Fer in *primaria*, the kind of good times that kids who grow up together have. That's why we loved each other, that's why I love him. There's one thing I'm really sure of: for a lot of people, my journey through life won't have been in vain.

Out of earth I come
and to earth I shall return.

I want to be called
earth, air,
fire, water
because that is
what I am.

I want to be called
north, south,

east, and west
because that
is where I am going.

I want to be called
sun, cloud,
lightning, and rain
because that is
where I am.

I want to be called
horse,
elephant, automobile
because I will travel.

I want to be called
Socrates, Plato,
Jesus, Marx, and Freud;
I want to be called human
because God is the Creator.

I want to be called
plant,
fruit, and shadow
because that is
what I'll go back to.

Out of earth I come
And to earth I shall return.

SARI
One afternoon when I wasn't home, Gaby cut her foot on the glass of the door to the garden. Nani didn't know what to do, and when I got home, I took Gaby to the Red Cross immediately. Her left foot was bleeding badly, just imagine, and I got very, very upset. It looked like she cut herself trying to open the door with her foot. By the time Nani saw her, the blood was pouring out.

FLORENCIA

Gaby's cousin Dinah had started to wash the dog, Connie, in the garden with the hose. Gaby didn't want her to, and so she kicked the door because she got angry, and that's how she cut herself.

SARI

We were all terrified. At the Red Cross, they wouldn't let me go into the operating room with her, no matter how much I explained that she wouldn't be able to tell them anything because she couldn't talk. But they said no, no one was allowed in, they were going to give her stitches, they were going to give her shots, they were going to sedate her — and I should calm down. But that only upset me more, because there are certain substances Gaby is not supposed to get shots of. Then I picked up the pay phone and tried to call Miguel and some friend or friends who might be able to give me some advice. In the middle of all that, a young man who obviously worked there came up to me and said, "Señora, may I help you with something?" I told him what was going on. He asked me to stay calm and then went into the operating room. A little while later he came out and told me that Gaby was perfectly fine, that I shouldn't worry, that she'd had the stitches in her foot, that she was in the recovery room, and that they'd bring her to me within the hour. Afterward I found out that he had stayed next to Gaby the entire hour, talking to her even though she could not answer, stroking her forehead, calming her the way he had calmed me. Then I asked him his name, and it was Luis del Toro.

FLORENCIA

After that happened, this young man Luis del Toro began to visit us. He was very easy to get along with, a very nice young man. He'd read to Gaby, talk with her, wait for her to answer on the ABC. He'd make her laugh, and he'd laugh too. A young person in the house. They'd talk about everything, but especially politics. In 1967 Señor Brimmer died, David ran away to the United States, and Luis del Toro became even more irreplaceable. He'd been coming over for almost a year when the student movement started up, and then, overnight, he stopped coming. We were wondering what could have happened to him. Gaby was already resigning herself to the idea that what happened with him was the same thing that happened with the other kids who'd come over once or twice or even five times and then never come back, when one night, she asked her mother to read us the list of young people who'd been taken to jail and there was Luis del Toro's name! We couldn't believe it. Gaby got very upset. She didn't sleep well, and the next morning she decided she'd go to see him no matter what, wherever they were holding him.

GABY

I was in my second year of *prepa* when the student movement began. Back then I believed in "law," in "order," in "justice." All of it had a tremendous influence on me. That was when I met Luis del Toro. One afternoon I was alone in my bedroom, and I tried to open the door to the garden with my left foot. But I broke the glass and cut myself. Mamá had gone to do some translation work at a German company, and Nani started crying, kneeling at my feet, crying and crying, holding my foot in her hands. She was still crying when my mother got home, and she was squeezing my foot to contain the bleeding. Mamá raced off with me to the Red Cross, and they gave me stitches there. The Red Cross was also where Luis came into in my life. He was a volunteer, and he came up to her while she was talking to Papá on the phone in German to tell her that I was fine, that his sick heart didn't have to jump around so much. He was already sick by then, and he died in August of that year, 1967. Luis del Toro went over to her, he offered to come see me in the recovery room, he sat down next to my bed, and started talking to me without waiting for an answer, sweetly and gently, not about me, not about my accident, but about life, about everyday things and all their little details, and I fell asleep — I don't know for how long, but it felt like I was at home, not in the hospital. Luis came with us when we went home. We became friends, and he began to come see me often. He'd bring books that we'd read together. We'd tell each other our deepest secrets, our problems, and before I knew it, I was in love with him.

> Erase you from my memory?
> I can't
> because you gave me
> a little happiness
> and hope.

It was that fast. I can't explain it. He was the first able-bodied guy who was kind to me. That's when the 1968 student problems began. Everybody knows it started as a simple fight between two schools, but on July 27 it became completely political. Nani and I went — without Mamá finding out — to the March of Silence. I went to some meetings in the University City, and I sat for hours listening to the news. That's how I realized that the press was lying and that the government wasn't going to give in on any of the six points.

SARI

Gaby had a woman take a letter to him, and Luis himself suggested, "Gaby, let your mother come first and decide whether this is an appropriate place to bring you." I went — I still remember seeing him there, I'll remember it to the last day of my life — and the next Sunday I brought Gaby. I was trembling, but I brought her.

GABY

I got kind of starry-eyed.

SARI

They never gave us a hard time. "I brought Gaby in a wheelchair to visit a friend," I would tell the guards, all women. I would chat with them because I viewed them as employees working for a branch of the judicial system, for the government, and we never had any problems. In fact, every so often a police- man would help me with the wheelchair.

GABY

We got to Lecumberri Prison early. I saw the main entrance with the police guards, who had faces like ogres. Mamá was smiling from ear to ear. We gave our name and my friend Luis's several times to several different ogres, and we were searched by policewomen to be sure we didn't have anything "bad" on us or in the food we'd made for Luis. Cellblock N was where we were going. We passed block after block of regular (not political) prisoners in blue uniforms, looking lonely. Some of them held their hands out past the bars, "Twenty centavos, a peso for cigarettes," and, as we went past, we felt embarrassed too. Others were waiting for their relatives, and a lot of them looked sad as they watched the visitors going by. At every block, two or three policemen shoved the prisoners back to keep them from begging. Finally we got to Block N, where another policeman asked us for our pass and our names. Block N felt different, it was another world, another world . . .

I felt overcome when I saw Luis, and I couldn't say a word. He was in Block N with hundreds of guys who were fourteen and older, waiting to be freed, because it would be impossible for all of them to be formally accused and then held there waiting for their trials to start. All my faith in the Law, in Justice, died there, and a terrible feeling of helplessness came over me:

> Five hundred miles and more
> separate me from you
> chasms of ideas and feelings
> come between us
> paths that are straight and parallel
> paths that will not meet.
> It is natural that I have had
> other loves
> other experiences
> that I won't forget.
> You know everything
> about my life,
> about my soul
> but I know nothing about yours. . .

SARI

When we went in, Luis took Gaby's shoes and socks off, put the ABC down in front of her, and started to hug her. He gave her a very brotherly kiss — always on the cheek or her forehead — and began talking with her. I left the room so they could be alone together, and while I was outside I looked up and down the cellblock, because it was such a different world. I made friends with someone who was in there because of drugs. I was struck by his white shirt, plus the fact that he was tall and very suntanned. After that, every Sunday when Gaby visited Luis del Toro, I would sit on a bench in the cellblock and talk with him. I was very fond of that young man, and he felt a lot of rapport with me.

GABY

Luis, would you like to know what I'm really like? I've changed a lot. When I was a kid, I was very cheerful, I had lots of nerve, I was playful, I caught on to things that were important, I played soccer with my brother and wrestled with him, too. Now, I have good days and bad days, I love to study, I love to find things out, and I like everything young people like. I'm a hard worker, I'm sincere . . . people say I'm understanding, and I say I'm too understanding; I don't like to be a pest, and when I ask somebody for something, I feel bad. I'm very sensitive to some things but not sensitive to others. Sometimes I hate people who complain about their lives and don't do anything to change them. I'm stubborn, I'm very critical, I don't think much of people who don't know how to help themselves. I'm nasty, I want to get back at the people who kill young people, get back at them in every sense of the word. But more than anything I want to live my life to the fullest. Sometimes I thank God that I'm physically different from everybody else, because when you're in my condition, you appreciate what you see and what you have. You appreciate life and death and love more. I'm more and more against being "immobile" physically and mentally. But if there's one thing in my favor, it's that I can't stop doing things. This has its pros and cons like everything else, because when my body tells me it's tired, my mind says I don't have the right to rest.

Mao says contradiction itself is a struggle, and that to resolve the struggle you have to understand that every situation brings with it a new contradiction that you must fight against all over again. Whoever doesn't accept this is fucked.

When I feel depressed, I scold myself: "Don't let yourself get knocked down, pick up your machete and clear the way. You're you, and don't you forget it, kid. Remember that you owe something to yourself. Study, study more than ever, because you're going to show the world — your world — that it doesn't matter where you are if your mind is *free*. What got into you to make you so depressed? To make you feel so sorry for yourself? Who are you to feel sorry for yourself if you have it in you to love yourself and to love others? If you stop being yourself, you stop being Gaby Brimmer, the fighter."

I chop down forests
me
with my machete
I cut down
obstacles and weeds
that block my path
I cut them down.
I chop down forests

That's me
and I destroy
evil thoughts
with my machete
and my reason.

Last night I curled up in my bed, and since I knew nobody could hear me, I tried to yell, "I feel bad, I feel alone." Who knows, maybe the reason I feel bad and alone and don't want to come out and say so is why I don't let anybody see me cry. But we've got to go on living, we've got to keep our strength up, get our energy from who knows where, put on happy "all is OK" faces — the way they say in English — so we don't make things hard for the people around us, because they've got their lives to live, too. I like the dahlias I bought on Sunday, they're such a beautiful purple. Like they say in English, "All is OK and why not? I believe in God so much that I must believe in His Help." . . . Shhhh. There are things that can't be denied, like the fact that I hear, I see, I sense what people feel (even though they may not answer). I think, I live, and that is a divine gift. And everything else? After that, nothing else matters. When I get my period, I'm screwed.

Now, as far as feeling inferior to other women goes, you know, it's not easy for me to tell you this, but sometimes I think my physical condition keeps people from thinking I'm nice. I think God has abandoned me, and I end up feeling bad. Do you understand what I mean? And I'm not speaking as a woman, but as a human being.

Here I am in my wheelchair, talking to you constantly, talking to myself constantly and feeling alone, talking to myself constantly and talking to you, alone, alone, because no one joins with me, no one sees me, even though I want to love everyone, everyone, everyone who walks by and never turns around to look at me, and if they do it's with a look of annoyance.

I miss you, love,
I miss your voice
explaining things to me.

I miss your look
that gazes harshly
upon injustice.

I miss your strong
presence.

I miss everything about you
and because I miss you so
I have no more love to give.

I learned to hate during that time. I didn't used to be aware of what was
going on, until what had happened started coming a lot closer to me. Then
I opened my eyes, and every day I got more depressed, and my hatred grew.
Pretty soon nothing was the same. Luis being in prison set my nerves on edge.
The situation in Mexico was making me very tense, and I was afraid of what
was going to happen to all of us young people. I know perfectly well that students are still being repressed after 1968, and that nothing and nobody have
been the same after 1968 except the repression. I got in to see the jail because
of a fluke, and I experienced the movement intensely. I sat listening to the
news for hours, and that's when I realized how the government was manipu-
lating the news in its favor, and that no would ever, ever learn the truth about
Tlatelolco. I saw familiar situations change, peoples' character change; I saw
my friends stop being friends because of ideology. You know? Sometimes,
when I don't feel like things are so tragic, I say to myself, "Well, not many
people have experienced this, and not many people in my physical condition
know what I know." I don't mean that I feel lucky to have had a friend in jail,
no way, but I do think I saw things that were new and different.

Tlatelolco means death
Tlatelolco means hate,
hate within my soul
hate within my mind.
Tlatelolco, city of the Aztecs
we can never forget.
No, I will not be silent
and I will forever say
that the massacre in Tlatelolco
is an example of inhumanity.

Who is to blame? Just one, only one
you cannot conceal the truth

it was the murderous government
a government gone mad
ordering the deaths
of students, adults, and children
who went to Tlatelolco
to demand that the government
give them a little freedom.
Tlatelolco means death
and death must be avenged.

I didn't kid myself about Luis, never did. I always accepted that he'd only see me as a friend and talk to me as a friend. I accepted reality because I lived it every day and keep on living it every hour, every minute. I always told myself, "You have to stay calm and not fantasize about anything outside your crappy real life, because they'll put a stop to it right away." I know Luis never said a word too much or too little. I knew there'd come a time when he'd get married, and of course not to me. No, not to me. I knew everything; I accepted it, like I accept having to eat so I don't die, and like I accept everything that happens because I have no other choice (and believe me, I'm writing this calmly).

Besides visiting Luis, I wrote him several letters that I never sent. Why didn't I send them? I still don't know.

March 6, 1972, Year of Repression,
second letter not sent to Luis.

Dear Luis:

I hope you're doing well. When we got home yesterday after I saw you, I kept thinking about the new position all of you took after the terrible assault you suffered at the hands of the regular prisoners on that terrible night of January 1, 1970. You, those of you who had joined forces with Víctor, have changed your revolutionary tactics. I know perfectly well that dialectics consists of change. And I know that we groups and individuals change a hundred thousand times during our lives. That's all fine. I'm not going to judge anybody, but don't you remember that you and I used to argue all the time about how to get more support from the workers, and you always denied the importance of first educating and organizing them, and then beginning the struggle at a particular time? I may not be into

politics like you, I may not know as much about economics or about anything like you do, but Luisito, I know where we live, and I understand the
defining character of the Mexican people. I know where they're going, and
I know that our people are deeply religious, that the only thing they believe
in is their Morenita, the dark-skinned lady, the Virgin of Guadalupe, and
that their religion verges on fanaticism. That's why I'm telling you that what
comes first is to educate people in the tiny, most isolated villages, not just
the people in factories in the cities. Watch out that you don't forget the
campesinos! They just may be the most important elements of the struggle,
because their boss doesn't hand them a paycheck every two weeks, and he
doesn't give them a bonus at the end of the year. Campesinos have to wait
till Mother Nature gives them what they need, they have to see if God will
help them out by making it rain on their land so there'll be a harvest, and
in the meantime they keep waiting, get drunk, and make babies like crazy.
When you get down to it, children are a campesino's prime asset, they're
his only source of wealth, because the seeds just get eaten up. Luis, the
campesino, the poor Mexican, has more faith in the priest, in "Father," than
in the politician, because "Father" always blames the heavens for any evil
and promises glory in exchange for so much suffering and poverty. All politicians do is cheat you, and they don't even promise heaven. A campesino
father enslaves his children and exploits them just like the government
exploits and enslaves him. The village cantina is the closest thing there
is to heaven, the only way of escaping from the harsh reality. Look, Luis,
I've listened to Nana's brothers and sisters, I've meditated a lot, I didn't
read three 650-page volumes of *The Indians of Mexico* — where I found out
about things more tragic than death —for nothing. No, Luisillo, don't take
me for an idiot, because I'm not. I still see and hear things, a lot of things.

You gave me some very valuable information when you told me about
the Open University, because if all you have to do there is study the sub-
jects in a particular degree program and then come in to take the exams,
that'll be terrific. To study at home with a book, work on a particular topic
with no time limits, and get my degree at the end of eight or nine years —
hey, that's not bad. I just have one question: will it work out?

I agree with you that the first thing to concentrate on is your getting out
of jail, and then we should reach an agreement about the issue I raised with
you: adopting a child. All I want from you is your name, and that's it.

Luis, I hope with all my heart that our friendship can continue once you're released. If it's not possible, I wish you all the best in life, because you deserve it. I hope for everything . . .

That's all for now. I'll give you these letters I didn't send when you come over someday.

I don't want to write more because I don't want to get sentimental.

Ciao,

I love you,

Gaby

P.S. I'm crazy, Luis. Don't pay much attention to me. That's just the way women are, you know. Nothing you can do about it.

Knowing that I admire you,
your name
is not a habit.
I have a confession to make:
Nothing is the way it was
before,
because of
constant separation
and time.
Time that destroys
what is greatest and strongest.

One day I wondered if I was lying to myself about Luis. Oh, come on! I thought, everybody lies to themselves to survive. I thought Luis must have been lying to himself whenever he said that the people were with them, that the socialist revolution would soon arrive, and that Mexico was ready for it. Whenever I disagreed with him, he'd refuse to back down, and he'd keep coming back with something dogmatic and with examples that were legitimate some of the time, but other times had no basis whatsoever. How can it be, I'd wonder, that I, someone who's shut away from the world, see reality better than he does? It's because I think things over, I draw conclusions. I don't believe Luis was completely swayed by dogma or that he was blind. It's just that when somebody's always isolated, when they're subjected to forced discipline, in a place where at the most they get two visits a week from people who are on a different wavelength from them, it makes them cling to unchanging beliefs.

For a friend who was a political prisoner in 1968

Help me, God
please help me,
let me not lose myself
in the anguish of death.
Lord, help me out of kindness
save me from loneliness.
Lord, I want to see him alive
to see him run free
all over the world,
help me see him like that.
God, I will seek your help always
to soothe my anguish
and the fear I feel for him.
God, as you care for your children,
care for him too.

I could give a lot of examples of people who lie to themselves because they're in jail physically or — what's kind of worse — they're in mental jails that won't let them be themselves. I loved Luis, but if God made me this way, I have to live with it and be good to myself and the people around me. Even if I have to fake it a lot of the time, and even if it hurts and I have to repress certain vital, natural impulses. There've been plenty of times I've had to jump through hoops to get just a few of the many things I've wanted. What's helped me the most is not to take myself seriously, at least not too much.

When I'd go to visit Luis in jail, Mamá and Nana used to criticize me. They'd tell me not to go, they'd talk like it was their job to judge everybody else, and my job to listen. They'd criticize Luis, they'd criticize me. Too bad for them! They don't understand that when you're young you break with all kinds of things: pride, vanity, envy. You try to live as natural a life as you can. You've got to live when you're young, because you have dreams that go up in smoke when you get to be an adult. If they could just understand that I love and forgive, but for God's sake, what do they think I am? A complete invalid?

I'm about to break the wall,
a wall of absence
of not being where I am
and being where you are.

I'm about to break the rock,
that resembles my stubborn head
that doesn't give in, that doesn't give up
even though it wants
to be where you are.

But if I did break the wall
or the rock,
Would you understand? Would you come?
For within these questions is pent up
a world of desire, yearning, and loneliness.

And if I don't break the wall or the rock
or the stubborn head or the silence
if I leave everything the way it is,
everything I have wished for will stay the same.
Silent, alone, and . . . change?
It will never come.

And life is action.

I became more aggressive during those jail years. Sometimes I'd even have a dish-breaking fit at lunch and start yelling at Nana for no particular reason. That's the kind of thing I used to do. When I wasn't, I'd be staring off into space, and no one or nothing would be able to get my attention. And Mamá? She was depressed like you wouldn't believe, because besides having to go with me to the jail, we had been abandoned by her beloved little boy, and it wasn't easy to live like this. "There are plenty of mothers whose children leave them," I used to tell her. "I know it's not much consolation, but being depressed all the time isn't going to help you straighten anything out." When I'd tell her to pull herself together, she'd get angry with me, so I liked it better when she went out. I almost suggested it.

Give me
a kiss

a caress
a flower.
I'm not asking for riches
or land, or a country, or sun.
All I'm asking for, Luis,
is love.

I wrote this poem about a guitar nine days after I saw Luis del Toro in jail, while I was listening to the folksinger Atahualpa Yupanqui play.

Guitar, play on, guitar,
for my sorrowful soul
weary
of loving.

Guitar, play on, guitar,
play a greeting for the pain
of being alive
and not at peace.

Guitar, play on, guitar,
as you soothe
my wounded heart
with your notes.

Guitar, play on, guitar
so that people
in the country and the city
will not cry alone.

SARI

All of you know that people manage to survive in jail. My daughter, Gaby, says Luis had just one motto while he was there: revolution. But I've reminded her that he studied French there. Although with Gaby the conversation took a different turn, of course! With her he talked about politics, tactics for fighting, strategies to follow, for hours and hours. I was surprised that Gaby knew about such things, but of course she'd heard about them in *prepa*. That's where she began to find out about Che Guevara and his comrade Camilo Cienfuegos, about Mao, about Castro. You know, the way all young people did.

GABY

He was trying to indoctrinate me. I think Luis had a lot of influence on my political ideas, but the first one to have any influence on me politically was my father.

SARI

More than anything else, my husband, Miguel, was one hundred percent Marxist. Marxism came before Judaism, and it had an influence on the children right away. He instilled Marxism in them, but he also instilled his love of music. We didn't ask the children whether they liked music, we just put it on and that was that. I remember that when we took David to his first concerts, he began to hate us. First his little head fell onto my shoulder, then onto my lap. It was logical for me to wonder whether we were making a mistake. But now David loves classical music and listens to it all the time, and so does Gaby.

GABY

In the street you can see
the students
marching.
Marching in search of
freedom.

In the street you can hear
cries for
freedom
for the people
thrown in jail
for telling the truth.

But the government turns a deaf ear
and there is but one truth:
that in Mexico
there is no freedom.

The students are armed
with reason
and not the rifles

that kill
in government fists.

I feel so good with short hair. Besides, my braid was just a rattail, and it had split ends. I cut it off so I wouldn't have to tie it back anymore, to feel more comfortable in the shower, and to change something on the outside, because it's hard to change on the inside. I hate anything that smacks of tying down. It's not something neurotic, it's just part of my character, part of my restless nature. Maybe it's because I'm tied down to this chair.

It doesn't matter to me if I lose you
my love,
because I already lost and won
by being born and dying
at the same time.

Watch out! people tell me
Does love really need
to be weighed and measured?
Does love really need
these terrible prejudices?
Does love really need
to be poured out drop by drop, my darling,
so it never runs out?

That's a lie!
Life is too short
and then comes death
dragging
hatreds, envies, loves, and labors.
To close your eyes and not wake up
that is death,
and during it all
we must learn to give.

It doesn't matter to me if I lose you
my love
if I can feel happy
for just a little while.

When Luis del Toro got out of jail, he didn't come to see me. Later I found out that he'd gotten married.

> I don't want to say anything to you,
> the pain of losing you is immense
> and I would rather silence myself with a sigh
> than tell you how much I've loved you.

> I'll silence the pain
> I'll walk the world with sure steps,
> I'll find another love.

> Here I am,
> you have taken away from me
> the refuge of your arms,
> your eyes' gaze
> has been stolen,
> yet I do not complain.
> I had you, I loved you
> and with that
> I will soothe the pain
> I carry inside me.

Nana is calling me to have cauliflower with hot sauce.

PART II

I'm not from here, or from there

I have no past or future

and being happy

is the color

that tells you who I am

FACUNDO CABRAL

GABY

All my life the question "What will happen to Gaby when we die?" has hung over me like the sword of Damocles. My family comes back to it year after year, and in 1970 I got a letter from my Aunt Betty and Uncle Otto in which they tried to persuade Mamá and me to go live in San Francisco, because there was a possibility my brother would come from Germany with his family. Betty and Otto are constantly obsessed with what will happen to me once the family has disappeared. Aunt Ana says Florencia is over fifty, that Mamá is very tired too, that it's not like we know so many people in Mexico City that I should feel very rooted there, that very few people come to see us, that I can't find anyone to read to me, that no one takes us out anywhere, that, that, that, that . . . that San Francisco has a lot of advantages over Mexico City. The first is that the family lives there, that's where my cousins Dinah and Miriam are. Miriam was born with asthma and is alive because of the tremendous effort Aunt Ana, a social worker who is half psychologist, has made. She's thirty years old, has a teaching degree, and has been married twice. I admire her because she accepts life in spite of her terrible illness. Dinah teaches immigrant children in San Francisco. She's twenty-four and a wonderful girl. I get along well with both of them, but I don't know why my relationship with Aunt Ana hasn't been as good or as close as with Aunt Betty, even though Ana has also been very good to me. I remember little things that hurt me from when Dinah and Miriam and I were little: one day when we were playing, I sat down on the ground and Dinah took my place in the wheelchair. Everything was fine, but then Aunt Ana showed up, and when she saw Dinah in the chair, she said something like, "Get out of that awful chair! God forbid you should be as handicapped as Gaby!" And she grabbed Dinah out of the wheelchair. I agree that no mother wants her child to be in a wheelchair, but I thought it was rude of her to say that in front of me. Another thing I remember Aunt Ana saying to me that made me laugh and cry at the same time was, "Listen, Gaby, tell me something. Why don't I ever see you get mad at the wheelchair, like other handicapped people?" I just stared at her and didn't say anything back. What does she know? All she could see was a little girl making jerky movements and dragging herself on her behind, and from so much dragging to get to where she wanted, she got a callus on her bottom that hurt, which kept her from being able to move by herself. The wheelchair was partly a blessing for me, because with my left foot I could move myself anyplace where there was nothing in the way, like steps or a staircase. Besides, what good does it do me to get mad at the chair if it doesn't solve anything?

Go to San Francisco? I told them that Aunt Ana's brilliant idea would only help Mamá if David brought his family there. Had she ever thought about what I'd do? David would live his life, and so would my cousins. But I don't know English well enough to get into college there, and I'm not at the right academic level either. I explained to them that I'd be like a parasite, waiting around at home for one of them to come take me out someplace and then bring me back after a few hours, pleased at having done an act of charity. Maybe they'd put me in a home, where they'd come see me once or twice a year? Besides, would people in a home be able to teach me anything useful that would make me feel comfortable? Would there be composition teachers or something like that, so I could keep writing? And what language would I write in? English? I told them I wouldn't be able to live the way they wanted, because I grew up in a normal environment. I've fought too hard in this life to end up as an index card or a file in some institution in the United States.

> To think of a sun
> of a dog
> of a boy
> of a field
> and to fall asleep
> on a clear night
> so you can think
> once more.

Do you know what kind of answer I got to my letter, not long after that? If I didn't want to settle down in San Francisco, they thought we should buy a condominium in the Jewish Home for the Aged on Calle Madero. They'd heard great things about the place. I could "try" to get used to it for my own good, "of course." It was decided. I'd go live at the home, Mamá and Nana would be close by, the climate was ideal. I'd have to give it a try. Ga-by-is-going-to-live-in-Cuer-na-va-ca. Letters came and went, but I was fed up with the family correspondence and kept quiet. Things weren't going so well at the university either. Nana was getting tired of so many stairs, but I kept on writing and writing to the people there. They refused to understand, and Nana would cry because she thought things were going wrong with me — especially in school — because she was so tired. The family had a point when they said she needed a good vacation, but then Nana cried even more, because they wanted to take me away from her. "In the Jewish Home, there will always be a nurse to take care of you if Nana's not there. All the old people there have someone to take care of them. Plenty of them are in wheelchairs, too, so they'll be very understanding of your problems." Pretty soon Nana felt shunted aside, not tired. If she was the one who'd been taking care of me and that was the most natural thing to do, if I was part of her life — a part of her, in fact — why did they want to separate us? They refused to understand that I was too young to go to Cuernavaca. Moving day was getting closer, letters came and went, and the apartment was getting built as fast as possible. Every day Florencia and I felt more depressed, more rejected and less understood. On June 30, 1972, I wrote the following in a monologue in English: I AM DOWN TODAY AND I WISH I COULD CRY OR RUN OUT. LET ME BE MATURE. I WILL SCREAM AT THEM IF THEY DON'T STOP WRITING THOSE UGLY LETTERS.

My brother, my cousin Dinah, Nana, and I never thought they should spend thousands of pesos for a room in an old-age home. We protested over and over, but adults never listen to young people. There they were, stubborn as mules, building an apartment in Cuernavaca, taking me out of the university, and moving me and Nana into a depressing environment, where you could smell death at every step, where the food was different because I wasn't brought up as an Orthodox Jew and I don't keep kosher or anything.

FLORENCIA
I liked Cuernavaca but just to go for a day or a weekend, not to live there for good.

SARI

This time I pinned all my hopes on Cuernavaca! I thought the climate was lovely. The Home was surrounded by flowers and plants, and it looked like an oasis — at least that's how I saw it — and I thought, since I'm always looking for a permanent roof over Gaby's head if I die, "Here she will be safe, here no one will harm her. All the elderly people here are harmless and there is a guard at the door, visitors are allowed every day, everyone has his own living space. It's ideal." Frankly, I got very excited about it, and there on the grounds of the Jewish Home we built a three-bedroom, three-bathroom apartment, with a living/dining room. It was lovely, with so many plants, all the natural greenery of Cuernavaca surrounding us. I sincerely believed I had found the solution. Once we had an exhibition of Gaby's paintings, and people came and bought them just like in a gallery. I made a price list with the titles of all the paintings, the materials used, everything. Anyway, I began to establish my life there. I tried to make friends, but it was strange to be with people who would vanish overnight, because at the age of eighty-five, people don't always wake up the next morning. There were many elderly German people there, and since Gaby understands German, she would realize that the woman talking to me one day no longer recognized me the next, even though I had been talking with her for quite a while. Gaby found this very depressing. Nani and Gaby got so depressed that I fell into a depression too. I did all of this with the best of intentions, because I wanted Gaby to have a roof over her head. The apartment is there now, without any furniture, abandoned, the windows closed, the weeds growing up the walls, pushing up the steps and into the cracks. We paid half a million pesos for it. We could — we should — go at least on the weekends, even one weekend a month, but Nani and Gaby get so depressed when they remember what it was like that we don't even go for one day a year. Who could live in an old-age home?

GABY

Sell it.

SARI

I don't even know how to sell it. I have no idea what to do, because the other elderly tenants each rent a room with a bathroom. None of them wants to get a bigger apartment, and ours is much bigger than most of the places people have in the home. I would have to speak with the president of the hundred-elderly-person Jewish community group there, but elderly people die, and the president changes over just like the president of a country does. Now I don't even know who the president is, so the long and the short of it is that I have not done a thing to take care of the apartment situation.

GABY

So just chuck it all, then — the apartment and my uncertain future.

SARI

I did everything in good faith, but of course I should have realized that a young, dynamic woman like Gaby would not be able to live in a home for the elderly. What was I thinking? And where would Gaby be able to live? Who would take care of her? The question was always there: "Where will Gaby live if I die too, now that her father is dead?"

GABY

Oh mother, don't start that again!

SARI

I got sick, and went to see my sisters in San Francisco, and then I went to Germany to see my other child, David. I left Nani and Gaby in the Jewish Home.

GABY

There were a few days in Cuernavaca when I felt triumphant, because in their letters Otto and Betty said they liked me better than their other nieces and their nephew (my brother, David). Until I thought, "I'm a disgusting egotist," and then I realized the price I was paying for being "the one they liked best."

A point in the distance
is what I've long been seeking
to comfort
the world I live in.
Whatever it may be
cries my soul
resting at night
going forth by day
in pursuit of a point in the distance.

The storm comes closer
the calm moves away
the sky is a blur
and the sea is rough.

The final judgment is near
but it won't hurt me at all
because I go forth in my world
in pursuit of a point in the distance.

The idea was that I'd get used to the Home gradually, not that I'd go live there all of a sudden. From the beginning, I knew that awful place wasn't for me or for people like me. That same night I said this prayer to God: "My God, I beg you, don't send me to a fate like this, take my life before I get old, Amen." I still say this prayer every night, and I pray for everyone's well-being. Believe me, before I went to live there, I wanted to live many years and grow old, like any other human being, and die whenever God called me to Him. But not any more. I think about death a lot. Every night I pray for God to take me, because I'm tired of living . . . don't let this confession scare you.

I'll fall asleep and dream
of being carried peacefully
down the river
that unites our bodies,
our souls,
swimming, the two of us together.

I don't feel like going on living in this shitty world, this contaminated world, this violent and insecure world. Tired of living? Yes. What does that mean? Tired of not being able to be me, tired of being dependent, tired of keeping so many things to myself. I know that nobody's going to help me with anything, and sometimes I think I can't even help myself the way I used to. I also know that what I want doesn't have a name, because you only live once, whether what you do is right or wrong. Fair or unfair, you've only got one life to live, and I'm not living the way I should be. I've also felt like killing someone and I've done it in my dreams, and even though it seems crazy, I've seen myself dead, covered by earth, turned into dust, violated by worms — the only things that would violate me — who devour me but can't destroy me.

Maybe that's why I want a little pine tree as my headstone instead of being buried in an ordinary grave, so that when my body decomposes it can fertilize a being that's living and beautiful and complete. I don't understand why bodies are shut into boxes and wrapped up in shrouds. Why are people so eager to preserve a dead body? It would be so much better to leave it free of all ties, cover it with earth (the only covering it really needs), and let it take its natural course toward putrefaction. In the end, wrapping a body in linen shrouds and putting it into a luxurious coffin won't keep it from disintegrating. I know people avoid talking about these things, but imagination is the channel through which people can express reality simply and cruelly. Listen, every time I write the word "reality," I think of Aunt Betty. When I'm depressed, I feel like getting into the car and driving up and down the highways without ever stopping, because when I feel low all I want to do is run to meet death. When I do meet death, my body will no longer react to anything and every single cell will say "no more." But I know God isn't going to hear me, because God gives and takes away when He feels like it. He's a good dictator, the most perfect of dictators. (God, give me back my ignorance of life so I won't feel as powerless as I feel now!)

Cover my face with a white cloth
so they won't see me cry.

The sorrow in my soul is vast
and my beloved is suffering.

Cover my face with a black cloth
because my end is near.

Weakened in the daily battle that brings us honor
that annihilates us before God.

The contradiction is pure
it is in man's soul
and the soul of every living thing.

Cover my face with a white cloth
so they won't see me cry,
cover my face with a black cloth
because my end is near.

In any case, I want you to understand that people simply can't put death out of their minds, and that death is inevitable. The truth is that I'm still raring to give the world a hard time. Thirty-one years can be nothing and they can be too much. It depends on how intensely you live them, which is why one day those of us who take life very seriously would like to rest.

I'm looking at the clock
so I can call you.

Time passes interminably
and my soul full of longing
see the clock as an enemy.

If I hadn't gone to live in Cuernavaca, I'd have swallowed that myth about old age. But since I was in the Home and I saw how they treat the people there, the way people's own children leave their parents all alone and how lazy the nurses are, I felt completely disillusioned. I've always been struck by the fact that nurses and relatives think that if their sick person doesn't talk, it's because the person doesn't feel anything. So they think they can treat sick people like pieces of luggage, as though they were nothing more than packages. They move them around, they move them aside if they're in the way, they put them to bed, they get them up, they never bother to say a word to them. Some children of people in the Home would come to visit, but then after a while they'd stop. First they'd miss one or two Sundays, and eventually they'd abandon their parents completely. A lot of the old people I saw didn't even know their own names; they were just being kept alive. Elderly people are totally dependent, they don't try or make any effort on their own. I saw a lot of people who would have been very capable of doing things for themselves, but they didn't because they just didn't care, and also because they were depressed, I think. Fun? There wasn't any. No distractions except for the television they would fall asleep in front of. I remember at the beginning there was an old lady who bragged — that's the word for it — bragged that her daughter would come to visit her every Sunday. It's true that we saw her on some Sundays walking around on the arm of a sturdy-looking woman, but the woman stopped coming, and the old lady began to fade and wither away. She stopped combing her hair, when before she always used to do herself up because "Tomorrow, you know, someone's coming to see me." She stopped doing herself up, she stopped everything. I felt sorry for her, but I also got angry at her lack of character. I wouldn't have given up. But who knows? The experience of being in the Home was what made my mind up, and I said to myself, "You've got to be realistic. If I start thinking about what my life would be like someday without Mamá or without Nana, I'd rather die young than end up back in the Home again when I really won't have the strength to fight anymore."

Sing the road
sing the pain
sing to everything
sing to mankind
for that is the song
that pleases the Lord.

Being in the Home was unbearable. But I still have nice memories of my days in Cuernavaca, where I met my best friends. One Sunday I was with the Gómezes for the first time, and there's a lot to tell about them. They took me to see Padre Wasson from the Nuestros Pequeños Hermanos children's home without telling anybody, and he said I could come to live there and they'd take care of me, and I could do something useful in return. I could type correspondence, reports, articles, write up what happened that day. I'd participate in community life, I'd be one of them. I'd only be around young people, boys and girls more or less my age — well, the whole thing would be a lot different than the Jewish Home. In those days I was feeling pretty insecure. At night I used to ask myself, "Where will I end up? What will happen to me? Nani is tired, and Mamá has infected me with her terrible pessimism." And like a stray dog I began to look for any opening in any door where I could stay. That's why when the Gómezes — Arturo, Marta, and Mario — told me about Padre Wasson, I went to see him right away. Two of them were spastics like me: Arturo, who's dead now, and Marta. The only healthy one is Mario, who works for Datsun and is studying accounting at the University of Morelos. We'd gone for treatment at the Cuernavaca Rehabilitation Center, and they invited me to their house. I saw a very united family. The father, Enrique, was the head of a construction crew, a conscientious man who stood behind his wife, María, one hundred percent. Then there were the children, Mario and Marta and the youngest, Arturo, who radiated energy in his motorized wheelchair and helped me so much because he infused me with a will to live. He had a strong character, he didn't let anything get him down, he was bossy and polite at the same time, the real head of the family. He used to get work for his father, and the people who hired his father looked up to him. "We have to marshal our strength, Gaby," Arturo always said to me. "And we have to organize a group to fight with the authorities for our rights, to get jobs, to make people listen to us and pay attention to us." The two of us set down three basic points for our association for crippled people:

1 We shouldn't be isolated or marginalized from the "normal" world.
2 Sources of work should be opened up for us so we can be financially independent, at least partly.
3 The issue of cerebral palsy should be publicized, so we can demand our rights from the authorities, like any other citizen can.

When Arturo died, I thought he wouldn't be able to help me any more, but when I need someone stronger than I am, I call out to him and remember him in his room, pouring strength into me, and I feel better, more sure of myself. Arturo knew there was no hope for him, but he didn't shut himself up at home waiting to die. He was a star that lit up his house and now lights up my life. He died in 1974, radiant, and the strange thing is that Marta, who had muscular dystrophy and was shy and had all kinds of complexes, became strong and charismatic after Arturo died, and she took over. That whole family was very interesting to me, but not to Mamá, who for one reason or another always had a splitting headache whenever we were going to go visit them or when they were going to come visit us.

I always wondered why Mario, who was so intelligent and not sick at all, was so self-absorbed, so spoiled, with no interest in what was happening in his country or in his family. He'd spend all day watching the junkiest programs on TV and listening to music. I understand all this, and I'm not criticizing him. I'm just making a comparison between someone who was supposedly healthy and someone else who was clearly sick: Arturo. I'd have liked you to have been able to meet him, because you'd have gotten to know a leader. Arturo outshone the entire world without trying, because he had incredible character, he was very strong, lucid, observant, attractive. All the people his father worked for would talk to him for hours, and when he died, they stopped coming over. Nobody went over there again. We human beings aren't good people. It hurts me to say it, but most of the time we put our own interests above everybody else's. And I'm not excluding myself from this vast majority.

I'd like to be a little girl
and have my father carry me on his shoulders
I'd like to forget my problems,
I miss my father, I need him,
ten rotten years without him,
ten never-ending years without him.
I'd like to be a little girl
so I could play with my dolls,
stare up at the stars,
it's been so long since I've seen them,
they say no one can see the stars
in the city any more.

On their foreheads children have
the star of innocence
but we adults
have no time to admire
the stars, or the leaves
fluttering on the trees

I'd like to be a little girl,
a good girl, a little star.

Padre Wasson told me to take a few days to think over his offer to come
live at Nuestros Pequeños Hermanos. I should "try it out" for a few months,
he said. I couldn't sleep thinking about whether this would finally be the solution to my future. I was about ready to say yes, but my Nanita's tears stopped
me. She was completely against it. What was she in my life for? she asked. She
also argued that the intellectual level there was way below mine, and that the
experiment with the Jewish Home, which hadn't worked out at all, was rob-
bing me of a lot of my self-confidence. All it took was the look of solidarity on
Nana's face, and my answer was, "No thanks."

Sun and light
when you're here
shadows and darkness
when you go.

When I saw what was happening to us in Cuernavaca, I wrote to Otto and tried to get him to understand our points of view. I told him that the fits of depression were pushing us under, that Nana had lost a lot of weight, that my life wasn't full of a thousand and one plans the way I was used to. Even though all the plans may not work out, they make me an active person. It's true that I had friends there — the Gómezes, my best friends — but there's more to all this than having friends. You need an entire environment that helps make life more bearable. Finally, as soon as we got an opportunity, we decided to escape, which was when Mamá had to go to Germany because my niece — David's daughter — was about to be born. That's right, break out of that jail, which was what the Home symbolized for Nana and me. I decided to move to Mexico City, without my family's permission and with Florencia's help, in April 1974. We knew the family would chew us out later, but I didn't care. The way those old people moaned and were neglected, frozen in their wheel-chairs, was killing us.

Just as I expected, the family got angry. Believe me, I love them, I under-stand their point of view. Before I moved, I thought about them and had some terrible dreams, but I also felt that if I didn't get Nana and Mamá out of that place, depression would finish all three of us off. "You have to stay in Cuernavaca, the apartment cost us half a million pesos, we're getting to the point where we can't handle much more, we don't have any more money or strength, we're old, we're going to die." My God, can I ever forget the bitter-ness that brewed during that hellish year in Cuernavaca, which caused Mamá's "nerves," Florencia to lose weight, and a lot of my own inner problems of not knowing what direction to go in?

Let Old Lady Death come
in her grim-reaper robes,
with her scythe
and her unwashed hair.

Let her come, let her come!
Let death come for me,
before my hair
turns to gray,
and my soul
perceives not

before my flesh gives way
and my eyes stop shining,
before all hope is gone
and there's no one to love,
before a thousand hours of agony
of being all alone!

Let that grinning skull come!
while I'm still young
when everything seems like a joke,
when a world
and lands unexplored
still remain,
when there's hope,
when something exists,
someone to love.

Let her come!
let her take me, let her take me
dancing to her monotonous beat
beneath the land and the sea.

There was no letter waiting for me from Uncle Otto when I came back from Cuernavaca. Anyway, he'd stopped writing frequently years ago. I understand why perfectly well, that he stopped because he was so busy, but it made me feel bad, and I thought the letter hadn't come because he was punishing me for being disobedient. "Gabriela Raquel," I thought, "don't be an idiot, he still loves you very much, even though you left Cuernavaca. It's just that the old lion can't show his love like before." That would be the worst — first I lose my father, then I lose Otto, a "father" who was fantastic. And that's why at night I say: "My God, don't, don't ever abandon me, not you."

Speed, beloved speed!
I love you for making me move
movement is life
warmth
love
being

everything
and all of it is G O D.

We moved into an empty house, one of the houses my mother rents out,
and you know how she reacted when she found us in Mexico City and not
Cuernavaca? I can sum it up in two words: unbearable and demanding.
Before I wrote this, I didn't think I wanted to give myself the luxury of accepting that my mother was a neurotic. All right, maybe we did spend a lot of
money, maybe I shouldn't have moved into a house that we can't "fix up with
taste." But what else could Nana and I do? What does Mamá think, that other
people don't have their own problems, and that they're all there just to wait
on her? Does she think she's the only person who's got a right to get tired
and exasperated? She still doesn't believe that Nana and I did everything we
could to adapt to the situation. Do you know what kind of tantrum she threw
the day after she got back, once we were alone together for a while? She got
so upset it was like she was going crazy. She put her head between her hands
and walked from one side of the room to the other, sobbing, and she started
saying she'd given birth to two completely useless children who she couldn't
rely on, that no one on earth had the kind of bad luck she had, that there was
no way out for her, none, none, none. Well, we already know that her son's
no good and neither am I, but listen, it's not her daughter's fault, and I don't
think you can blame David, because he never had anybody to teach him what
he was supposed to do. He was always allowed to do whatever he pleased, and
he was always given whatever he wanted.

> I will live.
> I am waiting for you, time.
> I am waiting for you, laughter.
> I am waiting for you, love.
> I am waiting for you, hate.
> I am waiting for you, vengeance.
> I am waiting for you, tranquillity.
> I am waiting for you, old age.
> I am waiting for you, death.
> I am waiting for you, life.

My family's main concern was still the same. They wanted to know whether
Mexico had what people call H O M E F O R G O O D in English — a kind of home
where sick people like me can stay when our parents die and we don't want

to be a burden on our brothers and sisters. But I've found a solution. I'll live in San Agustín, a working-class neighborhood where Nana's sisters have built a house. Simple people have always accepted me more than rich people, and they never get all worked up when they see me. They don't yell, "This is horrible! This is so awful, it's not right for terrible things like this to happen!" the way I've seen very upper-class people do, where relatives stage an honest-to-God Greek tragedy even though they're the audience at the same time. In San Agustín they accept me the way I am, period. I feel comfortable. In Mexico City, I decided — with Nana's consent, of course — to go back to the National Autonomous University, the UNAM. Since a degree in biology had already been ruled out, no use explaining why, and I'd definitely gotten it into my head that the only major that really interested me was exactly the one I could never work in, I decided to study journalism because as you know I'm in no position to choose, and since I'm good at writing and don't depend on anyone to do it for me, I said: journalism. I can spend hours in front of my typewriter, listening to music. If it were up to me, I'd already have spent years in a biology lab doing research, but when you can't do something, you shouldn't even dream about it, and I picked what I think I *can* do. I know I've been traumatized for a long time, I know about it all and I know why, but I wanted to give it another try for my own good and everyone else's. It's good to challenge yourself. Don't you think so? And I also said to myself, "Someday I'll have a book come out about this cruddy life I've managed to lead." Then people will see what a human being whose body practically doesn't function at all can do, somebody who is left only with a brain and her left foot to more or less live or survive in this crazy society that marginalizes anyone who can't "produce" salable items for someone else to consume for no reason at all.

FLORENCIA

Like I've said, I don't have time to think. I don't think about myself, I always feel like that's the way my life is, and that's all there is to it. I don't ever get to thinking about "If I was someplace else, what would my life be like?" I never did start thinking about that, because I think everyone's life happens according to fate, and everyone does what life has in store for them.

GABY

Okay. I enrolled in the UNAM. Fuckers! The teachers just as much as us, the students. So many courses that could have been useful but that weren't in the least because in some of them the teachers were afraid to engage in interesting political discussions, and in the others all anybody talked about was theory. Why the hell do we — the students — have a mouth or any thoughts? Very revolutionary and all, but we didn't protest a thing. Hah! Everything in this country is disgusting, I'm telling you, the educational system, the economic system, the political system. And books? Expensive, unbelievably expensive. Papers for our classes? Lots of them, and if we were living in some other kind of system they'd be used to improve it, instead of just being a way to give grades. But come on! They don't have any purpose at all. I was one of the many who followed along like sheep — it makes me feel disgusting! Besides, I could always feel so much political tension at the university, and I was a part of it too. So the *panchos*, who were students working undercover for the police, got into the Engineering Building during a rally in solidarity with the campesinos in the state of Morelos, and two of them ended up dead and some were wounded. All the schools in the university were afraid the *panchos* would do something to retaliate. Some other students have disappeared. The rector is only following government policy, he's the president's stooge, he's hankering after some political plum job, the UNAM is a trampoline, the waiting room for cabinet posts, whoever doesn't toe the line gets clobbered. Well, the few who dared to step out of line — students and teachers both — had their heads on the chopping block for sure. The government? Come on! Let's not kid ourselves, we're in a dictatorship. President Echeverría still isn't saying what happened when those student demonstrators were killed on June 10, 1971, and he never will.

I'm not saying that deep down I wasn't scared when I went to my classes, but more than anything I've got guts, and besides I'm not going to be like an ostrich that sticks its head in the sand and doesn't see what's going on around it.

I dreamt I was swimming in the sea,
Struggling between the waves and my soul,
I cried out for someone to save me,
but no one was there at all.

Will it be my fate to dream and never wake?
Will I never rest, not even in my dreams?
God! answer me,

and in the swirling whirlpool of my mind
all I hear is the sweet, overwhelming sound of the waves.

FLORENCIA

At the university, what people talk about the most, in the hallways, in the classrooms, between classes, is politics. At least that's what used to happen at the Faculty of Political and Social Sciences, where Gaby and I were. People were talking more about Echeverría and the Falcons secret police than about the political theory people study in books.

GABY

After my first semester in the journalism program, I couldn't decide whether I should stop going to school and concentrate on exercise, because my scoliosis had gotten worse from all the typing I was doing, and more than that I could see from what was going on around me that Nana, my right hand, couldn't do this any more. Her strength was fading, and I was a big burden to her. The kids in my classes always looked the other way when they saw us, and they never offered to help. Besides, Nana couldn't read to me as much as I needed for my classes and for doing the reports and assignments the teachers gave out. But on the other hand, I didn't feel like being around the house with Mamá because she gets so neurotic sometimes that I don't know where to go to get away from her. I felt unsatisfied, alone at school, without Luis, without any friends, nobody paid any attention to me, and I'm sure they were thinking, "This kid just gets in the way." I even started feeling like I wasn't interested in studying journalism any more, that it didn't matter to me at all. A lot of the reason I was feeling this way was because of the teachers, since they hardly came to class, and the ones that did come got there late a lot of the time, and they were boring. The people in my classes who actually talked to me are (or got turned into) real conformists, and when I'd tell them how mad it made me not to have anything to do all morning and that somebody ought to complain, they'd give me a little pat on the back and tell me not to worry, that you can't fight the system. Their condescending response made me even more frustrated, because I saw how passive all those kids were. "Just get your degree and get it over with," they'd tell me. Was my rebelliousness unfair or unfounded? Maybe consciousness-raising (mine, in this case) was bad for people? My parents didn't give me an education so that when I got out I wouldn't do anything with this "culture" and cost the country a lot of money. All of this — for what? To get up at seven in the morning and after Florencia drags the two of us up an endless number of steps, the teacher *didn't show up?*

FLORENCIA

What always got to me the most about the University was how disorganized it was, how completely apathetic people were about everything. Sometimes the whole morning would go by without a teacher showing up, and we were supposedly in one of the Faculties in the UNAM with the most energy, one of the newest, with the most going on.

GABY

We used to waste a lot of time, that's for sure. And then one day Florencia fell, and she didn't feel well. When she gets sick, which doesn't happen too often, it makes me feel very insecure to see her sunk into a big chair. And to top it all off, she feels like it's her fault and cries to herself! Well, it's like being in the middle of some horror movie spoof. Don't laugh, but we were like two characters out of the Addams Family or Addams Brothers or whatever they're called. Those monsters, dammit! And if you know you've only got one maid in the house to do the chores and your mother isn't going to start taking care of you and you hear Flor all upset because she thinks she's failing in her duty and you realize she's crying nonstop, then yes, you think there is no way you're going to be able to go to school.

> My ship is in danger
> my ship will run aground
> in channels unknown
> so I must save myself right now.

SARI

Sometimes I take care of Gaby, but I get nervous because she doesn't think I do things the way they ought to be done.

GABY

My reaction is to act like I'm calm, but inside only God and I know that I'm trembling. I get angry with her and even start swearing. That's how I try to keep the situation under control, because if I start to baby her, things get worse. Everything gets more anxious and out of control. That's what I learned when I was in those different hospitals and homes. Most of the doctors act that way, like nothing's going on, like everything's going normally. Since I couldn't take all the required courses in one semester, I had to pick just two or three. And I was always thinking it would take me such a long time to finish the damn degree. But Mamá has such faith that one day I'll earn money as a journalist that I want to believe it, too.

SARI

My faith in Gaby has been a salvation to me, even though I tend to be a pessimist.

FLORENCIA

Señora Brimmer went to different government ministries, to the Ministry of Public Education and the Ministry of Health, and she went through all the right procedures to get Gaby accepted into normal schools. She also sent articles and poems Gaby wrote to the United States, translated into English, so they'd get published in a magazine for handicapped people. That's why she says she's the father and I'm the mother, and don't give her anything on Mother's Day, but on Father's Day give her a tie.

SARI

Gaby was the one who did everything. Nothing happened because of me, I'm telling you, nothing. Not to put myself down, but to show the world, MAKE THE WORLD SEE, that a spastic can use her own strength to push her mother, her father when he was alive, her Nana, her brother, her friends, everybody, even those of you who are reading her words right now, who are holding her book in your hands. She could become a driving force and give meaning to her life; not only that, but she could give meaning to many other people's lives, the lives of other spastics and of people who seem to be healthy, like her Nana and me. What does "spastic" mean? you'll ask me. Gaby is spastic because cerebral palsy causes spasms. There are three kinds of spastics: rigid, flaccid, and athetoid, and Gaby is athetoid. Most spastics are very intelligent, despite the spasms. For example, my daughter communicates, she knows how to type, she paints, she knits, but she can't read a book by herself because when she has a spasm her head moves around and she loses her place, and she has a terrible time finding the next paragraph again. But she tries, she puts the book on the footrest of her wheelchair, on the ABC, she holds it down with her feet, and then she leans forward and keeps her head under control that way. She can read well, but you'd have to ask her what her neck feels like after she's been reading an hour or two, not to mention her back. A few years ago, Gaby said to herself, "Even though we're in wheelchairs, we can do things, too. I want to fight, not only for myself, but for everyone who's like me." An inner force was pushing her: "You don't know," Gaby says today, "what so many of us are capable of. Just like with healthy people, there are spastics who are efficient, not so efficient, and very efficient." Some are more capable than others. For example, my daughter is very gifted in languages and writing, but other spastics I know are good at knitting or painting or planning and organizing.

GABY

I know.
What do you know?
Actually, all I know is that I'm alive.
Why do you know you're alive?
Because I think.
About what?
About everything.
What does "everything" mean to you?
Me, God, and the world.
What do you know of God?
That He is in me
as I am in Him.
And the world?
I know the world is my native land
and because of that I know it is my home.
And finally
What do you know of yourself?
I only know one thing
but I know it well.
What?
I am alive.

People don't know what someone who has cerebral palsy is. Sometimes even the doctors don't know. They think we're mentally retarded, that we're half-wits, that somebody squashed us in the crib, that we have some congenital or contagious disease. They also think we might be crazy or dangerous, that we're epileptics, that we're going to have a fit, that we might rip up our clothes because we can't control our movements. All of this needs to be cleared up, in order to open the eyes of all the people who are blind and don't want to see our problem, who turn their backs on their fellow human beings — not just people who are physically handicapped, but so many normal human beings who also need help. Look, other people's attitudes have been a limitation on people with cerebral palsy, because their relatives won't dare take them to a restaurant, to the movies, or to any public place, because they're afraid of the reaction, which is always unfavorable. Nani and I used to go to the movies and sometimes to the theater, even though the people in the audience ended up watching me more than the actors. We don't go any more, especially because of all the practical obstacles that get in our way. It's hard for Nani to carry me with the chair and everything, to tolerate the stares, that attitude of no support at all, of rejection. I'm not some strange kind of insect. I just can't control my muscles, and I have spasms that make my body arch up and my head shake. This shouldn't be so hard to watch for people who understand what's going on and who are willing to understand people who aren't like them.

Many people say that cerebral palsy patients are aggressive and depressive in character. At the same time, however, we are very open to letting ourselves be loved. If we're aggressive (I do think I have quite a capacity for putting up a fight and that I ought to assert myself), it's because society's lack of understanding and constant rejection have made us that way. Being aggressive right back is the only way we have to defend however little — or however much — we're worth. Anger sparks a positive reaction in us. It makes us bristle with energy, and because of that we push the people around us to get what we want and need. We're also depressive because we're thinking creatures, and I think depression grows out of the thought process. My friend Arturo was beyond all hope, but he never let it get him down. He had a heart defect, and he knew that one day his heart would just give out on him. But he would come and go in his wheelchair, without thinking about death. He was always an optimist.

Did you love him? Yes I did,
with a love sublime
without passion, without desire,
now let him rest
at the Creator's side.

I've fallen in love not just once, but many times, although the strongest love
I felt was for Luis del Toro. Fernando gave me an African violet in a yogurt
container. This plant is so pretty, so generous with me that it hasn't stopped
growing and making little purple flowers. Since the guy who gave it to me
is named Fernando, I called it Fernanda. I get so excited watching my plant
grow, and it makes me so happy to see the tiny buds opening up. Taking care of
Fernanda makes me feel part kid, part explorer, and part botanist. Plants' lives
are just as complicated as peoples' lives. I feel responsible for Fernanda; she
can't eat or drink without me, and what's strange and beautiful about it is that
I don't feel tied down to her. She's not my possession, I just take care of her.

I also have some cacti that Quique gave me for my birthday, and they help
keep me going because when I see them, I smile, I go over to them, I give
them love and water every week. But I haven't named them yet. Maybe that's
because my relationship with Quique Marques is so unstable, even though
I love him. I guess I haven't talked to you much about him because I didn't
want to get more dramatic than usual, but I think it's time to turn that page.
Quique Marques is twenty-nine, and three years ago his girlfriend, Julieta,
who's a social worker, introduced him to me. All I saw was a boy who was
very serious, tall, strong, dark, and extremely withdrawn. To my surprise, he
came back to see me without Julieta, talked with me, and spent the entire
afternoon. He talked about Julieta and about his life, but mostly about the
illness he suffers from — epilepsy, though not the most serious kind. I don't
know why everybody picks me to tell their secrets to. It must be because they
think I can't talk. My friend Deborah hits me with all her problems too, without realizing that I end up alone, thinking about every sentence that comes
out of her mouth and about her problems, which have to do with parents and
hippies and drugs. Quique kept coming over without Julieta, as often as three
times a week. He told me he came back because of the tremendous force of
character he saw in me. As could be expected, the arguments began to start up
with Nana, who scolded me because, according to her, I was being disloyal to

Julieta. I got so upset that I quieted down and stopped telling Nana anything, but the fact is that I'd already fallen in love with Quique Marques.

FLORENCIA

Maybe it was a way of protecting her so she wouldn't suffer again, that's all. I always thought Enrique Marques behaved like a gentleman, but since Gaby suffered so much over Luis, I wanted to keep her from being disappointed again. Besides, Julieta would call up and tell me that Enrique didn't seem interested in her any more, that he wasn't as attentive to her as he used to be, and I saw that he was coming over here more and more often because Gaby, being as passionate as she is, began to worry about his epilepsy. She started writing to her Aunt Betty so she'd prescribe something for him too, she started looking for specialists at the Neurology Institute, she started cursing at her physical limitations because they got in the way of her being able to help him. When Gaby falls in love is when she gets the most exasperated about being in a wheelchair; she gets all upset, she feels anxious, and of course I try to keep that from happening.

GABY

After lunch, Quique and I listen to music, we read, I watch him sit down in an armchair and really let himself relax. Sometimes he falls asleep, and that makes me feel happy. When he wakes up, he looks around for me, and I get so excited that I can't fall asleep. We look at each other, we touch each other and hug each other; he knows how I've suffered and struggled just like I know how he has. Sometimes we laugh and cry together, we play at criticizing each other and criticizing society. If that damn medicine they give him, which doesn't do him any good anyway, makes him fall asleep, I let him sleep, and I watch him. If he's happy when he gets here, I share in his enjoyment. He looks at me with his brown eyes, and I feel a big fire burning inside me. Go a week without seeing him? I start cursing life out. I'm reading a good book, why isn't he here so we can read together? I wake up in the morning and think about him. At night, I pray for Quique first. If he's going through a crisis, I suffer when I think about what he's feeling. I get nervous, I kiss him wherever I can so he'll feel some affection, which I know he doesn't pick up on anyway. When I feel bad and depressed, he holds me or touches me affectionately, and I forget about everything. Yeah, I've figured it out, I'm head over heels, dammit.

If the soul wants to love
and give all of itself to you
but the body
doesn't respond
it is then
that the soul
tries to flee.

I get very frustrated, although I'd like to be able to ignore it. Quique's recently been studying English in some institute, and if he could find a job, I'm sure he'd feel a little more secure. For the moment, he's working at the Pemex refinery in Tula, about fifty miles away, but he's not happy there, and I want to help him find another job. Quique and I have been through everything. There've also been times when he leaves me very depressed, and I say to myself, "I can't take any more." But most of the time we're on the same wavelength. I can tell he really cares about me, and he knows I love him.

I would like to live with you
be your wife
have your child
and teach it what I know.

I would like to live with you,
I would like to give you a child,
but when I think about it
I immediately ask myself
What's the point of it all?

I'm not going to lose him, I've said it over and over, I'm not going to lose him. I know what I can and should expect from a relationship like this. I'm no idiot. Today is what's important, not to get my hopes up, not to build up useless expectations. I can't be sure if things will be the same tomorrow, or if something will change. Tell me, Quique, tell me everything, I'm listening to you, I understand you . . .

SARI
A gentleman, which is a word that encompasses a lot.

GABY

What I really regretted was when I got the idea of getting Deborah together with Quique. Deborah's a hippie, and her parents threw her out of the house. We've known each other more than ten years, and honestly I love her and understand her, and I even introduced her to Quique. Deborah's the only friend I have who suggests we take trips together, just us, without Nani. The only one who's willing to take care of me all the way. That's why we went to spend a week on a small farm in Oaxaca. Then we smashed up the car and had to stay another week, and one night she and Quique went to bed together. The next morning, I really made a scene. I told them they weren't going to make a fool out of me, and we went back to Mexico City. You think you're such a liberal, but shit! I couldn't hold back the way I felt, and I was afraid that might change my relationship with Quique. I realized that I loved him more every day, damn insecurity, and I was afraid he'd pull back from me because of Deborah. "I know he's started to fall in love with me," I'd already written to Aunt Betty. "When Nana isn't home, we give each other little kisses."

I'd like to see you
kiss your eyes
love you fully
but I can't.

I'd like to go to the country
and live my life with you
to see you my love
but I can't.

I love you, I truly love you
I'd like to be with you
and you have to know
that the love I give you is pure
I'd like to simply love you
but I can't.

My God, I love him! But does that mean I can't ever complain or feel bad? Aren't I like any other human being, who gets frustrated like anybody else? Please let this relationship keep going, and if it ends, give me the strength to cope, to keep feeling positive about things and not make the same mistake as

Mamá: believing she's the only one the worst things in the world happen to, and that everybody else has it great.

Enrique doesn't love himself. He wants to destroy himself, and it seems like I'm a part of it. He doesn't know what he wants. Hell! He's worse off than I am and . . . I'm nuts about him. Sometimes he spends the whole day here *sleeping*, and I just watch him. I also try to live life intensely, even if it hurts. What do I mean to him, really? At first, he felt like everybody was ostracizing him. Today, I can still say that — unfortunately — he hasn't been able to overcome his frustrations, but what hurts me the most is that his mother makes him feel more defeatist, because unconsciously it's in her interest to have him stay with her. Damn defeatism! Me, defeated before I put up a fight? Never.

At first I listened to him go on and on for hours about being lonely, being a failure, and having epilepsy. Then I fell in love, but I was already into the damn role of confidante and idiot, and I continued to accept it. Love either happens or it doesn't.

Beloved, hate me, respect me,
but be yourself through and through.
Accept for once
that life is harsh but beautiful
and that the sun is shining
for you.

Now I'd like to tell you about Deborah. Debo and I went to *prepa* together, but we never talked to each other. Our brothers were friends, and we didn't know it. Vicky (that's Deborah's mother) told my mother that Deborah felt drawn to me because I was such a fighter, but that she didn't dare have much to do with me at school because she was shy, and Vicky wondered whether it would bother me if Deborah came to visit, because she thought we'd really hit it off. And one day someone named Deborah came over to my house to see me. Since I didn't know anything about what our mothers had planned, I was pretty surprised that someone from school was coming to see me. We spent hours together, and that's how I found out that healthy, happy Deborah had a bunch of problems I'd never dreamed of, not even in my nightmares. My family is super-normal compared to hers. Her parents had tried to divorce each other several times, she had a lousy relationship with her brother, and her house was a constant shouting match. I was horrified, but out of all that we began to like each other, to talk over what was going on with the two of us. She was going to a psychoanalyst and was into smoking pot. I could see she needed me as much as I needed her. Deborah is very sensitive. She's been through a lot of disappointments, and along comes Gaby trying to push her forward. But I made the mistake of identifying with her too much, and instead of helping her I got so depressed that the day came when I told my mother that I didn't want her to come over any more. Mamá said that I absolutely shouldn't turn my back on Debi because she needed me more than I needed her, and that's how our friendship got stronger every day, even though it took a lot out of me. So when what happened in Oaxaca with her and Quique happened, I got mad at both of them, but it felt like Deborah was more understanding and cared more about keeping our friendship than Quique did. Debi is inhibited about making friends. It may seem strange, but the truth is that she is as shy as I am, and she's even shyer when it comes to making friends with women. Brother! Making friends with women is really hard for me too, and I don't know why.

If you tell me you don't love me
even then you won't
make me not love you.

The universe is love
we are just two particles
two stars.

Just two particles that catch on fire
when they collide
and burst into love.

Now my neck hurts, maybe because I'm tired. But today, though, the pain isn't because I'm repressing my urges to make living with me less annoying. I'm repressing my urges so I can put up with myself. Quique calls to tell me he's coming over and then he stands me up. A week later he calls again to tell me he's going to come by a few afternoons later, but he doesn't. But today I've got my impatience under control. Quique called. What's happening to me? Just hearing Quique's voice is enough to perk me up. Listening to him makes me feel better. What's happening to me? Oh Lord, don't ever let Quique feel pity or admiration for me. I don't want to be an object of either of those emotions from him. What I want is his love.

Sing, my soul
Sing, my psyche
for there is nothing new
but song.

Song is the murmur of the sea
or the river, small or large,
flowing with its centuries-old melody.

Sing, it won't matter if you repeat,
in being born we die
in beginning we end
to repeat what we know is no sin
the sin is not to sing.

Yesterday I was depressed, but not just because I was having my period. I don't understand why a relationship between two human beings has to end simply because one of them doesn't feel like going on, without taking the other one's feelings into account. Of course, I'm talking about Quique. I can think such awful things of this human being who's so fragile but so strong at the same time. As if the years of knowing him had always been a bed of roses. Oh no. Never in these three years have I allowed myself the luxury of calling him and saying flat out, "Come because I need you." I didn't want this gentleman to feel pressured or get angry. He on the other hand is completely free to make or break things whenever he feels like it. Who knows what kinds of ideas go through my stupid head, and if Nana knew that there've been lots of times I've wanted this relationship to end even though it might hurt me like crazy, she'd be amazed. Even Enrique can't imagine such a possibility. Just one look or gesture from him, and I melt. I start shaking even when I think about the possibility of it. Nana has her doubts about Enrique. Why? If he's faking it, then let him take it up with his conscience, and if he loves me, all the better. But at the end of the day, I'm not faking it and I'm not lying. I love him and I'll go on loving him. No one can take away the experiences I've had.

I love you, my child,
with a peaceful love
I never felt before.

I love you, and I'm not ashamed,
I love you and I plan on shouting it
from the mountains and the valleys,
from high in the pine trees

If you went away, my child,
by land and by sea,
I would know the paths to take
to find you once again.

You know, my child,
life is a short path
that we create,
inventing it whim by whim

One day I won, the day I met you,
one day I'll lose
but if you were to leave, my child,
I swear to you
I won't cry.

Someday I will no longer be able to fight my own physical handicap or his,
which is almost as serious as mine, even though he can come and go whenever
he feels like it. Someday what I built will collapse; my bricks of solitude, my
arches of isolation, my mortar of doubts and fears, the way I know he needs me
at the same time as he pushes me away; his lack of devotion because he's afraid
he won't know how to break the bonds afterward. Quique is like clay — clay
that allows itself to be modeled, but also to disintegrate in someone's hands.

Get out of my life,
my love,
because I don't want to love
or be hurt any longer.
The days when I accepted your violence,
the irony of your sleeping
here in my house,
while I would gaze at
your head on the pillow
are over.

Ideas about progress
are gone with the wind,
in the end, destruction
sweeps away our desires.
Get out of my life,
my love,
take away your violence,
your sack of frustrations,
and your self-pity,
take away the skin of your words
and leave me.
I want to keep all my desires
alive to the end.

This business of being a woman is really screwing me over. I don't want to curse anybody out, especially God, but what a cruel joke nature and then society played on us! I remember what I thought the first time I got my period: "Now I'll be able to have children just like you," as I faced the birds in their cages near me, with the nests we'd put inside so they could have their babies. I was sitting on the floor near them, watching them. I know I'm a woman, I've had orgasms. I have such strong desires that a single caress is enough to make me have an orgasm. I have them when I sleep, too, but I'm too young to settle for that; only loving halfway, never to the fullest. I know that the more I observe things, talk to people, read, study and get older, *the less rebellious I'll feel*. The only place I'll have children is in my poems, but maybe one day I'll be lucky enough to get them published, so that I'll live through them. Patience. Patience is the word I hate the most, a synonym for waiting and hoping, waiting and hoping, waiting and hoping. But what else is left for me?

I have you
but I don't feel you
I don't know you
well at all
and try as I might
I can't get inside you.

You haven't gotten inside me.

I see you up close
you're off in the distance
like this universe
that very few
know.

You haven't gotten inside me.

I hear you
but I don't understand you
all I hear is the voice
that calls me to the sea.

You haven't gotten inside me.

I have you
but I don't feel you
near.
I hear you
but I don't understand you.
And you, what are you thinking?

You haven't gotten inside me.

This love will pass like the others, quickly; and like always, only memories
will be left. This is what life is, I suppose, and I thank God and my own will
for not abandoning me because of my physical limitations, and for being able
to accept life as it comes.

From you, I expect nothing.
You took what I gave
and didn't offer
even a tiny bit of you
in return.
Everyone says,
"It's harder to give,"
and without your realizing it
I've given you everything,
everything out of love.

Life metes out
dangers, bitterness,
pain, and love.
Take from it what you wish
and leave me in peace
for the love I once gave you
I'll now take away.

FLORENCIA

Once Gaby went to Oaxaca by herself, with Ana and Raúl. They invited her for Holy Week and wouldn't let me come. They were going to take care of her. I stayed home and took advantage of the chance to get some cleaning done.

GABY

The trip when I had the best time was on May 26, 1976. I took a plane, by myself, without Nana, with the daughters of my friends Ana Solares and Raúl Quintero. Ana and Raúl were waiting for us at the airport, because they'd driven out from Mexico City before us. Raúl's family lives in Oaxaca, and we stayed with them. If there's anything I can't forget about Oaxaca, it's those women with aged, beautiful features, sitting like idols on the ground along the tree-lined boulevard. There they were, weaving, sitting at their beautiful, colorful looms, telling a chubby little kid whose stomach was sticking way out, who barely spoke Spanish, how much the fabric was so he could tell us. And the market — oh, what a market! It was like being in a swarm of bees, fast and precise. Old faces, young ones, children calling out for people to buy, selling bread, cheese, flowers, vegetables, chocolate.

When we went back to the house that night it was pouring rain. They put me to bed, and we all slept, exhausted. As I dozed, I thought life wasn't as bad as I sometimes think it is.

The next morning, the five of us went to Puerto Escondido in a light plane. From the window I could see the Sierra Madre Occidental covered with patches of green and brown, and then all of a sudden an expanse of blue on its shores that was embroidered with white lace. Puerto Escondido. We descended slowly, and it felt like my ears were going to pop when the airplane wheels touched down on the narrow, uneven, rustic runway. Raúl brought down the wheelchair, and then me. Tall, slender palm trees, laden with coconuts, and the salty sea, fierce, violent, and soothing, surrounded our tent. A feeling of being small and alone came into my soul, and the next thing I knew I had my bathing suit on. The water was rough, but we went in anyway, and a big wave knocked us over. I was happy having sand all over my body, but Raúl got scared, and the next day he took us to Puerto Angelito, where the water is calmer.

We had a good relationship right from the beginning. Of course, I had an easier time communicating with Ana and Raúl than with the little girls. Sure, we talked and used words, but at least for me it was easier to communicate with Raúl by looking at him, with smiles, gestures, and body language, which brought us together more than words did.

A rose is what I will give you,
a rose that is pure,
pure as my love.

The red rose I will give to you,
the yellow rose
I will keep.

The red rose is love,
the yellow rose is pain.
Which will it be?
Love and pain?
You take the love,
leave the pain for me.
Love on the beach
born of the sea.

She was a star,
you were a sun,
and fate brought you together.
But the star did not know
what your love could be
and everything came to an end.

Her vast love for you
was born on the beach, and there it died.
And I thought to myself, Sea,
Here too is where I will die.

At the beach, I smiled at the people around us who were curious and asked what had happened to me, while Ana told them a little about it. You have to be understanding and patient with people, and since sometimes it bothered me to listen to the ridiculous, far-fetched things some of them would ask (if I'd had a heart attack, if I had some awful disease, or a stroke, or a concussion, or had a rabid dog bitten me), I'd spend my time looking at the ocean and petting the dogs on the beach with my foot.

At Puerto Angelito, Raúl and Ana put a lifejacket on me and I went in swimming, and I felt truly liberated, not tied down, while the voices and exclamations of people who were amazed or intrigued that I could float alone in the water stayed at a distance.

I wouldn't trade those days for anything in the world. Even though I fell down a lot, was full of bruises, and got blood blisters, I also ate seafood, listened to salsa music, went swimming, and sunbathed under a sun that was so strong it had us drinking glass after glass of orange juice so we wouldn't get dehydrated. We also went skinny-dipping, and the way we communicated with everything was so natural, so free of all moral and social prejudice, that I realized how important it is to live everything to the fullest, and that for me life is a constant adventure, like a trip where you don't know how it will turn out, and then you start having a fantastic time.

FLORENCIA

Gaby came back all sore but happy. She had blisters all over her back, with I-don't-know-what-degree burns, but she didn't even notice.

GABY

Yesterday I dreamed that Mario Gómez and I were at a beach. I was walking along the shore with him, when the ocean rose up and formed shapes made of glass. Then I woke up and went back to sleep, and my dream continued: Mario and I were playing hide-and-seek outside a country house, I felt free, like a little kid running all over the place.

It's funny — in my dreams I'm almost always able-bodied. In a few dreams, I'm in a wheelchair. It doesn't make me feel good or bad to dream that I'm able-bodied, and I wouldn't want to live out what I dream, because I think I have a normal life anyway.

FLORENCIA

I put Gabriela to bed in her room, and she sleeps, and she's completely relaxed. In the morning, I go to get her up.

She can't do anything without somebody's help. I get her out of bed, I take her to the bathroom and get her dressed.

I'm always carrying her to do everything.

That's right, today I carried her to get her out of bed, give her a bath, get her into the wheelchair, everything.

GABY

I don't always dream I'm in the wheelchair, because Mamá says the wheelchair is in my head.

I thought I wasn't going to have any dreams because I took a Valium last night. I was very tense and upset for a lot of reasons. Mamá feels tormented about money, with the devaluation, with the cost of living going up, with owing money to Otto and her sisters who always help us out with expenses, the stupid apartment at the Jewish Home in Cuernavaca cost my aunts and uncles half a million pesos for nothing, is the money mine or not. Well, "mine" is saying a lot, because I still have trouble accepting that I'll always have to have an intermediary. Hell! I forget that legally I don't exist, and that at the bank I'm always down as incapacitated, and even though Mamá says this lousy money belongs to me, I personally can't take out a cent. That's having something belong to you? It's total bullshit! There was only one time I had a little money of my own, when I sold one of my poems to a group that played music about revolution. And they gave me three hundred pesos. They wanted more poems, but the problem is that I never write on assignment. I do it when I really feel what I'm writing, even though I'd like to be able to write when people want something, so I wouldn't have to be financially dependent on anyone. But it's clear that I don't have any business sense, because I always give my pictures away to the bazaars at the Rehabilitation Center. I always give away what I make.

In life I've known
traps.
Money is what puts people
in the most danger

because with money
even your enemies get paid.

Mamá is in the process of setting up a trust for me, even though she's made her will already. Wills traumatize me because the heirs are never satisfied, but if a trust can help my mother spare us all that bureaucracy, and even avoid the possibility of the government withholding my things because I'm "incapacitated," then let her go ahead and do it. I've always thought about giving up material things that will never be all mine anyway. I don't even want them. And then I'd have to make a will and leave what's not mine to my relatives, leave to them what I never touched so it would increase in value, and whatever I did touch, so it would decrease in value. In the end, though, man proposes and God disposes. But even with all that, I know I've been very lucky in life. I have friends and I also have enemies, I feel sure of myself, but unsure of the world I live in. I give my all to everything and hope I don't get hurt, and I try not to hurt anyone else. I want to take the measure of who I am, what kind of critical ability I have, and learn about the path I'm on.

I'd like to be able to say at the end of my life
that I was thankful I lived
and fought for a noble cause
like "human freedom,"
I, who am chained to this chair,
I, who am imprisoned inside a body
that does not respond.
That I loved my children and friends alike
and sang songs as night was falling.

I'd like to be able to say so many things
about my wounded soul
that lives in constant fright,
an anguish and restlessness that persists
without end
between dreams and wakefulness.

I'd like to be able to say in the end
that I was thankful
I could see, hear, smell, taste, and touch

above all, and in spite of it all
with this clumsy body,
in this wheelchair,
to have been able to reason and to love.

Mamá has been completely battered by the devaluation. Sure, it's affected every one of us financially, but does she have to take it so hard? This happens to her all the time, but in any case, I can't forbid her to get depressed. That's why I shut myself up in my study and don't let the bad vibrations in. I listen to a lot of music, we read, and I try to stay as far away from Sara as possible, even though I might get accused of not caring.

Mamá doesn't write to my aunts and uncles very much because she's always tired. Sometimes she's busy doing important things, and sometimes she's busy with things that aren't so important. There are days when she's so overprotective that it drives me nuts. Besides being a bundle of nerves, she infects everything around her with her fears and apprehensions. You can't live that way. I've got my defenses ready for those kinds of days. I just leave her alone and don't pay any attention to her.

FLORENCIA
The hard days never go on forever. I keep telling Gaby, happiness doesn't last, and sadness doesn't either.

GABY
Between the dentist, the lawyer, getting her car fixed because it keeps breaking down every half block, bank accounts, and insurance, Mamá is more worn out mentally than physically. It makes me feel bad, really bad, but all I can tell her is that's life.

People's feelings are an incredible hassle. I don't want my mother to be far away from me while she's alive, but I don't want to live with her either.

Mamá is so sensitive, the exact opposite of Aunt Betty. Poor thing, she thinks somebody's always hurting her and that she's the target of bad luck. She's constantly being hurt, beaten up by what people say to her, by what people do to her, by World War II, the persecution of the Jews. Whenever I'm around her, I can't stay on an even keel. There are times when I have to be so objective that I get too cold toward everything, but other times I have to take a more subjective approach in order to feel more human. Most of the time, though, I get to a point where I don't give a fuck about anything, and I just want them to let me die in peace.

I think I remember that forty-one million people died in World War II. How many in Vietnam? Of course, it's not about how many people died, but about who survived those horrible bombings, the napalm. They'll never be healthy physically, or mentally either. Are my parents healthy? Were they healthy after the war and the Nazi persecution? Maybe there's a difference. The Vietnamese people are in their country now, but the Jewish refugees aren't. . . . It's sensitive.

SARI

Even though the lawyers and the doctor agree that Gaby is completely lucid, they won't accept her signature, which means that we have to accept whatever demands any bank makes. If someone — the first bank employee we see — says, "I have no indication that your daughter is normal," then the entire process that Gaby has always been subjected to starts up: psychiatrists, psychologists, all sorts of doctors. No law protects her. We're lost, and that is why I want to set up a trust to protect her.

> With my forehead held high
> and a white cane
> I seek my way.
>
> Like all of us
> I've had a past
> and a present
> where fortune
> has been very kind to me,
> it's true.
>
> Setbacks
> bitterness and pain
> mounted up
> but I cannot deny
> that laughter and fun burst forth.
> With my forehead held high

and a cane in my hand
to lean on
I go seeking my way
and find it I will.

SARI

Miguel Brimmer was a selfless man. He worked long days, and when he came home at night, satisfied at having earned a day's pay and being able to support us, he would hug his children, play with them a little, and shut himself up in his room. The light stayed on until all hours of the night, because Miguel loved to study. I was always the one who was apprehensive, the one who was scared. Miguel was spiritual, I was material. I would be thinking that our money would not stretch far enough, that Gaby would always need to be taken care of. And David has never stopped asking me for money, and I haven't stopped sending it. I'm not his mother for nothing.

GABY

"You're asking a lot, nothing's ever enough for you, there's nothing more we can do. We're two old women, I don't have any strength left, I'm hard up, I'm drowning under these expenses, look how much pressure I'm under, last night I couldn't sleep, I'm tired, I woke up tired, I understand what you're saying but there's nothing more we can do," Mamá says. And I tell her that her argument is as valid as mine: "I just want to live a little."

I don't know, Mamá has very strange reactions to things. She turns cold and then criticizes the entire world. I see in her a lot of characteristics of a woman who is classist or only thinks about herself or however you say it.

Listen, Che, this anger is suffocating me. I have to let off some steam with you: What do you think Mamá did when my sister-in-law and my niece were here? She refused to make any effort to take them to the beach, and that makes me sick! It's not just that she's tired, but that she doesn't want to spend the money to give her daughter-in-law and her granddaughter Yael a few days of fun. Both of them deserve something more than having afternoon tea with a negative old lady who doesn't want to lift a finger to make them happy. I remember many scenes from my parents' marriage. Mamá was always cold to Papá, at least she was in front of me, of course. Dagmar and Yaelina's arrival here was a big thing for me, because while they were here, I wanted more and more to have a child. Having Yaelina around changed the whole environment. She was only here for a few days of vacation, enough to charm us all. Every day I found out new things about her, and she also found new people who were ready to love her, like me. Before she came, I wrote to my brother, David:

> There are two very important things I'd like to know for the wonderful way your daughter and I are going to hit things off. 1. Has she ever seen anyone in a wheelchair? 2. Have you talked to her a little about me, about what I'm like physically?
>
> The reason I'm asking is so I can figure out whether I'm going to scare her. Do you have pictures of me in the wheelchair that you can show her? I'm not saying this to emphasize that I'm different from other people. I'm doing it for your daughter, so she won't get "traumatized" (a psychological invention that makes life more complicated).

My relationship with my niece, Yael, was surprisingly good. Everything was the way it usually was, like nothing was going on, like she'd been seeing me her whole life. When we didn't have that little scamp around any more and everything went back to normal, I felt lonely and sad. As if it were normal to have a house without children yelling or talking! Hah! Silence is what adults do, and we adults are boring.

FLORENCIA
Gaby's always talked about adopting a child. Ever since she met Luis del Toro, that's when she got the idea. She wanted Luis del Toro to give his name to the baby.

GABY
The wind began to blow, the trees seemed like ballerinas. The clothes out on the line were rocking back and forth, sometimes just a little, and sometimes a lot, depending on the wind. And I wondered, "When am I ever going to rock a baby of my own?" The wind murmured back, "Maybe never."

SARI
I always understood Gaby's desire to be a mother, and I never opposed it. Far from it. I have always wanted my daughter's life to be as normal as possible, as complete as possible.

GABY

Oh God, yesterday I made the mistake of blowing up at Mamá! I hurt her when I said, "It's not that I'm not flexible, it's just that what's going on makes it look that way, I don't know what else to do." I pressed against her with my wheelchair, and I hurt her. I couldn't keep my bitterness or my resentment toward life under control. Even though she swears it didn't hurt, I know I did hurt her, and that made me feel so lousy that I wanted to heal her wound any way I could.

> Silence that is not silence
> noise stilled by the soul
> so as not to explode.
>
> The soul falls silent
> silent for fear of freedom
> silent for anguish at speaking
> silent for obsession with falling still.
>
> The silence of death
> is what I desire.
> Let life go on
> with its days of bitterness,
> its moments of happiness
> its desires and ambition
> the struggles suffered by one
> and all,
> its loves and its hatreds too.
>
> Silence and let the bells toll,
> silence, because I am tired
> silence for silence's sake
> silence. Leave me alone!
> Silence and ring down the curtain,
> the show is over. . .
> Silence!

In May 1977, all of my wishes to be a mother came true, almost without try-ing. A young woman was going to have a baby that for an endless number of reasons she couldn't keep or bring up. God was sending her to me, this was it. There was no time to talk things over with the family in the United States. The baby was born, a little girl who came into the world and waited for the exact moment I could take care of her. Mamá drove off to get her six hours after she was born and brought her home.

SARI

I rush everywhere, I go out to do my errands; the bank, the supermarket; the post office, because Gaby writes a lot of letters; and in the car on the way home, I think: "It's time for the baby to wake up," and I step on the gas because I'm longing to see my granddaughter. Gaby's happiness is more important than anything, anything, anything else.

GABY

I thought many times about adopting a child, and I talked about it with Florencia a lot. We spent entire afternoons making plans, and I remember that in 1969, I wrote a letter to Aunt Betty and asked her to ask her lawyer about the possibility of my adopting a child when I turned twenty-one and became an adult. Or if it wasn't possible then, maybe when I finished my degree and could show my diploma. I know what you're all thinking: nobody would ever give me a baby, but maybe if I could show I live under the protection of a community, I'd have a chance. I felt absolutely prepared (at least intellectually) to take responsibility for a child, and my nana Florencia always agreed. We wanted a *nunutzi*. I don't think there's anything more beautiful than little children.

I want a *nunutzi*
to bring joy to our house
and joy to my soul.
A *nunutzi* who talks
and also makes mischief.
I want a *nunutzi*
who has black eyes
to look at me with.
I want a *nunutzi*
with dark skin

and tiny hands
to stroke my hair with.
I want a *nunutzi*
who'll get under my skin
and bring joy to my soul.

(*Nunutzi* is or means "child" in the language of the Huicholes. I got it from
the book *Los indios de México*, about the different indigenous groups in Mexico. I liked the way it sounded.)

"Alma," I said to myself. I'll call her Alma, because it means "soul," and
"soul" is synonymous for being alive and being human.

SARI
Gaby's daughter is named Alma Florencia Brimmer.

GABY
We registered Alma Florencia under my last name. I did ask Quique Marques
to lend me his last name, and I kept telling him he wouldn't have any responsibility. But when I called him to get information about his parents, he left word
that he'd never let the baby have his name and I shouldn't get him involved in
this. That's why she'll have mine. She'll be my daughter under the law, and if
someday Alma wants to find her mother, the mother who gave birth to her,
I'll let her do it. I don't have anything to gain by not letting her do it, because
people always put more energy into running after what they're not supposed
to have. Tomorrow Alma will be two weeks old, and she's drinking three
ounces of milk. She's healthy and developing well, and she'll be a little dark-
haired beauty.

Morenita, little dark one, talk to me
I want to know about you
what you think
and what you see.

FLORENCIA
Every day I put Almita down for a little while next to Gaby's face. She pulls
on Gaby's nose, and pats her with her teeny-tiny hands. No, she's not scared
of her. I put her little head right up next to Gaby's. I do this a lot, and then I

let her stay there for a while, just lying down. The two of them look so happy, mother and daughter.

Gaby has wanted to have a baby in the house for such a long time. A little boy or girl, it didn't matter. She would talk about it with Señora Brimmer, with me, with friends, and she kept wanting it and wanting it and wanting it, and when the opportunity came, well, I don't think we had time to even think about it. We went off to get her and that was that. Now we have her here in the house, and we have to raise her. I never took care of such a tiny baby before, and I was scared those first few days. I told Gaby so, and we talked it over: "Now that I'm taking care of a baby, I'm not going to be able to be with you every second. We'll have to divide up our time, and I'm not going to be able to read to you like I did before," and Gaby told me, "If it's for the baby, I don't care, the two of us will take care of her."

GABY

At first I got jealous when I saw Nana spending so much time with the baby. Of course, we've stopped going out, stopped going to concerts; Nana can't read to me anymore, there are bottles to get ready, diapers to wash. Right now the sky is gray, the thunder sounds like there's going to be a storm, and a wind is coming up and blowing a row of diapers hanging on the clothesline we put in the garden. I can see them from here, from my study, where I'm sitting with Alma. We've got her lying down all comfy here on the couch, all covered with lots of blankets to protect her from the cold. It's started raining outside, and Alma Florencia has just woken up crying, she wants something to eat.

FLORENCIA

When the baby's awake, she eats here with Gaby. If we're going to be at the table, we take her and lay her down on two chairs pushed together. It's not a question of me shutting myself up with her to take care of her. The four of us live together.

GABY

I couldn't write to the family right away to tell them about Almita because — even though it may seem old-fashioned or abnormal — getting my period always has some effect on my mind and my nervous system somehow, and when I write to my family, I want my head to be clear. At any rate, whatever their answer is, Almita is here next to me, and no one and nothing is going to separate me from her. I waited many years to have her, and I know that in the future I can count on Nani's family; they accept me completely and they accept my daughter. They live in San Agustín, a poor neighborhood, and I like it there. They'll give me food and a roof over my head, for me and my daughter.

FLORENCIA
Two of my sisters live near Santa Clara, in a neighborhood called San Agustín. Gaby likes to go there and stay for a few days, and we already went there to show them the baby, and they liked her a lot.

GABY
The Morales family, Nana's family, live in a neighborhood in the State of Mexico called San Agustín, close to Mexico City. They really worked and worked to build their house. Four of them live there: Leonor and María, who are sisters, and their nephews Roberto and Teodoro.

These people are from the country. I've known them for years, and I've been able to see the way they've changed. Leonor, the older sister, takes care of things at home and has a little store — a little store where she sells groceries and things, right in the house. María, the younger one, works in a dressmaker's shop in Coyoacán, in southern Mexico City. The two nephews go to school and work to help pay for it.

The most important thing about this family is the way they're constantly trying to progress, financially as much as socially and culturally.

I think this is a much better environment for Almita than the environment in my own house, because in San Agustín kids are always running in and out, the way they do in all the working-class neighborhoods. They play and they run around, they deal with real issues that have to do with survival. They're not living in the middle of my mother's anxiety and depression. The kids make friends right away, and in very short order they begin the daily struggle of getting through life. That means they don't have time for fake problems, the ones that have more to do with the ego and psychoanalysis than with normal life, with what happens every day. I think it's a much more healthy environment for my Almita than the one I can give her at home, with three women who are only fairly happy despite the relative luxury. In San Agustín,

Almita would have friends her own age and normal relationships, not the solitude that Mamá, Nani, and I live in, because — and people can say what they
like — the three of us are always very alone. I like San Agustín, I feel comfortable there, even though the electricity might go off or else the current might
not work with my typewriter, and then I can't write. I'm making a lot of plans
for Alma. I'm starting to think about the day she'll start school, even though
I get apprehensive thinking about it because when we start to read and write,
we turn into different people, and sometimes it even ruins us. I think I'll send
her to the German school, because they teach them English and German
right from the start, and they instill discipline, which is very important for
the future. But then I get scared of that and go for another plan: a Montessori-
style school. But since Alma is dark, they might discriminate against her at
the German school or any other foreign private school. Besides, the tuition is
expensive, and if things continue to be so expensive, the German school will
only be for millionaires, and I'm no millionaire. So I'll send her to the public
schools I went to. But then when I see how tiny she is, I say to myself, "What
kind of dope are you? She's not even eight months old, and you're already
thinking about what school to send her to. Have a good time with her, and let
time take care of the rest!"

FLORENCIA
I have my two daughters, the big one and the little one.

GABY
Bringing up a human being is so complicated that sometimes you don't know
which way to turn. And everything gets a lot more complicated when you've
got an only child and you want to give her everything. You end up completely
putting your foot in it — you blow it, as people say. In the time we've had Alma
with us, we've changed the way we're bringing her up thousands of times so
we don't blow it. Every day is an experience, both for Alma and for the three
of us. Her crib is next to my bed, and in the morning if it's not cold or I'm not
feeling lazy, I take my foot out from under the covers and put it between the
bars of her crib to play or tickle her or just so she knows I'm there. If she's in
a good mood (and she usually wakes up happy), she sits up, moves over to
my foot, kisses me, and we start to play. If she wakes up in a bad mood, she
ignores me completely, and I take my foot away as a sign of respect. Little

things like that will make for good or bad upbringing, and we're not just trying to bring her up, but to learn from her, too.

SARI

No one can resist a baby's smile, and Alma smiles a lot when you look at her, when you talk to her. She looks good in white, pink, blue, and all of this penetrates my every pore and doesn't stop. Later we'll know whether it was worth it, but for me it is already worth it to see the happiness in Gaby's face, in Nani's face, in the face of this little girl who is smiling from ear to ear.

GABY

Everybody is telling me to start writing poems to her, but I maintain that poetry is born, not made. It's as delicate as she is. The seed of a poem comes from the feeling that someone or something sparks within us. Alma is sparking many things in me that still don't have a name. They're frozen inside my head, but someday they'll start moving and come gushing forth on paper.

> Like a rosebud
> like a fresh wildflower
> a human flower grows, lovely and healthy.
>
> Growing in my house,
> Growing in me,
> like a turbulent sea not at peace.
>
> Tiny bud, don't cry,
> Alma big and small,
> don't cry because you'll make me cry too.
>
> Sleep, go on, go to sleep,
> sleep, because that's how you'll grow
> healthy, strong, and beautiful
> a rose from the rosebush you'll be.
>
> Almita is a little bud,
> a bud that will open
> to become a flower.
>
> Alma, Alma
> dream and dream,

the world goes around
and you
in your crib
go around the world.

FLORENCIA

The baby fills me up so much. There's no room in my head for anything besides running to take care of her, even though I don't spend the whole day doing it because she does let me make meals, do laundry, and sew. Just a little while ago I put her to bed, but she started crying so I brought her downstairs and here I am with her. Otherwise I'd be asleep.

GABY

She's so big, with those two shining eyes that gaze out as though they already understood so much of what's happening in the world. She talks in her own way, and she's growing normally. If she was born of her parents' fleeting love, they don't know what they're missing out on. Every day I marvel at the simple fact of seeing a child grow. Maybe Alma Florencia is always going to lack a father figure, but she'll have more than enough love, care, dedication, and schooling. I hope everything stays like this, and that life will also give her love and security. Sometimes I wonder, Where do we get security in this lousy world that has such an uncertain future? And I answer, "Take life as it comes, today and tomorrow, and God will decide." But God always remains silent. I'm no nihilist — I love life and everything about it. It's just that in my thirty-one years, I've experienced life and had to accept our world for what it is. I haven't liked having to do that, but what else is left for me?

Few can match my parents for their fighting spirit and work ethic. If my father hadn't had to work since he was a boy, he would have been a philosopher. That's right, get this, everybody, my father had an exceptional brain and memory. At night, when all of us were asleep, he'd spend hours reading, and sometimes I'd see a light on in his room early in the morning, because his room was next to the one where Nana and I slept. After he died, nothing was the same for me. The person who'd given me security, love, and wisdom was gone; the person who'd given me the most encouragement to fight had disappeared. I accepted his death because I didn't have a choice, and then I accepted physical and intellectual separation from my only brother, who abandoned us — especially my mother — when we needed him the most. She thought she'd always be able to lean on him, but then she had to fight on alone. I couldn't help her. Then we had to accept 1968 and the Corpus Christi massacre on June 10, 1971. We had to accept that politics is the dirtiest thing that exists in this world, that politicians are a bunch of bastards, and that people are killed or discriminated against because of ideology, religion, or — in most cases — economic power. I was lucky in some ways: I got to experience the environment at the university, some friends come to visit me, I have Nana with me, and I'm seeing my daughter grow up. I maintain a vast correspondence, and I can see, hear, feel, and smell.

SARI

Nani's family near Mexico City consists of two sisters who haven't married and who are like her — strong women, wise, exceptional. Both of them have promised me that they will never abandon Nani or Gaby, and now that includes baby Almita, too. I wonder, "And if the sisters die first?" That is the biggest source of anxiety in my life, along with the other things that cause me anxiety. Now I know that Gaby definitely does not want to go to the United States.

GABY

Almita is here with me. It's cold and she's got the hiccups, but she won't take her eyes off me. She looks at me as though she were saying, "What could that lady be doing making that strange noise with that big, huge thing?" And someday maybe she'll be using that big, huge thing, which is the typewriter. All of a sudden she starts making noise, and I think it's time for her banana with orange juice. I'll turn off the typewriter for a while and concentrate on her. I try not to meddle with her personality, but I always make sure to give her stimulation so that she'll be the one who looks for things, finds things, falls down, gets up. I let her find things out, strew the records around, grab books; I follow her with my eyes, I watch her attentively. You're going to tell me I can't manage her, and you're partly right. I can't even give her a hug. But on the other hand, I give the orders, and Nana carries them out. Let's say Almita can move around more easily when she's face-down. Sometimes Nana puts her the other way, so then I tell my Nanita to turn her over. I keep track of her meals, and I decide what she's going to have so that she'll have a little of everything, with the result that she's already eating what we eat, but put through the blender. I took her off Gerber's because I don't like processed foods. Naturally, Alma thinks Nanita is the one who's most important, and in fact she is because she's the one who does everything for her, but she loves me too because I keep her entertained while Nana has to cook and leaves her next to me on an air mattress. Almita loves my mother because she just does; I suppose she perceives a lot of good things about Mamá, because every time she sees her, her whole face lights up, and then Mamá takes her into her arms. Besides, since Almita has a wonderful personality, she wins people over just by looking at them. You're going to say I'm a mother who's madly in love with her daughter, and I'm not about to deny it. But when you've been wanting a son or a daughter for ten years or more and then all of a sudden you really have one — of flesh and blood, with a teeny little bit of a neck — it's the least you deserve. I'm crazy about her. After all, I had the example of two women who devoted themselves to me body and soul. Besides, Almita is a darling that I've nicknamed "The Hurricane," while Nana calls her "The Castanet." Believe me, both of them fit: "The Hurricane" because if you leave a book on the floor for her, she crawls over, picks it up, and destroys it in order to figure out what it is, and "The Castanet" because she's always happy.

Yesterday something wonderful happened. Almita stood up in her crib for the first time.

This happens to all children who are physically and mentally healthy, but you know what, everybody? When you watch a child develop day after day, and you realize the kind of progress that child has made in eight months, you get excited and surprised when you see the way that, little by little, the child is becoming an independent being. Maybe it doesn't mean as much for an ordinary mother to see her child stand up in her crib as it does for a handicapped mother. But for me, seeing my daughter standing up on her two legs, straight as straight can be, plump and strong, makes up for so many years in a wheelchair. Do you understand what I'm trying to tell you?

Very soon I'll want to take her to the sea too, to watch her run along the beach. If you take a trip and cross the sea, remember how much I love it all, because that's where life was born; when you're out on the water, send a pure white thought to Gaby the seagull.

AFTERWORD

The book *Gaby Brimmer* had an enormous impact on Gaby's life. In the widely distributed newspaper *Novedades*, Elena Poniatowska promised that Gaby's extraordinary strength and love of life would surely touch readers' hearts.[1] The main book party was held at Mexico City's magnificent Palacio de Bellas Artes, where in the presence of distinguished intellectuals, celebrated actor Susana Alexander read segments from the text.[2] Gaby felt "in the clouds . . . like in a dream."[3] Indeed, the book was received enthusiastically by Mexican readers and critics, and the fanfare and warm acceptance made the book a best seller.[4]

Television cameras, interviewers, and telephone calls following the book's appearance turned the Brimmers' home into a "madhouse."[5] Many visitors, including curious strangers, arrived to see Gaby. The house attracted new people and friends, what Poniatowska came to call Gaby's "fan club." Although she sometimes tired of the public attention, Gaby enjoyed the new celebrity status, which expanded her horizons, enabling her to come into contact with intellectuals, artists, and politicians. Soon she would use her fame to become a leading activist on behalf of Mexico's people with disabilities.[6]

For Gaby, the real novelty the book created was in revealing "the new Gaby." She became more cheerful, confident, and demanding of herself. Now defined publicly as a writer, she could allow her writing to play a more central role in her life. The emotional and intellectual processes writing involved were enormously significant to her: "Each white sheet was a challenge . . . it was like being born and reborn," Gaby wrote.[7] She focused on her own experiences, while inserting in the texts opinions on just about everything: "She got herself involved with the entire world in her writings," said Florencia. "Literature is my life," Gaby asserted, "and I wouldn't know how to live without it."[8] Indeed, after *Gaby Brimmer*, two more books by Gaby came out. In 1980 Grijalbo published *Gaby, un año después*, a collection of poems, which sold twenty thousand copies in two editions.[9] In 1982, *Cartas de Gaby* was published, containing letters from 1977 to 1981, half of them to Poniatowska.[10] In 1986, a small press printed *Disfraces y otros cuentos*, an anthology of autobiographical stories Gaby wrote in the first half of the 1980s about "women who lived different situations, but with one common denominator, which is loneliness and lack of options."[11] A collection of later poems was never accepted by a publisher.[12]

Writing helped save Gaby from the low moods that settled upon her from time to time. Yet during the early 1980s, when she felt she had lost her creativity, and for most of the 1990s, when she developed a paralysis in her left foot and could not use it to write, she sank into depressions that could last for months: during those periods, she barely wrote.[13] When Gaby later recovered some foot movement, learned to dictate short texts orally, and also received a donated special computer from IBM, she immediately returned to her writing.

One of the most exciting consequences of *Gaby Brimmer* was that in 1980 Gaby was approached with proposals to turn the book into a feature film. She accepted an offer from director Luis Mandoki, the son of Mexico City Hungarian Jews.[14] More important for Gaby, however, was that he was a son of her radical generation, known in Mexico as the "Generation of '68," whose members preserved the memory of the massacre of Tlatelolco and held left-wing views.[15] Gaby herself worked on the script, which she decided to structure as an introspective examination of her life, rather than as a traditional linear narrative.[16] In the end, Gaby was satisfied with the ninety-two single-spaced pages she wrote, despite finding it painful to again relive many of the events and emotions of her life. So exhausted was Gaby after five months of work, that she wrote to her brother Henry in San Francisco that she felt as if she was left with nothing to say.[17]

The final film script melded Gaby's work with versions prepared by other screenwriters.[18] However, the film had to wait for a producer until 1985, when Mandoki at last raised funds from a U.S. investor and began production in Cuernavaca, a colonial city near the capital.[19] The role of Gaby was played by Rachel Levin (known today as Rachel Chagall), who initially prepared for it by spending time at a United Cerebral Palsy center in New York City. Levin also stayed at Gaby's home, where they reviewed Gaby's movements and voice, which helped her play the role for which she was to receive a Golden Globe nomination.[20] The other central parts were given to two eminent actors: Norwegian Liv Ullmann as Sari, and Argentinean Norma Aleandro as Florencia, a role for which she was nominated for an Oscar. *Gaby: A True Story* was premiered in 1987 in Mexico and throughout the United States. At the first premiere in Acapulco, accompanied by family and friends, Gaby was ecstatic. With a love of partying and tequila, she celebrated long into the night. Elegance and glitz characterized the premier in Hollywood, where later the movie itself received an Oscar nomination. Gaby's San Francisco family, including her brother Henry, attended the event with her.[21]

The film portrayed Gaby as a woman with a significant disability who challenges hostile social attitudes through individual rebellion and positive thinking. It can be categorized as belonging to what historian Paul Longmore calls the "drama of adjustment" genre. The emphasis is on "achievement and success," as "disability does not inherently prevent" people with disabilities, like the heroine Gaby, "from living meaningfully and productively and from having normal friendships and romantic relationships."[22]

In real life, Gaby had begun to sharpen the social critique she had first voiced in the book. In the 1980s she increasingly spoke about disability not as a random condition and individual tragedy but as a shared social identity. In her view, society at large, the political authorities, and the medical establishment, needed to stop treating people with disabilities as ill, and to remove all physical and social barriers to their participation in society.[23]

Gaby also continued to fault the families of people with disabilities, along with other nondisabled people, for adopting oppressive mind-sets and behaviors. While people with disabilities often sought access to the world, she contended, overprotective families kept them isolated or neglected, thereby impeding their progress in education, employment, and family life.[24] The sexual rights of people with disabilities were especially important to Gaby and she used her own experiences to help society better understand the complexity of this taboo as a social matter.[25] She thought of herself as a "complete woman," as her blind friend Raquel Carrillo comments, just as people with disabilities were "lovers no different than other human lovers."[26] She was furious with a nondisabled man's suggestion that her "body was sick, and to desire it would be another sickness."[27] Nondisabled men who merely "wanted her soul" and "platonic love" hurt her.[28] On the other hand, when a love affair between Gaby, then in her late thirties, and a man with disability was terminated by his parents, Gaby railed against parental authority over an adult son and bitterly commented that he "seemed like a doll tied up to his family with a rope."[29]

In a public address, Gaby noted that it had "not been easy at all" for her to become an activist: "I was accustomed to a life more dedicated to literary labor and work as a mother." Yet she became integrated "slowly, painfully, and beautifully into the cause."[30] Ultimately, it was the movie — which was shown in theaters throughout Mexico and Latin America at a time when people with disabilities in those countries had begun to agitate for their rights — that propelled Gaby's "international takeoff" as a "world figure" in the disability community, according to Mario Ávila Delgado, a movement leader.[31] Even before that, however, Gaby had begun to act on her hope of creating an activist group in Mexico that would grow into a social movement.[32]

One of the first organizations Gaby was connected to since its formation in Guadalajara in 1973 was the Asociación de Lisiados de Jalisco (ALJAC, or Jalisco Association of Crippled People). She knew the group's founder, Arturo Heyer, as well as Mario Ávila Delgado, who became its president and in the late 1970s included Gaby as a contributor to its journal, *Superación*.[33] As it increasingly became an honor for disability groups to be associated with Gaby, she was also invited to the Asociación Universitaria de Minusválidos (University Association of the Handicapped) at the Universidad Nacional Autónoma de México (UNAM, or National Autonomous University of Mexico), founded in 1986 by wheelchair sports activist Martha Heredia and Ernesto Rosas, the blind leader of the Mexican branch of the Organización Nacional de Ciegos de España (ONCE, or Spanish National Organization of the Blind).[34] That same year, the ALJAC became the impetus behind the founding of the Confederación Mexicana de Limitados Físicos y Representantes de Deficientes Mentales (COMELFIRDEM, or Mexican Confederation of People with Physical Limitations and Representatives of the Mentally Handicapped), with Ávila Delgado as its first president. The COMELFIRDEM's goal was to unite local and separate disability groups under a single "cross-disability" umbrella organization, fighting to eliminate physical, cultural, and social barriers, and promoting government policies, reforms, and laws to ensure the integration of people with disabilities into society. As a national confederation, it soon joined the Canada-based Disabled People's International (DPI).[35]

Building on the success of the book *Gaby Brimmer*, in the early 1980s, a group of UNAM students drawn to Gaby — Imelda Quezada, Flor Díaz de

León, Martha Heredia, and Jesús Esquinca, among others—organized campus lectures for her. Then, as a result of the movie's publicity, the growing excitement of those people who surrounded Gaby led to the founding of the Asociación para los Derechos de Personas con Alteraciones Motoras (ADEPAM, or Association for the Rights of People with Motor Disabilities), an organization whose goals she had already outlined in the text of the book. In 1987, as volunteers, they routinely went to movie theaters where the film was being screened, selling the book, collecting donations, and explaining to the audience that Gaby was a real woman living in Mexico City. Consequently, more people, with and without disabilities, flocked to Gaby. Meetings held once a month on Saturdays crowded Gaby's house and garden. Besides playing music and dancing, people at the gatherings discussed how best to fight for the removal of all discriminatory barriers.[36]

As Gaby explained, the ADEPAM was organized for "free-minded" people with disabilities.[37] Initially the organization was supported by funds from Avon's Zazil Prize, awarded to Gaby in 1988 as the outstanding woman of the year for humanitarian work. Gaby's income from the film also made it possible to purchase a used wheelchair-accessible van, which Henry brought into Mexico from the United States for Gaby's and the ADEPAM's use.[38] Originally the ADEPAM was managed by persons with disabilities, such as Gaby's childhood friend Vicente Martínez as secretary; Jorge Pineda as treasurer; and Gaby herself as president. In 1989, the ADEPAM became legally registered as ADEPAM Gabriela Brimmer, A.C. ("Asociación Civil," indicating charitable/not-for-profit status under Mexican law), and it immediately became affiliated with the COMELFIRDEM. In 1991, it changed its status to "Institución de Asistencia Privada" (I.A.P., or "Private Assistance Institution") to benefit from Mexico's Private Assistance Board's prestige, fundraising administration, and financial supervision.[39]

The following year an activist familiar with disability politics and programs, Fernando Rodríguez, founder of Mobility International Mexico, and his wife, Marina Hernández, joined the staff.[40] During that period, the ADEPAM was searching for direction. Initially, its activities consisted of helping its low-income members gain access to employment and health services.[41] Decision-making was based on the principle of "participatory democracy," in which all members debated and voted in the general assembly. Gradually, members who did not need services ceased to attend the assembly, which was finding it increasingly difficult to make concrete decisions. Gaby wanted the ADEPAM to lead a social struggle, but as president she also had difficulties taking it in a clear direction. Over time, others in the organization, who had easier access to political functionaries and people outside of the ADEPAM, took over some duties and decisions.[42] Also, despite Gaby's wish that the ADEPAM not become involved with the government and politics, it turned out to be impossible to prevent individual members from participating in party politics.[43]

Frustrated about the obstacles the ADEPAM faced as an activist group for the rights of people with disabilities, Gaby was ready to resign as president in 1994, but her associates, refusing to envision the ADEPAM without her, talked her into staying.[44] In 1995, the organization began slowly to shift its emphasis to rehabilitation. Physician Teresa García and Angélica Herrera, Gaby's physical therapist, joined the staff, and with Gaby's renewed optimism, the ADEPAM became a rehabilitation center for children with motor disabilities. Rejecting the antiquated conception of disability as pathology, the ADEPAM's comprehensive approach provided physical therapy along with language and psychopedagogical therapies and family social work. Although that was far from the group's original activist goals, the people close to her felt that Gaby was pleased.[45]

The 1990s were also years in which Gaby's involvement with the COMELFIRDEM increased, reflecting her leadership on a national level. Central to the organization's work were the Jornadas Culturales y Deportivas (Cultural Symposia and Sports Events), which took place once or twice a year in different cities throughout Mexico. The COMELFIRDEM's affiliated and unaffiliated national and regional organizations were invited to take part. By the mid-1980s, there were already groups in states such as Jalisco, Nuevo León, Colima, Oaxaca, Baja California, Chihuahua, Guanajuato, Durango, Coahuila, and Tlaxcala. These gatherings included lectures, roundtable discussions, and workshops on topics related to disability and the rights of people with disabilities. Wheelchair sports games and a party closed each event. One of the main goals was to promote activism throughout the country and gain influence over local and state political functionaries. Equally important to the COMELFIRDEM was being able to draw the attention of Mexico City groups to the activism that was taking place far away from the capital. Finally, the organizers used the local media to disseminate information on disability issued by the United Nations and other international organizations among the participants, the politicians, and the general public — material otherwise barely available in Mexico.[46] As the COMELFIRDEM's "moral representative" and "pillar" in the capital, Gaby participated in almost all the events in these series. Not only did she lend them her prestige; she also helped the COMELFIRDEM to build relationships with major Mexico City organizations and politicians.[47]

Gaby was also a star participant in DPI's Fifth Latin American Seminar, held in Mexico City in 1989 and cosponsored by the COMELFIRDEM. This was the COMELFIRDEM's first international event, and it used the occasion to push for federal disability policies and propose a national rehabilitation commission, to be installed by the next administration, which would take office in 1994.[48] Four years later, Gaby and the ADEPAM were major organizers of DPI's Fifth World Assembly, hosted by the COMELFIRDEM. The presence of high-ranking politicians, as well as more than two thousand representatives from Mexico and around the world, allowed the assembly to have a significant political impact.[49] In recognition of her stature and work for the COMELFIRDEM, Gaby was named vice president of its executive board in 1996, and in 1998 she was elected to the Committee of Women with Disabilities for DPI's Latin America Region.[50]

Gaby's leadership role also involved accepting important invitations from abroad. In San Juan, Puerto Rico, in 1989, she was a guest of Futuros, a consortium that worked with the private sector to offer employment to people with disabilities. In 1992, she was invited to visit a cerebral palsy organization in Bergamo, Italy. She also went to Havana, Cuba, in 1997 for the Second International Conference on the Rights of People with Disabilities as a special guest of the Asociación Cubana de Limitados Físico-Motores (ACLIFIM, or Cuban Association of the Physically Handicapped).[51] Also in 1997, Judy Heumann, then the assistant secretary for special education and rehabilitative services at the U.S. Department of Education, invited Gaby to address the International Leadership Forum for Women with Disabilities, in Bethesda, Maryland.[52] This forum further raised Gaby's feminist consciousness, helping her to recognize the specific disadvantages women with disabilities encountered, such as double discrimination, greater physical dependency, and confinement to the "sad and narrow space of home."[53]

Now an icon of disability rights, Gaby continued to receive and accept invitations to appear throughout Mexico, where she addressed local organizations and met with people with disabilities and their families. Everywhere she was honored with awards, receptions by high elected officials, press conferences, and wide coverage by the local media. On some occasions, a visit consisted of naming a school, a rehabilitation facility, or a cultural center after her.[54] Often, she conversed with admiring people with disabilities, some of whom thanked her in writing. These letters, along with most of the press coverage of Gaby throughout the 1980s and 1990s, expressed affection and respect for Gaby in ways that still reflected antiquated thinking about disability, a view through a lens of pity or self-pity. Many letters and articles referred to Gaby as a source of inspiration, a woman who had triumphed over the limitations of her body, a woman of stoic courage, and a model of human will.[55] For example, in 1993 a blind woman handed Gaby a letter that read, "My life is very sad, but when courageous people like you appear, I know I should never let myself be defeated.... I felt ashamed of the thoughts of anguish I sometimes have.... I admired you, and from now on, I will not allow myself to be defeated."[56] Indeed, it proved to be difficult for the leadership of the disability rights movement to transform the social, cultural, and medical attitudes rooted deeply in Mexican society.

In February 1994, Mexico's disability rights movement initiated a direct action it had never tried before: the Marcha de la Amistad (Friendship March) was the country's first national demonstration of people with disabilities. Organized by the group Acceso Libre (Free Access), and headed by Gaby as the symbol of the movement, some three hundred people using wheelchairs, crutches, and canes spent three hours advancing from Mexico City's Revolution Monument to the nation's congressional headquarters. Gaby presented the movement's petition for equal rights to the legislators who met the group gathered at the foot of the stairs, because the building had no access ramp. The main message was: "We ask neither for charity nor gestures; we demand total integration."[57] The march was a model for two identical marches organized later that year by the COMELFIRDEM, in Puerto Vallarta, Jalisco, and Irapuato, Guanajuato.[58] All of these marches demonstrated that the disability movement was determined to fight, especially in the atmosphere of political change and human rights discourse that was occurring in the Mexican political and institutional mainstream. In her testimony at the National Human Rights Commission in 1996, Gaby's timely message was that, similar to those of other marginalized groups, the rights of people with disabilities must also be included within the framework of human rights.[59]

This period signaled an increased recognition of the rights of people with disabilities, as advocated by President Ernesto Zedillo's administration since taking office in December 1994. The United Nations' 1993 Standard Rules on the Equalization of Opportunities for Persons with Disabilities, which in Mexico was monitored by the Comisión Nacional Coordinadora (National Coordinating Commission), had some influence on the political establishment, as did the Mexican disability rights groups' activism, and the expansion of disability rights struggles worldwide.[60] During Zedillo's six-year administration, the federal government for the first time recognized its obligation to develop policies for the inclusion of people with disabilities in society. At the core of official policy was the Programa Nacional para el Bienestar y la Incorporación al Desarrollo de las Personas con Discapacidad (National Program for the Welfare and Incorporation of People with Disabilities into Development), also called CONVIVE. It was established in 1995 and headed by the Sistema para el Desarrollo Integral de la Familia (DIF, or Family Development Agency), the government's authority for social services and welfare benefits. CONVIVE was responsible for working with the nongovernmental organizations to promote jointly, in the president's words, "a culture . . . of sincere inclusion and dignity for people with disabilities."[61]

CONVIVE, as a program, rejected the medical model of disability and adopted instead a human rights and social development model.[62] Across the country promotional service offices were created, each headed by a person with disability, whose job was to apply the CONVIVE programs locally through the DIF departments.[63] Following the United Nations' recommendations, the category of disability was included in the 2000 Censo Nacional de Población y Vivienda (National Census of Population and Housing). Many state laws concerning disability were enacted and others reformed in the years 1996 and 1997. Also, in 1998 the government's health system adopted official guidelines for comprehensive attention to people with disabilities, and in 2000, the Instituto Mexicano del Seguro Social (IMSS, or Mexican Social Security Institute) published accessibility standards for people with disabilities, adapting all its facilities with ramps.[64]

Despite the application of the United Nations' Standard Rules, however, the advances gained during the Zedillo administration were limited. CONVIVE was not anchored in a legal framework and therefore its implementation was partial, and dependent on the will of politicians. Implementation was also uneven among autonomous local authorities, and it was difficult to evaluate the real impact CONVIVE had on the lives and rights of people with disabilities.[65]

Gaby's remarkable role in the campaign waged by the Mexican disability rights movement received plentiful official acknowledgment during her lifetime. In April 1995, she received her highest honor, the Medalla al Mérito Ciudadano (Civic Merit Medal) from the Assembly of Representatives of the Federal District (Mexico City's legislature), for her humanitarian work and her struggle for the rights of people with disabilities. Gaby was the first woman to receive this award. In a solemn ceremony at the assembly chamber, in the presence of government officials, family, friends, and associates with disabilities, the medal was presented to Gaby by the chairman of its special commission. He admitted that Mexican society had been unjust to people with disabilities, forcing them to suffer cruelty and rejection, but praised Gaby and the ADEPAM for their efforts to fight this injustice.[66] In the address that was read to the assembly by Marina Hernández, Gaby called for equal opportunities and the right to education, training, recreation, and love. Of Mexican society she said: "We have the creativity and determination with which to build a more democratic, just, and humane Mexico, where all grievances by people with disabilities are listened to and resolved."[67] A month later, when President Zedillo introduced the CONVIVE program, some of his words about the rights and needs of Mexicans with disabilities were identical to Gaby's at her award ceremony.[68]

During the 1980s and 1990s, through good times and bad times, family and friends accompanied Gaby's rise to the leadership of the disability rights movement in Mexico. Gaby commented that Sari had been the real "motor" behind her, though she continued to feel a mixture of love and resentment for her mother until Sari's death from cancer in December 1982.[69] Similarly, Gaby expressed both a deep emotional connection with and an ambivalence toward her relationship with Florencia: "We are condemned to depend on each other because you without me have no life and I without you would not make it to the door. Your almost perfection . . . helps me, gives me security and at the same time causes me anguish."[70]

Gaby, Florencia, and Alma—five years old when Sari died—constituted a tight family in a complex set of relations. Gaby mothered Alma, while Florencia combined the figures of mother and grandmother to Alma, and caregiver for Gaby. Indeed, Florencia provided direct care for everyone, while Gaby made many of the major decisions for the family and became a public figure.[71]

In 1985, a new living arrangement was established in the Brimmer-Morales household. Rosalinda Ávalos, Gaby's confidant and therapist at the time, her physician husband Raúl Rodríguez, and their daughters moved in. The intention of the move was to provide Gaby with additional assistance and to re-create a large family in a lively home.[72] Alma welcomed a man and playmates around the house. However, the experiment of living together became difficult and lasted only one year.[73]

Gaby was also surrounded by devoted friends, most of whom were nondisabled, during the 1980s and 1990s: Helen Himmelfarb, who lived in Mexico City and was a cousin through marriage, Angélica Herrera, Imelda Quezada, Paulina García, and Flor Díaz de León. Each about twenty years her junior, the latter three especially developed a strong emotional and intellectual connection with Gaby, as she talked to them about their search for inner discovery and personal liberation. Gaby loved their company, and they ensured that Gaby would enjoy the things she loved: travel, the beach, parties, and clubs. Friends who accompanied Gaby on trips and adventures — a beach vacation in Cuba with Helen, whitewater rafting in Oregon with Imelda, and excursions around Mexico City with Paulina — concur: "This woman's energy was incredible."[74]

As politically radical as Gaby was, she was also a spiritual person. She believed in God and at the same time confronted God when she felt emotionally tormented.[75] With hardly any Jewish religious influence from her parents, as a child Gaby was exposed to Catholicism through Florencia. As an adult, Gaby was not religious in the ordinary sense, yet in 1988 she converted to Catholicism. More than converting for merely theological reasons, she satisfied in this way her radical political convictions, her belief in God, and her deep-felt spiritual needs.[76] Gaby was drawn to radical Catholicism after many conversations with her friend Father Sergio Méndez Arceo, famous as "the revolutionary priest" for his involvement in agrarian struggles and the 1968 student movement. He preached an alliance between Christianity and socialism, an idea Gaby was attracted to, in addition to feeling drawn to the simple vitality of his message. His words, Gaby wrote, reached the soul, "entering into the body like osmosis."[77] On Holy Saturday 1988, Gaby was baptized at his church, known as "the poor people's church," in Cuernavaca, in the presence of some of the people dearest to her.[78]

By the late 1990s, Gaby seemed to be fulfilled in many areas of her life, but at the end of 1999, she told Imelda that she had a feeling she would soon die. To Flor, Florencia, and her sister María Asunción Morales, she said something to the effect that it might no longer be worthwhile for her to live.[79] On the night of January 3, 2000, Gaby died unexpectedly in her sleep at home, just one night after a joyous New Year's party at Rosalinda and Raúl's home.[80]

Many eulogized Gaby.[81] At a tribute organized by the Junta de Asistencia Privada del Distrito Federal (JAPDF, or Private Assistance Board of the Federal District), its president spoke about Gaby's legacy of firm discipline, unbreakable will, and enormous hope. Gaby was an inspiring example not only to people with disabilities, but to everyone, beyond time and borders, he said, repeating the conventional description of Gaby as an exceptional individual, but making no mention of the activist dimensions of her struggle. By comparison, Mexico City's secretary of social development mentioned Gaby's influence on the social agenda and her having become a symbol for cultural and ethical change in Mexico and throughout the world.[82]

President Zedillo read a eulogy for Gaby on his January 15 radio program, revealing that he and Gaby had met and discussed the progress of his government's programs. He mentioned achievements such as additional rehabilitation units, improved physical mobility and access, increased integration of children and youth in regular schools, and expanded job training programs and employment for people with disabilities. He also declared that the Zapata Rehabilitation Center for children with cerebral palsy in Mexico City would be named after Gaby. Two months later, when he unveiled a bust of her there, the president formally announced the creation of the Premio Nacional de Rehabilitación Física o Mental (National Prize for Physical or Mental Rehabilitation) in Gaby's honor, as well as a scholarship for artists and writers with disabilities, saying: "We will never forget the lessons of courage, tenacity, and triumph she gave us with her life and work."[83]

In his own eulogy, Gaby's friend Mario Ávila Delgado wrote about the qualities everyone admired in her: love, bravery, sensibility, spirit, and intellect. Mario also saw in Gaby what those who knew her well understood to have made her an extraordinary woman: she was at the same time rebellious and humble. Gaby dared to fight for a complex cause under difficult conditions. Her fight brought her recognition and power; yet she was never interested in power and was never presumptuous. We "thank Gaby for teaching us to be humble," Mario wrote. "I hope you keep being rebellious, as you were on earth."[84]

ACKNOWLEDGMENTS

I wish to thank Gaby's family in Mexico City, Florencia Morales and Alma Brimmer, for welcoming me into their house and allowing me to interview them, and for making their collection of Gaby's writings available to me. Angélica Herrera spent hours telling me about Gaby and the ADEPAM, allowed me to use the organization's archive, and introduced me to many of Gaby's friends, associates, and relatives, whom I interviewed. I am grateful to all the people who agreed to talk to me: Boris Albin, Rosalinda Ávalos, Mario Ávila Delgado, Raquel Carrillo, Flor Díaz de León, Paulina García, Teresa García, Mimi Greisman, Raúl Hernández, Martha Heredia, Helen Himmelfarb, Lily Margolis, Vicente Martínez, María Asunción Morales, Imelda Quezada, Raúl Rodríguez, Ernesto Rosas, Dinah Stroe, and Santiago Velázquez.

Alicia Ronay encouraged me constantly and was of great help during the interviews. At the Center for Social Research, University of Colima, I especially thank my assistant Edwin Mayoral, as well as Patricia Sánchez, Nora Ríos, Guadalupe Chávez, and Cecilia Chávez who, with Edwin, efficiently transcribed the interviews.

Finally, I am grateful to the Hadassah-Brandeis Institute, which supported some of our work through a Research Award, as well as the University of Colima's Ramón Álvarez-Buylla Fund.

NOTES

1 Elena Poniatowska, "La Nueva Ana Frank Será Gaby Brimmer," *Novedades*, December 10, 1979; Elena Poniatowska, "Gaby la Gaviota: Gaby Brimmer," *Comunidad Conacyt*, January 1980, 16–17.

2 "Jaime Sabines Señala el Amor a la Vida de Gaby Brimmer. Niña con Parálisis Cerebral que Ha Llegado a Escribir Poemas," *Excelsior*, December 15, 1979; Patricia Zama, "Elena Poniatowska presentó dos nuevos libros en el Fonágora: *Gaby Brimmer* y *De noche vienes*," *unomásuno*, December 14, 1979.

3 Gaby Brimmer, "Argumento de la película 'Gaby Brimmer,'" November 26, 1980, 70, Gaby Brimmer Manuscripts, Brimmer Family, Mexico City (hereafter cited as Brimmer MSS).

4 Elena Urrutia, "Dos libros de Elena Poniatowska," *FEM*, January–February 1980, 101–102; Emma Rizo, "La hermosa gente: Gaby Brimmer," *Ovaciones*, December 27, 1979, 2; Fabianne Bradu, "Pista del tesoro," *Revista de la Universidad de México*, n.d., 41–42. The book was sixth on leading Mexican bookstore chain Librerías de Cristal's bestseller list January 4–10, 1980, rising to first place February 22–28, and then dropping to second place March 21–27.

5 Brimmer, "Argumento de la película," 69–70; Gaby Brimmer, "Resumen o sinopsis del argumento de la película 'Gaby Brimmer,'" December 11, 1980, 9, Brimmer M S S; Elvira García, "Gaby Brimmer: una extraordinaria pasión por la vida," *Claudia*, May 1980, 48.

6 Elena Poniatowska, "La muerte de Gaby Brimmer," *La Jornada*, January 4, 2000; Florencia Morales, interviews by author, Mexico City, February 2 and 21, 2008; María Asunción Morales, interview by author, Mexico City, March 24, 2008; Mario Ávila Delgado, interview by author, Guadalajara, March 17, 2008; Dinah Stroe, interview by author, Mexico City, April 3, 2008.

7 Gaby Brimmer, "Disfraces," in *Disfraces y otros cuentos* (Mexico City: Ediciones y Creatividad, 1986), 125.

8 Brimmer, "Disfraces," 88, 105, 108, 120; García, "Gaby Brimmer," 48; Florencia Morales, interview, February 21, 2008.

9 Gabriela Brimmer, *Gaby, un año después* (Mexico City: Editorial Grijalbo, 1980); advertisement, *Novedades*, March 1, 1981; Gaby Brimmer to Elena Poniatowska, June 25, 1979, in Gaby Brimmer, *Cartas de Gaby* (Mexico City: Editorial Grijalbo, 1982), 24; Florencia Morales, interview, February 21, 2008.

10 Gaby Brimmer, *Cartas de Gaby* (Mexico City: Editorial Grijalbo, 1982).

11 Gaby Brimmer, *Disfraces y otros cuentos* (Mexico City: Ediciones y Creatividad, 1986); Guadalupe Esquivias, "Gaby Brimmer, mujer de lucha y tenacidad," *Todo México Somos Hermanos*, n.d. http://www.anunciacion.com.mx/periodico/contenido/59.html (June 1, 2008).

12 Florencia Morales, interview by Juan Pablo Berlanga and Alejandro Orozco, *Foro de celebridades, estrellas, personajes*, Canal 9, Nayarit, videocassette, 1994.

13 Gaby had already started to write of depression in 1979; see, for example, Gaby Brimmer to Elena Poniatowska, October 3, 1979, in Brimmer, *Cartas*, 36; other periods are recounted in Gaby Brimmer, manuscript, Mexico City, July 8, 1981, Brimmer M S S; Alma Brimmer, interview by author, Mexico City, April 3, 2008; Flor Díaz de León, interview by author, Mexico City, March 25, 2008; Imelda Quezada, interview by author, Mexico City, March 24, 2008; María Asunción Morales, interview.

Gaby's ability to move her left foot started deteriorating in 1991, to the extent that she was unable to type or use the ABC board. In 1993, IBM donated a computer, of the kind already used by people with cerebral palsy, which she could use by lightly pressing a switch with the toe. But Gaby missed her typewriter, used the computer minimally, and in 1995 stopped writing altogether. When a slight movement was observed in her right foot in 1997, Gaby, hoping she could write again, immediately asked her physical therapist to sit her at the computer. For accounts of or reflections on the events involving Gaby's left foot or her feelings about her typewriter, see Gaby Brimmer, "Prólogo," radio script, August 26, 1982, Brimmer MSS; "Resumen o sinopsis del argumento de la película," 16; Gaby Brimmer, "Catarina Soledad," in *Disfraces*, 9; Brimmer, "Disfraces," 108; Alice Thornton, "The Woman Inside," *Register-Guard*, May 28, 1992; Kimber Williams, "Author Hopes to Regain 'Voice,'" *Register-Guard*, May 29, 1992; "Gabriela Brimmer," *Siglo 21*, December 4, 1995; and Angélica Herrera, interviews by author, Mexico City, February 20 and March 24, 2008.

14 Brimmer, "Resumen o sinopsis de la película," 1–2.

15 Brimmer, "Argumento de la película," 82; Gaby Brimmer, "Los elefantes iluminados," radio script, March 30, 1982, Brimmer MSS; Gaby Brimmer, "Hacia el Zócalo. ¿Servirá para algo?" radio script, June 28, 1982, Brimmer MSS. Gaby supported the opposition United Socialist Party of Mexico (PSUM) founded in 1981, until 1989, when she embraced the new left-wing Party of the Democratic Revolution (PRD). See Herrera, interview, March 24, 2008; Raúl Hernández, interview by author, Guadalajara, March 17, 2008. Gaby's radio scripts for Education Radio were rejected as politically "inappropriate." See Gaby Brimmer to Elena Poniatowska, July 8, 1980, in Brimmer, *Cartas*, 5; Gaby Brimmer, "Prólogo," August 26, 1982, Brimmer MSS. See twelve rejected radio scripts, Brimmer MSS; Sergio Zermeño, *México, una democracia utópica: el movimiento estudiantil del 68* (Mexico City: Siglo Veintiuno Editores, 1978).

16 Brimmer, "Resumen o sinopsis del argumento de la película," 3; Brimmer, "Argumento de la película," 88–89.

17 Brimmer, "Resumen o sinopsis del argumento de la película," 4, 8, 11; Gaby Brimmer to Henry Brimmer, September 14, 1980, Brimmer MSS; Gaby Brimmer to Henry Brimmer, May 25, 1981, in Brimmer, *Cartas*, 62, 109–110. The film script was signed as completed on November 26, 1980. See Brimmer, "Argumento de la película," 92. Gaby wrote thirty-four pages of additional scenes to the original script in the following year.

18 Raquel Peguero, "Vicisitudes de un mexicano en Hollywood," *La Jornada*, October 30, 1994, 28.

19 Peguero, "Vicisitudes de un mexicano," 28; Raquel Peguero, "Ser director de Hollywood no es la gran cosa: Mandoki," *La Jornada*, October 29, 1994, 25; José Antonio Fernández F., "Entrevista con Luis Mandoki," *Revista Telemundo*, June 19, 2006, www.canal100.com.mx/telemundo/entrevistas/?id_nota=6100 (July 17, 2008).

20 Michael Buckley, "Rachel Levin," *Films in Review* (March 1988): 154–156; "Once-paralyzed Rachel Levin Gets a Fresh Start in *Gaby*," *People Weekly*, December 21, 1987, 64. See Florencia Morales, interview, February 21, 2008.

21 *Gaby: A True Story*, dir. Luis Mandoki (Tri-Star Pictures, 1987). For reviews, see Michael Buckley, "Gaby," *Films in Review* (January 1988): 41–42; Janet Maslin, "Film: 'Gaby,' Story of Determination," *New York Times*, October 30, 1987; Guillermo Aguilera, "Gaby Brimmer: Una vida de película," *Contenidos*, February 1988, 64–67. One of the highlights of the premiere in Los Angeles was a television interview Maria Shriver did with Gaby for NBC TV. See Stroe, interview; Mimi Greisman, telephone interview by author, May 20, 2008; Helen Himmelfarb, interview by author, Mexico City, March 26, 2008; Florencia Morales, interview, February 21, 2008.

22 Paul Longmore, "Screening Stereotypes: Images of Disabled People in Television and Motion Pictures," in *Images of the Disabled, Disabled Images*, ed. Alan Gartner and Tom Joe (Westport, Conn.: Praeger, 1987), 70–72.

23 Gaby Brimmer, "Conferencia, Facultad de Medicina UNAM," August 3, 1988, ADEPAM I.A.P. Manuscripts, Mexico City (hereafter cited as ADEPAM MSS); Gaby Brimmer, address, San Juan, Puerto Rico, March 1–5, 1989, ADEPAM MSS; Esquivias, "Gaby Brimmer"; Gaby Brimmer to Elena Poniatowska, March 14, 1980, in Brimmer, *Cartas*, 45; Gaby Brimmer, "Barreras," *Superación* (Guadalajara, Jalisco), June 1980, 3, ALJAC A.C. Manuscripts, Guadalajara, Jalisco.

   It should be noted that Gaby did seek out physical therapy — as opposed to "medical treatment" — at various points in her adult life. (Rosalinda Ávalos, interviews by author, Mexico City, March 25 and April 2, 2008; Raúl Rodríguez, interview, April 2, 2008; Herrera, interview, March 24, 2008; Paulina García, interview by the author, Mexico City, March 26, 2008.) In 1992, she went, through Mobility International USA, to the organization's headquarters in Eugene, Oregon, to be fitted for appropriate assistive devices. A physician at the University of Oregon's Rehabilitation Center explained that Gaby's pains were caused by her typing method and poorly designed wheelchair. A donation of a state-of-the-art custom-built wheelchair was obtained by the center's therapists and wheelchair experts, with a special head rest, upholstered seat, armrest tray, and foot plates. Gaby was also offered a choice of computers with writing and voice systems. Because of its high price, however, Gaby could not obtain this device until the following year, when IBM donated a computer to her for writing. ("Gaby's Trip to Eugene," May–June 1992, videocassette, ADEPAM MSS; Williams, "Author Hopes to Regain 'Voice'"; Hope Nealson, "Poet Speaks with 'Her Left Foot,'" *Oregon Daily Emerald*, May 29, 1992; Quezada, interview.)

   In addition, as of 1994, Gaby's physical therapist, Angélica Herrera, worked with Gaby on her speech. Gaby began to pronounce sentences, enabling her to speak and dictate short texts, which was especially important during the period when she could not type. (Ávalos, interview, March 25, 2008; Herrera, interviews, February 20 and March 24, 2008.)

24 Gaby Brimmer to Elena Poniatowska, October 18, 1980, in Brimmer, *Cartas*, 57; Gaby Brimmer, address, CEDI, April 11, 1989, ADEPAM mss; Gaby Brimmer, address, Xalapa, July 15, 1989, ADEPAM mss; Gaby Brimmer, address, Guanajuato, November 14, 1994, ADEPAM mss.

25 Brimmer, "Argumento de la película," 91; Gaby Brimmer to Elena Poniatowska, July 8, 1980, in Brimmer, *Cartas*, 53; María del Pilar Cruz Pérez, "Mujeres con discapacidad y su derecho a la sexualidad," *Política y Cultura* 22 (2004): 147–160.

26 Raquel Carrillo, interview by author, Mexico City, March 24, 2008; Gaby Brimmer, "Carta de amor," March 17, 1987, 1, Brimmer mss.

27 Brimmer, "Argumento de la película," 91.

28 Brimmer, "Disfraces," 108.

29 Brimmer, "Argumento de la película," 84; Brimmer, "Carta de amor," March 17, 1987; Paulina García, interview.

30 Brimmer, address, San Juan, Puerto Rico, 5.

31 Ávila Delgado, interview.

32 Brimmer, "Argumento de la película," 70–71, 92; Stroe, interview; Brimmer, address, Xalapa, July 15, 1989; Brimmer, "Resumen o sinopsis del argumento," 10.

33 Gaby Brimmer, "Artículo para Superación," *Superación*, December 1977, 4; Gaby Brimmer, "¿Cómo se Libera una Muchacha Lisiada Gravemente?" *Superación*, June 1978, 1, 8; Gaby Brimmer, "¿Qué Hacer? ¿Qué Decir? ¿Qué Cambiar?" parts 1 and 2, *Superación*, June 1979, 2, 7; Gaby Brimmer, "Editorial," *Superación*, June 1980, 8; Gaby Brimmer, "Barreras," *Superación*, June 1980, 3; Ávila Delgado, interview.

34 Martha Heredia, interview by author, Mexico City, March 25, 2008; Ernesto Rosas, interview by author, Mexico City, March 24, 2008.

35 Ávila Delgado, *Lo que me tocó convivir*, 14; Rosas, interview; Hernández, interview; Diane Driedger, *From Vision to Making History: The First Decade, Disabled People's International* (London: C. Hurst; and New York: St. Martin's, 1989), 94–114.

36 Gaby Brimmer to Henry Brimmer, September 14, 1980; Gaby Brimmer, "Resumen o sinopsis del argumento de la película," 10; Brimmer, "Argumento de la película," 78, 89–90; Vicente Martínez, interviews by author, Mexico City, February 20 and April 3, 2008; Quezada, interview; Florencia Morales, interview, February 21, 2008; Florencia Morales, interview by author, Mexico City, March 24, 2008; Díaz de León, interview; Himmelfarb, interview.

37 Esquivias, "Gaby Brimmer."

38 Alma Brimmer, interview, April 3, 2008.

39 Angélica Herrera, interview by author, Mexico City, February 27, 2008; Mario Monroy, Eugenio Ibarolla, and Miguel Alessio, Notarios, incorporation records, Mexico City, March 2, 1989, ADEPAM MSS.

40 Angélica Herrera, interview by author, Mexico City, June 18, 2008.

41 Martínez, interview, February 20, 2008; Florencia Morales, interviews, February 21 and March 24, 2008; Herrera, interview, March 24, 2008; Esquivias, "Gaby Brimmer."

42 Herrera, interview, February 20, 2008; Martínez, interview, April 3, 2008; Ávalos, interview, March 25, 2008; Teresa García, interview by author, Mexico City, April 3, 2008; Santiago Velázquez, interview by author, Mexico City, June 18, 2008.

43 Ávila Delgado, interview. Gaby was offered high political positions by the Institutional Revolutionary Party (PRI) in the 1990s. She declined because she believed the disability rights movement had to stay away from party politics in order to maintain its independence. See Hernández, interview.

44 Florencia Morales, interview, *Foro de celebridades, estrellas, personajes.*

45 Herrera, interview by author, Mexico City, April 3, 2008; Teresa García, interview; Florencia Morales, interview, February 21, 2008.

46 Ávila Delgado, *Lo que me tocó convivir*, 15–21; Ávila Delgado, interview; Velázquez, interview.

47 Ávila Delgado, interview; Ávila Delgado, *Lo que me tocó convivir*, 15–21, 124–127; Hernández, interview.

48 Ávila Delgado, interview; Ávila Delgado, *Lo que me tocó convivir*, 21–23; Rosas, interview.

49 Angélica Herrera, interview by author, Mexico City, February 21, 2008; Herrera, interview, March 24, 2008; Carrillo, interview; Ávila Delgado, interview; Velázquez, interview; Hernández, interview.

50 Ávila Delgado, interview; Velázquez, interview. Gaby received an offer to become the Confederation's second president, but she declined, understanding the position would require her to function as a consensus builder and not leave her free to speak her mind and assert her opinions. See Hernández, interview.

51 Ávalos, interview, March 25, 2008; Alma Brimmer, interview, April 3, 2008; Herrera, interview, June 18, 2008.

52 Kathy Martinez to Gabriela Brimmer Dlugacz, Washington, D.C., February 27, 1997, ADEPAM MSS; Gaby Brimmer to Judy Heumann, June 25, 1997, e-mail message, ADEPAM MSS; Gaby Brimmer to Christopher Button, Mexico City, June 26, 1997, ADEPAM MSS; Quezada, interview; Gaby Brimmer, "Right of Women with Inability [*sic*]," May 9, 1997, ADEPAM MSS; Laura Hershey, "The International Leadership Forum for Women," http://newmobility.com/articleViewIE.cfm?id=25 (June 22, 2008).

53 Gaby Brimmer, "Y Gabriela Brimmer dice," 1991/1992, 5, Brimmer MSS.

54 "La ejemplar misión de Gabriela Brimmer," *Diario Yucatán* (Mérida, Yucatán), January 15, 1993; "Gaby, Mujer que logra vencer a la adversidad," *Novedades Yucatán* (Mérida, Yucatán), January 15, 1993; "Crear Conciencia y Sensibilidad Hacia los Discapacitados: Meta de Gaby Brimmer, *El Sol de Irapuato*, June 11, 1993; Ricardo Baeza Ramírez, "Gaby Brimmer Recorrió Instituciones," *El Sol de Irapuato*, June 12, 1993; Teresa Miranda de Navarro, "Infinito amor muestran los irapuatenses a Gaby Brimmer," *El Centro* (Irapuato, Guanajuato), June 12, 1993; Juanita, "Integrantes del Centro Social Israelita Ofrecieron un Convivio a Gaby Brimmer," *El Mexicano* (Ensenada, Baja California), November 1, 1993. In Tijuana, at the Centro Social Israelita (Jewish Social Center), Gaby was received by the rabbi and the meal included "delicious dishes from Jewish cuisine." "Siempre Gaby," *La Tarde de Baja California* (Tijuana, Baja California), November 1, 1993; Jesús Soto Martínez, "Gabriela Brimmer, un Ejemplo a Seguir," *El Heraldo de Baja California* (Tijuana, Baja California), October 26, 1993; Aída Suárez, "Gaby, superó las barreras," *El Sol de Hidalgo* (Pachuca, Hidalgo), March 27, 1994; Isabel Juan, "Gaby Brimmer en Oaxaca: Inspiración de lucha," *El Imparcial* (Oaxaca, Oaxaca), July 29, 1994; José López Gutiérrez, "Gaby Brimmer, Invitada Especial en la Presentación del Grupo 'Arte Para Todos,'" *El Sol de Irapuato*, October 27, 1995; Adolfo Morales Manchada, "Testimonio: Foro Regional de Discapacitados," *El Sol de Tijuana*, n.d., 1995; Virginia Fernández, "Demandan los Discapacitados Acceso a la Educación e Integración al Sector Productivo," *El Mexicano*, n.d., 1995; "Una esperanza para todos," *Centro de Rehabilitación Integral "Gaby Brimmer"* (Ciudad Acuña, Coahuila), April 15, 1996, 2–8; "Gaby Brimmer," *Gaceta Municipal, La Federalista* (Ciudad Acuña, Coahuila), April 1996, 1–3; Dora Isela de la Cruz de León, "Concluyó con Éxito el Taller Sobre Discapacidad," *El Heraldo de Irapuato*, June 19, 1999.

55 Laura Galaviz to Gaby Brimmer, Irapuato, Guanajuato, June 1, 1993; Maximino Elizarrarás to Gaby Brimmer, Irapuato, Gto., June 4, 1993; José Luis Rosas to Gaby Brimmer, Irapuato, Gto., June 4, 1993; Raúl Tafoya to Gaby Brimmer, Irapuato, Gto., June 5, 1993; Andrés Ramírez to Gaby Brimmer, Irapuato, Gto., June 5, 1993; Miguel Angel Diosdado to Gaby Brimmer, Irapuato, Gto., June 5, 1993; Javier Martínez to Gaby Brimmer, Irapuato, Gto., June 10, 1993, ADEPAM MSS.

56 Lupita Rubalcaba to Gaby Brimmer, Irapuato, Guanajuato, June 5, 1993.

57 María Eugenia Antúnez and Andrés Balcázar, *Diagnóstico sobre discapacidad en México* (Mexico City: Antúnez-Balcázar Consultores, 2005), 23; Ávila Delgado, *Lo que me tocó convivir*, 66–67; Ávila Delgado, interview; Heredia, interview; Rosas, interview; "Marcha de discapacitados para plantear demandas," *La Voz* (Montevideo, Uruguay), March 1994, 6, reprinted in Ávila Delgado, *Lo que me tocó convivir*, 90–92.

58 Ricardo Baeza Ramírez, "Demandan Discapacitados Igualdad de Derechos," *El Heraldo de Irapuato*, November 18, 1994, 1, 8A; Ávila Delgado, *Lo que me tocó convivir*, 75–76; Ávila Delgado to author, July 9, 2008, e-mail message.

59 Gaby Brimmer, "Derechos Humanos. ¿igual que derecho a la vida, a la dignidad, a la justicia?" Mexico City, May 6, 1996, ADEPAM M S S.

60 Ávila Delgado, *Lo que me tocó convivir*, 62–63, 68, 93–94; Ernesto Rosas Barrientos, "Una convención para armonizar," in *Memoria del Seminario Internacional Convención sobre los Derechos de las Personas con Discapacidad: Por Una Cultura de la Implementación* (Mexico City: Secretaría de Relaciones Exteriores, 2007), 219–230; Rosas, interview; Herrera, interview, June 18, 2008.

61 "Palabras del presidente Ernesto Zedillo, durante la presentación del III Informe de Avances del Programa Nacional para el Bienestar y la Incorporación al Desarrollo de las Personas con Discapacidad," August 11, 1998, http://Zedillo.presidencia .gob.mx/pages/disc/ago98/11ago98.html (August 14, 2008).

62 "Palabras del presidente Ernesto Zedillo," August 11, 1998; Antúnez and Balcázar, *Diagnóstico*, 6, 9; Rosas, interview.

63 "Palabras del presidente Ernesto Zedillo"; Antúnez and Balcázar, *Diagnóstico*, 21.

64 Antúnez and Balcázar, *Diagnóstico*, 19, 26–27, 57–64; "Palabras del presidente Ernesto Zedillo"; Ávila Delgado, *Lo que me tocó convivir*, 64.

65 Hernández, interview; Antúnez and Balcázar, *Diagnóstico*, 52–53.

66 Alonso Urritia, "Otorgan la Medalla al Mérito Ciudadano a Gabriela Brimmer," *La Jornada*, April, 25, 1995; Ávila Delgado, *Lo que me tocó convivir*, 102–104. According to Angélica Herrera, it may have been Fernando Rodríguez who, with his political connections, worked behind the scenes with the PRD, then the party in power in the Federal District government, for Gaby to get the medal. See Herrera, interview, February 20, 2008.

67 Claudia Ramos, "Galardonan a Brimmer," *Reforma*, April 25, 1995; Alberto Rocha, "El Olvido no Puede ser Destino Para Nadie: Gabriela Brimmer," *Excelsior*, April 25, 1995; Sandra Puente, "Brimmer: la sociedad debe saber que existimos," *El Universal*, April 25, 1995.

68 Elena Gallegos, "Pone en marcha el Presidente un programa para discapacitados," *La Jornada*, May 13, 1995, 21; Antúnez and Balcázar, *Diagnóstico*, 21.

69 Brimmer, "Disfraces," 87, 90; Ávalos, interviews, March 25 and April 2, 2008; Rodríguez, interview; Alma Brimmer, interview by author, Mexico City, March 25, 2008; Stroe, interview; Greisman, interview; Boris Albin, interview by author, Mexico City, March 27, 2008.

70 Brimmer, "Argumento de la película," 77.

71 Ávalos, interview, March 25, 2008; Stroe, interview; Himmelfarb, interview; Quezada, interview; Alma Brimmer, interview, April 3, 2008.

72 Ávalos, interviews, March 25 and April 2, 2008; Rodríguez, interview; Stroe, interview; Himmelfarb, interview; Albin, interview.

73 Brimmer, "Disfraces," 94; Alma Brimmer, interviews, March 25 and April 3, 2008; Herrera, interview, April 3, 2008; Ávalos, interview, April 2, 2008; Rodríguez, interview.

74 Himmelfarb, interview; Stroe, interview; Paulina García, interview; Quezada, interview; Herrera, interview, February 20, 2008; Florencia Morales, interview, February 21, 2008; Ávila Delgado, interview; Velázquez, interview; Carrillo, interview; "Gaby's Trip to Eugene."

75 Gaby Brimmer to Elena Poniatowska, July 9, 1980, in Brimmer, *Cartas*, 54; Ávalos, interview, March 25, 2008; Quezada, interview; Paulina García, interview; Gaby Brimmer, manuscript, December 16, 1981, Brimmer MSS.

76 Ávila Delgado, interview; Stroe, interview; Greisman, interview; Himmelfarb, interview; Martínez, interview, April 3, 2008; Ávalos, interview, March 25, 2008; Florencia Morales, interview, February 21, 2008; Díaz de León, interview; Gaby Brimmer to Blanca, June 4, 1973, in Brimmer, *Cartas*, 69; Gaby Brimmer, "Verónica," in Brimmer, *Disfraces*, 52–53; Brimmer, "Disfraces," 106, 117.

77 Ávalos, interview, April 2, 2008; Rodríguez, interview; Zama, "Elena Poniatowska presentó dos nuevos libros"; Carlos Fazio, "Don Sergio Méndez Arceo: Patriarca de la solidaridad libertadora," *Adital*, March 17, 2004, http://www.adital.org.br/site/noticia_imp.asp?cod=11382&lang=ES (May 21, 2008); Brimmer, "Disfraces," 117–118.

78 Martínez, interview, April 3, 2008; Ávalos, interview, April 2, 2008; Rodríguez, interview; María Asunción Morales, interview.

79 Irma Hernández, "Gaby Brimmer se Siente Realizada como Mujer," *El Sol de Irapuato*, June 18, 1999, 1, 7A; Florencia Morales, interview, February 21, 2008; María Asunción Morales, interview; Quezada, interview; Díaz de León, interview.

80 Florencia Morales, interview, February 21, 2008; María Asunción Morales, interview; Alma Brimmer, interview, April 3, 2008; Ávalos, interview, April 2, 2008; Rodríguez, interview.

81 Poniatowska, "La muerte de Gaby Brimmer"; América Juárez, "Deja su ejemplo Gaby Brimmer," *Reforma*, January 5, 2000; Mauricio Matamoros, "Amigos y familiares despidieron a la escritora," *unomásuno*, January 5, 2000; Rebecca Rosen Lum, "Disabled Writer Whose Life Inspired Film Bio Died at 52," *Jewish News Weekly of Northern California*, January 14, 2000, http://www.jewishsf.com/bk000114/obbrimmer.shtml (April 28, 2002); Eileen Girón Batres, "Gabriela Brimmer Left Us with the Century," *Disability World*, April–May 2000, http://www.disabilityworld.org/April-May2000/IntntalNews/Gaby.htm (May 27, 2008); "En Homenaje a una Gaviota, Gaby Brimmer," *Lev Kadima* (Spring 2004): 11–12.

82 Alejandro Ainslie de Font Réaulx, *Boletín Informativo de la Junta de Asistencia Privada del Distrito Federal*, October 2000, 9–11; Clara Jusidman Rapaport, *Boletín Informativo de la Junta de Asistencia Privada*, 18–19.

83 Ernesto Zedillo, "Homenaje Póstumo del Presidente de la República a Gaby Brimmer," *Pláticas del Presidente*, January 15, 2000, transcribed in Ávila Delgado, *Lo que me tocó convivir*, 109–111; "Llama EZP a redoblar esfuerzos para apoyar a las personas con discapacidad," *Nosotros*, March 2000, http://informatica.issste.gob.mx/website/comunicados/nosotros/marzo2000/LlamaEZParedoblar.html (July 17, 2008).

84 Mario Ávila Delgado, "A Gabriela Brimmer Dlugacz," January 28, 2000, transcribed in Ávila Delgado, *Lo que me tocó convivir*, 124–129; Ávila Delgado, interview.

TIME LINE

Selected Events in Mexican Disability Rights History
(Including Information on Concurrent International Developments)

Special thanks to Mario Alberto Ávila Delgado and Martha
Heredia Navarro for their assistance in compiling this time line.

1870   Escuela Nacional de Ciegos (National School for the Blind) founded in
       Mexico City by politician and statesman Ignacio Trigueros. Escuela Nacional
       de Sordos (National School for the Deaf) founded in Mexico City during the
       same era.

1940   Instituto de Capacitación del Niño Ciego del Estado de Jalisco (Jalisco State
       Training Institute for Blind Children) founded in Guadalajara.

1949   Sociedad de Ciegos de Monterrey (Monterrey Society for the Blind, today
       known as the Sociedad de Invidentes de Monterrey) founded.[1]

1959   Comité Internacional Pro Ciegos (International Committee for the Blind)
       established in Mexico City as a not-for-profit assistance organization, build-
       ing on initial efforts begun in 1922.

1967   Federación de Deportes para Sordos (Sports Federation for the Deaf)
       founded.

1970   Asociación Pro Personas con Parálisis Cerebral (APAC, or Cerebral Palsy
       Association) founded in Mexico City.

1972   First wheelchair games organized in Mexico.

1973   Asociación de Lisiados de Jalisco (ALJAC, or Association of Crippled
       People of Jalisco), Organización de Invidentes Unidos de Jalisco (United
       Organization of the Blind of Jalisco), and Fraternidad Cristiana de Enfermos
       y Limitados Físicos (FRATER, or Christian Fraternity of the Sick and Physi-
       cally Handicapped) founded in Guadalajara.[2]

Instituto Francisco de Asís, an assistance organization for low-income people with intellectual disabilities, founded in Mexico City.

Rehabilitation Act of 1973 signed into law in the United States by President Richard Nixon.

1976   Reglamento de Prevención de Invalidez y Rehabilitación de Inválidos (Regulations for Prevention of Handicaps and Rehabilitation of the Handicapped) issued by President Luís Echeverría.

1979   Consejo Nacional de Recursos para la Atención de la Juventud (CREA, or National Council of Resources for Youth Services), under the leadership of disability activist Fernando Rodríguez, opens the first school to train people with disabilities for jobs in industry. This program ended after President José López Portillo left office in 1982.

Grupo Latinoamericano para la Participación, la Integración y la Inclusión de las Personas con Discapacidad (Latin American Group for Participation, Integration and Inclusion of People with Disabilities, or GLARP-IIPD) granted status as a not-for-profit organization in Mexico.

1981   International Year for Disabled Persons proclaimed by the United Nations.

Mobility International USA founded in Eugene, Oregon, and Disabled People's International (DPI) in Winnipeg, Manitoba, Canada.

1982   Proclamation of United Nations Decade for Disabled Persons (1983–92).

1983   Mexico signs the U.N. World Programme of Action concerning Disabled Persons. As part of this program, Rehabilitation International works with Mexico's healthcare sector to organize disabilty-related events and projects in Mexico during the U.N. Decade for Disabled Persons.

World Institute on Disability (WID) is founded by Judy Heumann, Joan Leon, and Ed Roberts in Oakland, California.

1985   Mexico joins the Organización Nacional de Ciegos de España (National Organization of the Blind in Spain, or ONCE), through the Fondo de Cooperación de ONCE con Latinoamérica (ONCE Latin America Cooperation Fund).

1986   Ley sobre el Sistema Nacional de Asistencia Social (National Social Assistance System Act) signed into law by President Miguel de la Madrid.

Asociación Universitaria de Minusválidos (University Association of the Handicapped) founded at the Universidad Nacional Autónoma de México

(National Autonomous University of Mexico, or UNAM), remaining active through the early 1990s.

Confederación Mexicana de Limitados Físicos y Representantes de Deficientes Mentales (Mexican Confederation of Persons with Physical Limitations and Representatives of the Mentally Handicapped, or COMELFIRDEM) founded in Guadalajara.

1987 COMELFIRDEM becomes a member of DPI.

1988 Asociación para los Derechos de Personas con Alteraciones Motoras (Association for the Rights of People with Motor Disabilities, or ADEPAM) founded in Mexico City by Gaby Brimmer and her friends and colleagues.

1989 Fifth Latin American Seminar of DPI organized in Mexico City by DPI and COMELFIRDEM.

Libre Acceso (Free Access, a national organization that works to promote accessibility and the rights of persons with disabilities) founded in Mexico City.

ADEPAM becomes affiliated with COMELFIRDEM.

1990 Movilidad Internacional México becomes affiliated with Mobility International USA.

Americans with Disabilities Act (ADA) signed into law in the United States by President George H. W. Bush.

1992 GLARP-IIPD, recognized as a not-for-profit organization in 1979, forms a Mexico chapter whose members begin to organize activities and programs for people with disabilities.

1993 International Day of Persons with Disabilities (December 3) celebrated for the first time in Mexico, after initial declaration by the United Nations in 1992.

United Nations adopts the Standard Rules on the Equalization of Opportunities for Persons with Disabilities.

1994 Marcha de la Amistad (Friendship March), national march of people with disabilities to the Palacio Legislativo de San Lázaro (Mexico's congressional headquarters building) in Mexico City, to present a petition for equal rights to legislators.

1995 Programa Nacional para el Bienestar y la Incorporación al Desarrollo de las Personas con Discapacidad (National Program for the Welfare and

192 ❧ Time Line in Mexican Disability Rights

Integration into Development of People with Disabilities) introduced by President Ernesto Zedillo.

Ley para las Personas con Discapacidad del Distrito Federal (Persons with Disabilities Act of the Federal District) approved by the Asamblea de Representantes del Distrito Federal (Federal District Representative Assembly, today known as the Asamblea Legislativa del Distrito Federal).

1997   International Leadership Forum for Women with Disabilities held in Bethesda, Maryland; attended by Gaby Brimmer and other Mexican women with disabilities.

1998   First forum on "Liderazgo y Derechos de las Mujeres y Niñas con Discapacidad" (Leadership and Rights for Women and Children with Disabilities) organized in Mexico City by DPI's Comité de Mujeres con Discapacidad/ Región Latinoamericana (Committee of Women with Disabilities/Latin American Region).

"Multiple Disabilities . . . Multiple Challenges" international conference organized in Mexico City by the Confederación Mexicana de Organizaciones en Favor de la Persona con Discapacidad Intelectual (CONFE, or Mexican Confederation of Organizations for People with Intellectual Disabilities).

Fifth DPI World Assembly held in Mexico City.

2000   January 3. Gaby Brimmer dies in Mexico City.

Plans for the Premio Nacional de Rehabilitación Física o Mental (National Award for Physical or Mental Rehabilitation) announced by President Ernesto Zedillo during his eulogy for Gaby on his radio program "Pláticas del Presidente."

"Normas para la accesibilidad de las personas con discapacidad" (Accessibility Guidelines for People with Disabilities) published by the Instituto Mexicano del Seguro Social (Mexican Social Security Institute).

Oficina de Representación para la Promoción e Integración Social para Personas con Discapacidad (Office for the Advancement and Social Integration of People with Disabilities) established by President Vicente Fox.

Mexico ratifies the Organization of American States Inter-American Convention on the Elimination of All Forms of Discrimination against Persons with Disabilities.

2003 Ley Federal para Prevenir y Eliminar la Discriminación (Federal Discrimination Prevention and Elimination Act) signed into law by President Vicente Fox. Establishes the Consejo Nacional para Prevenir la Discriminación (National Council to Prevent Discrimination, or CONAPRED), which is empowered to receive and resolve complaints of discrimination.[3]

Mexican government launches Internet portal www.discapacinet.gob.mx.

2004 Ley de Asistencia Social (Social Assistance Act) signed into law by President Vicente Fox. National Social Assistance System Act (1986) abrogated.

2005 Ley General de las Personas con Discapacidad (People with Disabilities Act) signed into law by President Vicente Fox, establishing the Consejo Nacional de Personas con Discapacidad (National Council of People with Disabilities), which replaces the Office for the Advancement and Social Integration of People with Disabilities. The new council is headed by the Ministry of Health, which some disability activists regard as a return to the "medical model" for disability and therefore a step backward.[4]

2006 Inclusion International holds biannual General Assembly in Acapulco.

Mexico City government approves regulations for Persons with Disabilities Act of the Federal District.

2007 Ministry of Economy announces approval of Norma Oficial Mexicana (Official Mexican Standard), which requires that public buildings constructed in Mexico be accessible.

Mexico's Senate approves Ley General de la Infraestructura Física Educativa (Physical Infrastructure for Educational Buildings Act), which includes provisions for monitoring accessibility adjustments.

Mexico City mayor Marcelo Ebrard introduces accessibility manual for local buildings.

Mexico City metro system signs anti-discrimination agreement with CONAPRED, targeting increased awareness of accessibility issues.

2008 Mexico's Ministry of Public Education announces Mexico's federal Chamber of Deputies approves change to Ley Federal de Trabajo (Federal Labor Act), requiring businesses to guarantee accessibility.

Mexico City mayor Marcelo Ebrard announces approval of construction of Line 12 of the city's subway system, planned to be accessible.

Comisión Nacional de Derechos Humanos (National Human Rights Commission, or CNDH) and the Federación de Colegios de Arquitectos de la República Mexicana (Federation of Architects' Associations of Mexico) sign an agreement to undertake accessible construction, communications, and transportation projects. Ebrard also announces other accessibility goals for the city, including a 20 percent increase in accessibility for the public transit system and improved accessibility of streets.

NOTES

1 Today, there are approximately eight hundred organizations in Mexico devoted to providing education and training, physical therapy, and other related services to people with disabilities, as cited in María Eugenia Antúnez Farrugia and Andrés Balcázar de la Cruz, *Diagnóstico sobre discapacidad en México* (Mexico City: Antúnez-Balcázar Consultores, 2005), 23. Some are mentioned in this time line, but it is obviously impossible to list them all here.

2 Many early organizations of people with disabilities were "based on Christianity and were formed in nine Latin American countries. These organizations, called Christian 'Fraternities' of disabled people, had originated in France, having been started in 1942 by Monsignor Henri François"; Diane Driedger, *The Last Civil Rights Movement: Disabled Peoples' International* (London: C. Hurst; New York: St. Martin's Press, 1989), 17.

3 For more comprehensive information on Mexican federal legislation that guarantees various rights to people with disabilities, see Antúnez Farrugia and Balcázar de la Cruz. Mexico's state and local governments also have disability-related legislation and regulations, too numerous to list in this time line.

4 Antúnez Farrugia and Balcázar de la Cruz, 6.

READING LIST

Primary Sources

ADEPAM Manuscripts, ADEPAM [Asociación para los Derechos de Personas con Alteraciones Motoras] Gabriela Brimmer I.A.P., Mexico City.

Ávila Delgado, Mario Alberto. *Lo que me tocó convivir.* Guadalajara, Mexico: privately printed, 2008.

Brimmer, Gabriela. *Gaby, un año después.* Mexico City: Editorial Grijalbo, 1980.

———. Selected articles and poems, including articles published in *Superación*, 1977–80: "Artículo para *Superación*" (no. 10, December 1977); "¿Cómo se Libera una Muchacha Lisiada Gravemente?" (no. 12, June 1978); "¿Qué Hacer? ¿Qué Decir? ¿Qué Cambiar?" (no. 16, June 1979); "Breves Notas Breves" and "Editorial: De cara al sol" (no. 18, December 1979); and "Barreras" (no. 20, June 1980). ALJAC Manuscripts, Guadalajara, Mexico; "Dejadme sufrir," *Rehabilitation Gazette* XV (1972): 38 [poem, in Spanish with English translation] and "Mexican Poetess" [article in English], ibid., 37–38; "Of Life and Love," *Northern California Foreign Language Newsletter* XXI, no. 82 (October 1972): 9 [poems, in Spanish with English translation].

Brimmer, Gaby. *Cartas de Gaby.* Mexico City: Editorial Grijalbo, 1982.

———. *Disfraces y otros cuentos.* Mexico City: Ediciones y Creatividad, 1986.

———. Manuscripts. Brimmer Family, Mexico City.

Secondary Sources

Antúnez Farrugia, María Eugenia, and Andrés Balcázar de la Cruz. *Diagnóstico sobre discapacidad en México.* Mexico City: Antúnez-Balcázar Consultores, 2005; available at http://scm.oas.org/pdfs/2007/DIL00140s.pdf and http://www.abc-discapacidad.com.

Barnartt, Sharon N., and Richard K. Scotch. *Disability Protests: Contentious Politics 1970–1999.* Washington, D.C.: Gallaudet University Press, 2001.

Brown, Christy. *My Left Foot.* 1954. London: Vintage, 1998.

Center for Reproductive Rights. *Briefing Report: Reproductive Rights and Women with Disabilities: A Human Rights Framework.* January 2002.

Charlton, James I. *Nothing About Us Without Us: Disability Oppression and Empowerment*. Berkeley and Los Angeles: University of California Press, 1998.

Cimet, Adina. *Ashkenazi Jews in Mexico: Ideologies in the Structuring of a Community*. Albany: State University of New York Press, 1997.

Cotter, Anne-Marie Mooney. *This Ability: An International Legal Analysis of Disability Discrimination*. Burlington, Vt.: Ashgate, 2007.

Driedger, Diane. *The Last Civil Rights Movement: Disabled Peoples' International*. London: C. Hurst; New York: St. Martin's Press, 1989.

———, Irene Feika, and Eileen Girón Batres, eds. *Across Borders: Women with Disabilities Working Together*. Charlottetown, Prince Edward Island, Canada: Gynergy Books, 1996.

——— and Susan Gray, eds. *Imprinting Our Image: An International Anthology by Women with Disabilities*. Charlottetown, Prince Edward Island, Canada: Gynergy Books, 1992.

Fine, Michelle, and Adrienne Asch, eds. *Women with Disabilities: Essays in Psychology, Culture and Politics*. Philadelphia: Temple University Press, 1988.

Finger, Anne. *Past Due: A Story of Disability, Pregnancy and Birth*. Seattle, Wash.: Seal Press, 1990.

Fleischer, Doris Zames, and Frieda Zames. *The Disability Rights Movement: From Charity to Confrontation*. Philadelphia: Temple University Press, 2001.

Franco, Jean. *Plotting Women: Gender and Representation in Mexico*. New York: Columbia University Press, 1989.

Frank, Gelya. *Venus on Wheels: Two Decades of Dialogue on Disability, Biography, and Being Female in America*. Berkeley and Los Angeles: University of California Press, 2000.

Gillespie-Sells, Kath, Milchette Hill, and Bree Robbins. *She Dances to Different Drums: Research into Disabled Women's Sexuality*. London: King's Fund, 1998.

Hillyer, Barbara. *Feminism and Disability*. Norman: University of Oklahoma Press, 1993.

Jacobson, Denise Sherer. *The Question of David: A Disabled Mother's Journey through Adoption, Family, and Life*. Berkeley, Calif.: Creative Arts, 1999.

Jörgensen, Beth E. *The Writing of Elena Poniatowska: Engaging Dialogues*. Austin: University of Texas Press, 1994.

Kaminsky, Amy K. *Reading the Body Politic: Feminist Criticism and Latin American Women Writers*. Minneapolis: University of Minnesota Press, 1993.

Lesser, Harriet Sara. "A History of the Jewish Community of Mexico City: 1912–1970." Ph.D. diss., New York University, 1972.

Lewis, Cindy, and Susan Sygall, eds. *Loud, Proud and Passionate: Including Women with Disabilities in International Development Programs*. Eugene, Ore.: Mobility International, 1997.

Linton, Simi. *Claiming Disability: Knowledge and Identity*. New York: New York University Press, 1998.

Longmore, Paul. *Why I Burned My Book and Other Essays on Disability*. Philadelphia: Temple University Press, 2003.

Mathews, Jay. *A Mother's Touch: The Tiffany Callo Story*. New York: Henry Holt, 1992.

Medeiros-Lichem, María Teresa. *Reading the Feminine Voice in Latin American Women's Fiction: From Teresa de la Parra to Elena Poniatowska and Luisa Valenzuela*. New York: Peter Lang, 2002.

Poniatowska, Elena. *Massacre in Mexico*. Translated by Helen R. Lane. New York: Viking Press, 1975; Columbia: University of Missouri Press, 1991.

Rousso, Harilyn. *Women and Girls with Disabilities: An International Overview and Summary of Research*. New York and Oakland, Calif.: Rehabilitation International and the World Institute on Disability, 2000.

———, Susan Gushee O'Malley, and Mary Severance, eds. *Disabled, Female, and Proud! Stories of Ten Women with Disabilities*. Boston: Exceptional Parent Press, 1988.

Saxton, Marsha, and Florence Howe, eds. *With Wings: An Anthology of Literature By and About Women with Disabilities*. New York: The Feminist Press, 1987.

Schaefer, Claudia. *Textured Lives: Women, Art, and Representation in Modern Mexico*. Tucson: University of Arizona Press, 1992.

Schuessler, Michael K. *Elena Poniatowska: An Intimate Biography*. Tucson: University of Arizona Press, 2007.

Scotch, Richard K. *From Good Will to Civil Rights: Transforming Federal Disability Policy*. 2nd ed. Philadelphia: Temple University Press, 2001.

Shaw, Barrett, ed. *The Ragged Edge: The Disability Rights Experience from the Pages of the First Fifteen Years of the Disability Rag*. Louisville, Ky.: Advocado Press, 1994.

Shapiro, Joseph P. *No Pity: People with Disabilities Forging a New Civil Rights Movement*. New York: Times Books, 1993.

Sienkiewicz-Mercer, Ruth, and Steven B. Kaplan. *I Raise My Eyes to Say Yes*. Boston: Houghton Mifflin, 1989.

Smith, Bonnie G., and Beth Hutchison. *Gendering Disability*. New Brunswick, N.J.: Rutgers University Press, 2004.

Stone, Deborah A. *The Disabled State*. Philadelphia: Temple University Press, 1984.

Umansky, Lauri, and Paul Longmore, eds. *The New Disability History: American Perspectives*. New York: New York University Press, 2001.

Webb, Ruth Cameron. *Journey into Personhood*. Iowa City: University of Iowa Press, 1994.

Zola, Irving K. *Missing Pieces: A Chronicle of Living with a Disability*. Philadelphia: Temple University Press, 1982.

CONTRIBUTORS TO THE
ENGLISH-LANGUAGE EDITION

TRUDY BALCH is a freelance writer, editor, and Spanish- and Ladino-to-English translator based in New York City. She has also worked as a translator and journalist in Guadalajara, Mexico. Her translations include *Women Writers of Latin America: Intimate Histories*, *The Poet King of Tezcoco: A Great Leader of Ancient Mexico*, *My Ocean: A Novel of Cuba*, and the English subtitles for the Ladino dialogue in the film *Novia que te vea*. Her articles have appeared in such publications as *Américas*, the *Forward*, and the *New York Times*.

AVITAL BLOCH is research professor and director, Center for Social Research, University of Colima, Mexico. She has published on U.S. intellectual history, feminism, and multiculturalism, and guest taught in these areas around the world. With Lauri Umansky, she is editor of *Impossible to Hold: Women and Culture in the 1960s*; her other books include *Política, pensamiento e historiografía en Estados Unidos contemporáneo*, and, as editor with Rogelio de la Mora and Hugo Cancino, *Public Intellectuals in Contemporary Latin America*. She serves on the executive board of the International Federation for Research on Women's History.

JUDITH E. HEUMANN, prior to assuming her current position as director of the District of Columbia Department on Disability Services, served in numerous national and international capacities, including as the first advisor on disability and development to the World Bank, and assistant secretary for special education and rehabilitative services of the U.S. Department of Education during both terms of the Clinton administration. She has helped draft a broad variety of disability-related legislation in the United States, has won numerous awards for her collaborative work on diversity and human rights issues, and is a board member of many public policy and service organizations.

JORGE PINEDA is currently the accountant for the National Council on Independent Living, having previously worked in a similar capacity for the National Association of Developmental Disabilities Councils and for firms in the San Francisco Bay area, as well as in his native Mexico City, where he also collaborated with Gaby Brimmer on many disability-related projects. These included the founding of the ADEPAM, for which he was the first treasurer. He is on the board of the National Technical Assistance Center for Latinos with Disabilities and the Latin American Youth Center in Washington, D.C., and is an active conference participant.

LAURI UMANSKY is professor of history and associate dean of the College of Arts and Sciences at Suffolk University. With Paul Longmore, she is editor of *The New Disability History: American Perspectives* and the History of Disability Series at New York University Press. Her books include *Motherhood Reconceived: Feminism and the Legacies of the Sixties*, and, with Michele Plott, *Making Sense of Women's Lives: An Introduction to Women's Studies*; with Avital Bloch, she is editor of *Impossible to Hold: Women and Culture in the 1960s* and with Molly Ladd-Taylor, *"Bad" Mothers: The Politics of Blame in Twentieth-Century America*.